Klintman begins with the assumption that the social, economic, and evolutionary sciences share a concern with human interests but that few cross-disciplinary lessons on human interests have been learned, then unpacks each discipline's contributions to our understanding of human interests whilst carefully excavating the often hidden and ignored distinction between manifest and latent interests. Readers willing to engage in some heavy intellectual lifting will in the end arrive with Klintman at an important conclusion – that the human sciences aspire to contribute to the improved welfare of humans, non-humans, and the planet, yet their own biases, shortsightedness, and resistance to cross-disciplinary learning have perhaps derailed them from their own explicit goals.

Dr Stephen Zavestoski, *University of San Francisco, USA*

Ever since Albion Small introduced the notion of interest into sociology hoping that it would serve the same purpose as the notion of atoms has served in the physical sciences, theories of interests have been disputed. Mikael Klintman's new book not only equips readers with a much needed overview of similarities and differences of interest concepts across the social and human sciences, but also delivers basis for integration while preserving disciplinary diversity. This book is a milestone in our understanding of the stuff that human beings are made of.

Matthias Gross, *University of Jena and Helmholtz Centre of Environmental Research, Leipzig, Germany*

Sociology is at its best when it rubs up against other human sciences. Klintman opens the doors of sociology to non-sociologist thinkers from Pinker to Piaget. Every page will stir controversy and, one can only hope, a shoring up of the foundations of sociology.

Jerome H. Barkow, *Emeritus Professor, Dalhousie University, Canada*

For the past century, the human sciences have experienced an astounding – and increasingly confounding – process of fragmentation as disciplinary knowledge has become more recondite and more insular. Mikael Klintman describes how we are beginning to move in a new direction, one that is simultaneously deepening and integrating. Progress in forging meaningful interdisciplinary collaboration is the foremost challenge of the twenty-first century and can help to bring into view a world that is more socially equitable and ecologically sustainable.

Maurie J. Cohen, *Professor of Sustainability Studies, New Jersey Institute of Technology, USA*

Human Sciences and Human Interests

Within the disciplines of social, economic, and evolutionary science, a proud ignorance can often be found of the other areas' approaches. This text provides a novel intellectual basis for breaking this trend. Certainly, *Human Sciences and Human Interests* aspires to open a broad debate about what scholars in the different human sciences assume, imply, or explicitly claim with regard to human interests.

Mikael Klintman draws the reader to the core of human sciences – how they conceive human interests, as well as how interests embedded within each discipline relate to its claims and recommendations. Moreover, by comparing theories as well as concrete examples of research on health and environment through the lenses of social, economic, and evolutionary sciences, Klintman outlines an integrative framework for how human interests could be better analysed across all human sciences.

This fast-paced and modern contribution to the field is a necessary tool for developing any human scientist's ability to address multidimensional problems within a rapidly changing society. Avoiding dogmatic reasoning, this interdisciplinary text offers new insights and will be especially relevant to scholars and advanced students within the aforementioned disciplines, as well as those within the fields of social work, social policy, political science, and other neighbouring disciplines.

Mikael Klintman is Professor of Sociology at Lund University, Sweden, and Visiting Academic of St Anthony's College, Oxford University, UK. He studies obstacles to knowledge exchange across the human sciences in issues of environment and health. Klintman's previous publications include *Citizen-Consumers and Evolution* (Palgrave, 2012).

Routledge Advances in Sociology

Human Sciences and Human Interests

Integrating the social, economic, and evolutionary sciences

Mikael Klintman

LONDON AND NEW YORK

First published 2017
by Routledge
2 Park Square, Milton Park, Abingdon, Oxon OX14 4RN

and by Routledge
711 Third Avenue, New York, NY 10017

First issued in paperback 2017

Routledge is an imprint of the Taylor & Francis Group, an informa business

British Library Cataloguing-in-Publication Data
A catalogue record for this book is available from the British Library

Library of Congress Cataloging in Publication Data
A catalog record for this book has been requested

ISBN 13: 978-1-138-48492-4 (pbk)
ISBN 13: 978-1-138-89798-4 (hbk)

Typeset in Times New Roman
by Wearset Ltd, Boldon, Tyne and Wear

Contents

Acknowledgements

I would like to thank the people who have greatly helped me with my work. They have done so by reading drafts, discussing its ideas, or in other ways provided support: Alexandra Nikoleris, Andreas Olsson, Anna Jonsson, Anna-Lisa Lindén, Britt-Marie Johansson, Christofer Edling, Christopher Swader, Gert Spaargaren, Göran Djurfeldt, Johan Sandberg, Johannes Stripple, Karin Bäckstrand, Kim Jepsen, Lars J. Nilsson, Linda Soneryd, Lisa Eklund, Magnus Boström, Maria Grafström, Matthias Gross, Peter Oosterveer, Rolf Lidskog, Steven Yearley, Thomas Lunderquist, Tullia Jack, and Ylva Uggla.

Olle Frödin deserves special thanks for many passionate discussions and valuable recommendations concerning the subject of this book. I very much hope that we'll continue our dialogue and collaboration long after this ink has dried.

Furthermore, I'd like to recognise a few organisations (and their members) with communities that have provided me with many ideas and insights for this book project: The Department of Sociology, Lund University, RC24 within the International Sociological Association (ISA), RN12 within the European Sociological Association, and St Antony's College, Oxford University. As to the latter, particular thanks go to Dominic Johnson and the Board for inviting me not just formally to be a Visiting Academic at St Antony's from 2016, but also to take part in the informal, intellectual debate and collaboration.

My thanks also go to the organisations that have funded parts of this book project: The Swedish Research Council for Environment, Agricultural Sciences and Spatial Planning (Formas, Dnr. 2013–308, coordinated by Johannes Stripple), The Foundations for Humanities and Social Sciences (RJ, FSK15–1081:1, coordinated by Anna Jonsson), and the Magnus Bergvall Foundation (Dnr. 2015–00973).

Finally, I want to express the warmest thanks to my wife Jenny, our boys Matti, Fred, Bruno, and Leo, my mother Lillemor, and my in-laws Ingegerd and Hans for their support, patience, and inspiration. Without them, the idea for this book would have remained just that.

Introduction

Problem background

What might scholars and students from the human sciences (here the social, economic, and evolutionary sciences) have in common across the disciplines? If we ask, chances are that they will sooner or later mention the following: a concern with, and about, human interests. Many of us human scientists forget this apparent bottom-line reason for doing human science when we are in the midst of our daily, relatively technical tasks of which much of our work consists (collecting data, computerising, analysing, reporting). This forgetting of the main *why* behind our daily endeavours is strictly tied to the fact that explicit analyses and discussions of human interests are strangely missing from large parts of the human sciences.

The topic of human interests falls partly within what is sometimes referred to as 'axiology': the role of interests and values, both of scientific communities and values that the human sciences prescribe to the people – 'subjects' inside and outside the studies in question (Bunge, 1996). Without an in-depth understanding of the interests and values that underlie or are at stake concerning a certain societal problem, how could human scientists then explain or suggest in a well-founded manner how it could be handled? Moreover, without thorough reflection about the interests and values underlying claims and recommendations of human scientists themselves, usually strongly tied to their disciplinary identities, how then would it be possible to fully understand and assess these claims and recommendations? Courses and debates within all the human sciences usually recognise the importance of relating to 'ontology' (what exists), 'epistemology' (what can be known and learned), and 'methodology' (how to gain knowledge). Axiology (what are the underlying values and interests) is typically absent outside the philosophy and to some extent psychology departments, at least as a formal topic within the human sciences, although it is arguably at least as important an element as are others. My obvious claim is that axiology, in the sense noted above, ought to be incorporated into standard university courses and scholarly debates in the human sciences and beyond. In addition to the analytical insights the incorporations of axiology may entail, it helps human scientists to provide satisfactory responses to the devastating question so often raised concerning their research and findings: 'So what?'.

What, then, are human interests? The book seeks to investigate and explain this complicated and largely overlooked question. It would be fruitless to try to define it beforehand. However, this would not be fruitless in the sense of redundancy, such as what this common phrase reflects: 'it can't be defined, but you know it when you see it'. Nor is it fruitless as in impossible to understand for some people, which is a point sometimes brought up concerning fine art. A famous example is how the iconic jazz musician, Louis Armstrong, responds when he is asked to define jazz: 'if you gotta ask, you ain't never gonna get to know'.

For our purpose, a core intuition about human interests will do in this early part of the book, as long as our intuition is open to interests that go far beyond selfish, material interests. There is a rich history of ideas surrounding interests, and the term seems to have oscillated between a narrowly economic meaning, and a much wider sense that includes human passions. An excellent book by the economist Hirschman (1977/2013) goes in-depth in studying seventeenth and eighteenth century ideological reasoning about material interests. Instead, the point of departure of our book is, again, to analyse human interests in a far wider sense, echoing the French philosopher, de Silhon's list of human interests, and, informed by the social, economic, and evolutionary sciences, possibly adding a few as well: 'Interest of conscience, interest of honour, interest of health, interest of wealth, and several other interests' (Silhon, 1661, 104–5).

Nonetheless, as straightforward as the question – what are human interests – may seem, two things – at least – are puzzling about it. I have already mentioned the first thing: Aside from important examinations in philosophy and psychology in relative isolation, the question is rarely subject to systematic, empirical investigation and debate in large parts of the human sciences. Why? It seems that human interests are rejected from (self-)critical discussions in several human sciences, since human interests – beyond the most basic physical ones – are seen as raising only 'ideological' issues or as being a matter of personal taste. However, assumptions among scientists about human interests are central to how we formulate research questions, gather data about people and groups, and analyse the results. Human scientists can never ignore human interests. What happens is instead that most disciplines within the human sciences carry and reproduce implicit assumptions, intuitions, and common sense notions about human interests, without allowing these understandings to be scrutinised and revised.

Second, while the social, economic, and evolutionary sciences share a concern with human interests, and whereas the relevance of these disciplines to human interests is one of the raisons d'être of these disciplines, their mainstreams have so far been highly unreceptive to cross-disciplinary lessons on this matter. This has been the case even where such lessons would entail an advancement of knowledge.

These are only three among several examples that the book provides:

Sociologists sometimes join the complaint among the general public about the inherent greed of corporate leadership (Clements, 2013; Lorenz, 2012). Although the result of corporate bonus and salary systems is often perverse inequality compared to the resources of ordinary employers, sociologists often fail to see the underlying mechanisms. Evolutionary psychology as well as new developments in economics focusing on 'the economy of esteem' can be applied to the case in question: The core interest among corporate leaders is accordingly to be placed higher on the media list of successful corporate leaders than their colleagues in other corporations (Brennan & Pettit, 2004). Thus, vanity and relative success is the human driver here, not a fundamental interest in becoming infinitely rich. Greed and perverse inequality in relation to the general public are perhaps best described as (only) a symptom and a negative side effect. Instead of resigning, since one can rarely hope for a change of heart among business leaders, sociologists could discuss, based on the lesson from evolutionary, how the stable human interest in social status among business leaders – and among the rest of us – can be redirected – for instance through policy changes – to more constructive societal struggles. Whereas human vanity can never disappear, it may indeed be channellised in more humanitarian directions (Klintman, 2012a).

Scholars with their academic background in traditional economics try to analyse people's 'willingness to pay' for offsetting their CO_2-emissions (Brouwer, Brander, & Van Beukering, 2008) or for improving the welfare of animals before slaughter (Kehlbacher, Bennett, & Balcombe, 2012). However, such studies sometimes rest on the assumption that willingness to pay reflects a relatively stable human interest. The assumed, relatively stable willingness to pay is based on the assumption of a stable economic rationality of seeking the maximum utility for one's contribution of money, time, or other efforts. Instead, sociologically informed research shows that human interests behind, for instance, people's willingness to pay are highly flexible between and within cultures, strongly influenced by volatile, situated social norms and conventions. Thus, the freshness date (and place) of willingness-to-pay studies run the risk of being extremely limited, unless they are coupled with sociological insights and longitudinal analysis.

Scholars and policy makers with a narrow rational choice approach continue to call for more information about the health risks of sugar, fat, and smoking (Dallongeville, Dauchet, de Mouzon, Requillart, & Soler, 2011). However, such prescriptions, unless supplemented with other policy instruments, ignore the finding in evolutionary and social sciences that humans, to be sure, express interest in reducing such health risks. At the same time, people have a (more) fundamental, latent interest of sharing habits and conventions with our peers and with those with whom we want to identify ourselves (Confer *et al.*, 2010). Thus, to further improve individual knowledge about health risks is insufficient for motivating individuals to reduce those risks unless the impact of people's cultural setting is brought into the picture (Bolsen, Leeper, & Shapiro, 2014).

All three examples suggest that each human science has been highly disinclined to learn from the other human sciences. This compartmentalisation is reflected in, for instance, the evolution-oriented science writer Shermer's grossly over-generalising claim: 'historians, sociologists, and many in the humanities are "cognitive creationists" who assume that the mind, including intelligence, emotions, beliefs, and attitudes, is immune to laws of nature' (Shermer, 1996, 66). From the other side, the eminent sociologist Collins reveals his a priori rejection of the evolutionary approach: 'I am not interested in either pursuing or arguing with a rival research program *that seems to me* [my italics] to have limited explanatory resources' (Collins, 2005, 227). Why this 'proud ignorance' and even intellectual xenophobia, as both these quotes imply? It would be naïve to believe that different approaches to human interests are merely different intellectual viewpoints in an innocent sense. Rather, their relation – or non-relation – reflects competition between rivalling cultural groups for the domineering explanatory story of, in this case, human interests and, by extension, competition for resources. While competition that is based on mutual learning can be creative and progressive, competition based on proud ignorance embraces the status quo, as in a continuous intra-disciplinary recycling of knowledge claims. Moreover, it is old wisdom that one cannot fully understand even one's own approach, unless learning with an empathetic mind-set about rival approaches. Mill is probably still to this day correct about 'ninety nine in a hundred of what are called educated men':

> they have never thrown themselves into the mental position of those who think differently from them, [something that would necessitate supplying their real or imagined opponents] with the strongest arguments which the most skilful devil's advocate can conjure up ... and consequently they do not, in any proper sense of the word, know the doctrine which they themselves profess.
>
> (Mill, 1869, 68)

In some cases, incommensurability is, of course, a valid concern to avoid fundamental contradictions when some theories are combined. In other instances, however, claims of incommensurability might be based more on an instinctive fear of mixing intellectual cultures. This is probably a reason for the rarity of in-depth comparative studies across rival research programmes.

The academic rivalry for humans

For understanding humans and society more broadly, the strongest delineations go between: (a) what this book labels 'mainstream social science', henceforth 'social science', stressing a critical role of socialisation, social institutions, and how human interests are somewhat independent of genetic evolution (Berger, 2011; Tooby & Cosmides, 1992); (b) evolutionary science with focus on humans and society, henceforth 'evolutionary science', such as evolutionary anthropology, evolutionary psychology, and neuroscience (Dawkins, 2005; Pinker, 2002; Trivers, 2011); and (c) economics, henceforth 'economics', 'economic science' or traditional economics (Friedman, 2002; Smith, 1776/1843); for alternatives, prefixes are used, such as 'behavioural' in Thaler and Sunstein (2008).

Although the three approaches differ in points of departure – social structure/ institutions, economic utility, and 'human universals', all three aspire to understand and explain partly similar social problems. Yet, when scholars of each approach categorise the other sides' scholarly efforts as based on 'social reductionism', 'economic reductionism', or 'genetic determinism', the risk becomes severe of scholars from all three directions entering with a limited or flawed understanding of human interests. This risk was materialised in the examples above, and further examples will be discussed throughout this book. Moreover, when users of human scientific results, users such as policy makers, are to apply scholarly findings they cannot be expected to have the resources to do the cross-scientific analyses needed to capture the most significant findings about human interests. Instead, there is a risk of destructive policies founded on weak, academic knowledge claims of one approach only, claims that have not been scrutinised constructively by neighbouring approaches.

Aim

Through a close comparison of how core dimensions of human interests are implied, described, and explained in mainstream social science, economics, and in evolutionary science, this book aims to provide new knowledge about weak points as well as potential lessons and influences between the human science disciplines for better understanding human interests, particularly in issues of health and environment.

By extension, the book develops the basics of an integrative framework for understanding human interests. This framework is formulated as a number of distinct and clearly marked propositions throughout the book. The purpose of this framework is to give the social, economic, and evolutionary science supplementary, analytical tools for assessing their studies and results in the context of human interests. When I have examined the theoretical and empirical work in social, economic, and evolutionary science for this book concerning human interests, one (multifaceted) type of rationality turns out to have a higher explanatory value than other types of rationalities, or than complete irrationality: something that I call 'social rationality'. The book argues and explains that the logic of social rationality underlies all the themes of human interests that this book investigates, namely interests that mainly exceed the most essential physical needs.

Although the characteristics of social rationality are investigated and explained throughout the book, a few words of initial explanation are needed. The general term 'rationality' is used in an immense variety of ways in philosophy, psychology, sociology, economics, and political science. In one of my previous books (Klintman, 2012b), I try to make a very simple and general working definition of rationality. It reads as follows: 'actors or groups having, or with the potential to have, certain goal(s) for which they are motivated to use their resources (according to their hierarchy of preferences)' (Klintman, 2012b, 19).

Various disciplines have used similar core definitions, yet tailored for the specific analytical purposes of each discipline. Purposes may include understanding according to what rationalities politics, private firms, and bureaucracy operate, through for instance administrative rationality and economic rationality). Alternatively, it has been done for normative purposes (to prescribe what rationalities such institutions, or society as a whole, ought to operate on, such as discursive rationality, ecological rationality, and deliberative rationality. It is beyond the scope of this book to analyse or summarise this plethora of perspectives on rationality. Instead, the book examines the explanatory value of what can be called social rationality. I develop and scrutinise the following argument: The reason that we humans live today is that our ancestors during some 6 million years have, by natural selection, evolved to be adapted to survive and reproduce in hunter-gatherer societies. By contrast, people have lived for only the last 12,000 years in agricultural and urban societies. To survive and reproduce successfully, the genetically rooted social motivation has been key to our ancestors, and continues to be as deeply rooted in us today universally. Social motivation implies our endless interest in social bonding, cooperation, developing intimate relationships, and in influencing as well as imitating others. On the other hand, social motivation also implies preventing being exploited or cheated by other individuals and groups. Without a social rationality to better seek, unconsciously and consciously, fulfilments of this motivation, our ancestors – and thus we – would never have been able to survive or reproduce. At the same time, our social motivation entails several tendencies that were adaptive to a hunter-gatherer society but are maladaptive to today's advanced, urban society (Buss, 2000; Runciman, 2005). This mismatch helps to explain much of the disinclination for individuals, organisations, and states to make sufficient effort to reduce environmental harm, for fear of losing social positions, of having to alter society's infrastructure substantially, or having to abandon current lifestyles. By gaining an in-depth understanding of social motivation and social rationality at all levels of society, the knowledge basis could become much improved for more efficient and realistic choices of efforts to organise society and develop policies and social norms through which members of society may reduce various societal harms as positive side effects of satisfied social interests.

> Proposition 1: people, organisations, or (other) actors in the political realm should not be expected to have reductions of harm to common resources, such as the environment, as their overriding interest. Social rationality implies that only where activities of reduced harm function as positive side effects or means to social ends (bonding, distinction, esteem, or in some cases monetary gain) can actors be expected to make full efforts in this direction.

Three themes

To make it possible to manage the enormous range of potential human-interest factors in a single book, the book concentrates on three fundamental themes:

- manifest and latent interests;

- culturally specific and universal interests;
- interests, continuity, and change.

I have selected these themes since all of them have turned out to be highly relevant for elucidating differences and similarities of the three scholarly approaches, theoretically and empirically. All themes, separated as three parts of this book, include concrete, empirical examples. The examples are intended to show how, and why, scholarly assumptions about human interests make an analytical as well as practical difference, regarding the explanatory value of the studies. There are several types of examples in this book. The main criterion for selecting the examples is that they should show the practical relevance of how the human sciences conceive of human interests within the themes that the book investigates. Almost all examples concern environmental and health-oriented issues. Within these immensely broad problem areas, human interests concerning transportation and food are paid particular attention. In addition, health issues concerning violence are also subject to examples in this book.

Previous literature

What previous efforts have been made to create bridges and communication between social, economic, and evolutionary sciences?

They-should-be-like-us literature

There is abundant literature written by evolutionary biologists, ditto anthropologists, psychologists, and evolution-oriented behavioural economists, discussing human interest from the evolutionary perspective of 'human nature'. Much of this literature includes the objective of criticising social, economic, as well as modern society in general for a lack of understanding and consideration of evolutionary thought (Barkow, 2005; Dawkins, 2006; Pinker, 2002). Scholars and science writers very active in the public debates have written the literature on this theme on evolution. Some of this literature – and indeed the titles mentioned above – are scientifically ambitious. Several titles are also written in a non-technical and accessible style, more so than the works by social scientists.

To the extent that this stream of literature addresses those parts of the social and economic sciences that do not have an evolutionary basis, the former is typically developed from an us-them outlook, 'us' being evolutionary science disciplines and scholars and 'them' being social and economic scientists. There are pros and cons of this outlook. A possible advantage is a sober perspective that the outsider's eye may ideally provide social and economic scientists with, the latter ones having for too long isolated themselves in their respective intra-disciplinary debates. Such intra-disciplinary debates too often turn into hair-splitting or debates between 'trends' in social science and economics, rather than between new substantive findings. A potential problem with the us-them outlook is that evolutionary science scholars from, for instance, psychology and biology, by not being experts in standard social science and economics, run the risk of extrapolating specific arguments and statements from marginal niches of social science to entire disciplines. The richness, nuances, and subtle influences that nonetheless exist between, for instance, parts of social science and other sciences are typically ignored. Similar to situations where an organisation may have guest speakers who give their outsider worldview, the literature written by evolutionary scientists and writers has probably been as inspirational and provocative to social scientists as to the general public. Yet, it is fair to say that the claims made by these evolution-oriented scholars have contributed mainly to the general public debate (particularly on evolution vs creationism).

We-should-be-like-them literature

During the last couple of decades, a limited number of social scientists have taught evolutionary thought to modestly interested social scientists (Lopreato & Crippen, 2002; Runciman, 2009; Sanderson, 2014). These social sciences have in several cases made excellent efforts in helping social scientists, and economists, open their eyes to evolutionary science. If I should mention a risk here, the eagerness to incorporate evolutionary thinking into the social and economic sciences seems to lead, in part, to defensive reactions from these two sciences. For instance, I have personally witnessed such reactions, implied in questions such as 'isn't there anything in the centuries of accumulated knowledge in the traditional, social and economic sciences that is worth building on and sharing with evolutionary scholars?' Of course, there is – tremendous amounts, theoretical and empirical!

In economics, alternatives to the mainstream view of economic rationality have had more success in the vast field of economics than alternatives to mainstream social scientific assumptions have had in social sciences (Ariely, 2009). Behavioural economics has made impressive progress in widening the discussion within economics about human decision making. Moreover, this sub-field has rapidly been applied in a broad range of sectors of society to improve decision making concerning health, food habits, environmental concern, and – of course – financial planning. Whereas behavioural economics has connections to evolutionary thought, parts of the traditional view of the economic aspects of rationality still seem to exist in this subfield too. Subsequent chapters expand on this.

Despite-partial-incompatibility-there-is-ample-room-for-mutual-learning literature

Aside from these two categories of literature aimed at human scientific dialogue, there is a third category that is much less well developed than the other two: books which, in addition to identifying factors that are incompatible across the rivalling approaches, strive towards identifying overlaps as well as the potential for partial integration. The book *The Economy of Esteem* is a good example

(Brennan & Pettit, 2004). Others include the books by the sociologist Mazur (2005) *Biosociology of Dominance and Deference*, and the book by Turner and Maryanski (2016), entitled *On the Origin of Societies by Natural Selection*. Both the latter books walk the reader through the entire human history using the lenses of sociological and evolutionary thought. The three books have in common that they, although influenced by evolutionary science, are firmly positioned within the writing style and culture of their respective mother discipline: sociology and economics. There is arguably a need for more books that, in similar ways, maintain the integrity of the traditional discipline, while at the same time being open to new insight from outside.

This is one of the things that this book tries to do on human interests. Having spent years in the fields of sociology, consumer research, policy research, philosophy of science, and evolutionary thought, I have long noticed an absence of constructive competition and mutual learning across human scientific disciplines. Yet, it has been increasingly evident how 'dialogues' (i.e. between two disciplines, such as the social and evolutionary sciences, or the economic and evolutionary sciences) are too limited to provide a wide, human scientific knowledge sharing about human interests. Therefore, this book has broadened the 'conversation' into a trialogue, between social science, economics, and evolutionary science. In doing so, the book is intended to open up channels of communication across these so far largely compartmentalised approaches. I hold that intellectually curious communication and closer competition will be necessary for them to maintain and increase their societal relevance.

Assumptions and position

Here follow some further clarifications about the position and assumptions in this book: What should be done within and across the three approaches to improve knowledge about human interests, and in turn to better understand and improve society?

First of all, I do not claim that social, economic, and evolutionary sciences should replace their business-as-usual with cross-disciplinary collaborations wherever possible. Instead, a message of this book is that conventional analyses within disciplines should be broadened in certain respects, doing justice also to deeply rooted, often-latent dimensions of social rationality, and to (other) cross-disciplinary lessons about human interests.

Second, the diverging and contested approaches to human interests found in the human sciences are not analogous with fighting children, whom we all should try to turn into dearest friends. Nor does this book call for assimilation. It only calls for integration, which presupposes contact, knowledge sharing, collaboration as well as competition. In fact, fights are good, as long as they help the rivals increase their contact with, and curiosity about, each other. To reach this stage, wrestling is better than slingshotting from a distance. So far, cowardly slingshotting has been the primary means of communication between the three approaches. This, for instance, can be seen when examining how scholars that have gained a reputation as intellectual giants in the respective approaches reveal an astonishing ignorance and incuriosity about the other schools of thought when commenting on the explanatory value of the other approaches to understanding humans and society. This was exemplified earlier in this chapter. The book tries to indicate how this cross-disciplinary incuriosity could be cured, partly by correcting misconceptions about the others, and by highlighting important commonalities and synergies.

Still, this book aspires to go further than this. All claims about humans and human interests are not equally valid. Human interests should for none of the three approaches be only a matter of perspective, mere cleverness, taste, or even moral view (the latter reflecting what various scholars consider that human interest should be, in a normative sense). Through wishes and impulsive claims of scholars, certain misconceptions have been turned into 'common wisdom' about human interests – erroneous knowledge claims with highly negative societal consequences.

The reader is likely to wonder what criteria should be used for identifying misconceptions about human interests. I willingly admit that the position of this book is not an entirely even one across the three approaches. The degree of unevenness rests on my view of scientific knowledge as placed on levels of emergence. This is an old and well-established view, with some different versions (Moll, 2004; Polanyi, 1968). Emergence is a process where something new emanates at a higher level, that mechanisms at lower levels cannot explain. The scientific discipline of physics is the foundation that lies underneath chemistry, which in turn is the foundation underneath biology. Biology and evolutionary psychology provide knowledge about the evolutionary basis for human life. The key to human life is social life. Human life would be inconceivable and impossible without a social context. This is a fundamental lesson, not only in social science but also in its underlying discipline: evolutionary psychology. Humans live on this earth today because our ancestors were adapted genetically to their ancestral social and physical environment. Humans have evolved genetically to hold our social interest closest to our heart, 'instinct', which has made it possible for us to cooperate, survive, and procreate. This implies that fundamental principles of evolution ought to serve as the basis for social science and economics. Human (biological) evolution should be understood as the foundation of human sociality and social life. The process of emergence, in sum, refers to these two factors: The first factor is that properties at the level of social and economic organisation cannot be reduced to, or entirely explained by, lower levels, such as evolutionary psychology or biology. This factor runs the risk of being overlooked by evolutionary science. For instance, processes and properties in the biological world may be constrained (albeit not contradicted) at the social level. This is the reason several cultural patterns and expressions may differ across cultures; the cultural levels have supervened and constrained biological and evolutionary psychological levels (although the cultural levels are still consistent with the lower levels). The second factor, in contrast, tends to be forgotten by the social and economic sciences, and it was mentioned in parentheses above.

Principles (and research results) at the higher levels ought to be consistent with, and should not contradict, principles at the lower scientific levels (Salthe, 1989). One of the founders of sociology, Durkheim, sees by the turn of the nineteenth century as his mission to establish this discipline as examining 'social facts' – about norms, consequences of norm violation, and so forth – that cannot be reduced to the 'lower levels' of psychological or biological facts (Durkheim, 1895/1982). To be sure, he convincingly identifies a number of social facts that arguably cannot be reduced to facts at the lower levels. Such social facts include the need for deviance and a certain degree of crime in order for a society to clearly define and highlight the prevailing social norms. However, he – and many subsequent social scientists – overlooks the other side of the coin, although it is a truism: That the emergent properties, such as social facts, remain highly dependent on the properties at the lower levels. The social facts and mechanisms of society would look extremely different if its underlying building blocks, humans, were genetically equipped in different ways and variability than they are. When comparing the 'social facts' of human and non-human societies, such as ant societies or groups of chimps, we may note certain similarities and certain differences. Both similarities and differences reflect to a significant degree the genetic similarities and differences between humans and non-humans. This hopefully illustrates how social facts in human societies are dependent on human, genetically based properties. Without a basic, scientifically grounded, understanding of these properties, human scientists have little chance of under-standing and explaining the emergent properties of society and its economy.

The dependence of emergent levels of society and its economy on human psychology and genetics means that we should expect compatibility between the most fundamental principles of the 'lower' disciplines of neuroscience, evolu-tionary psychology, and the 'higher ones', such as social and economic sciences. Stated more clearly, social or economic scientific claims that are logically incon-sistent with fundamental, evolutionary lessons should demand particular scrutiny. Still, there is, of course, ample room, and need, for the social and eco-nomic sciences to develop explanations of social and economic phenomena in the vast areas where, for instance, evolutionary psychology is insufficient. The social and economic sciences have an especially important role to play in exam-ining and explaining the emergent properties of the social group or the market as a system, properties that are far more than the sum of each individual in the group or system (Pratten, 2013). Evolutionary science is itself a continuously developing field (several disciplines and fields, in fact), just like social science and economics. Thus, particularly the more specific claims in evolutionary research should be received with a similar analytical reserve, and be scrutinised in repeated studies, as should specific claims in social sciences and economics.

The structure of this book

Chapter 1 introduces the main conceptual distinctions on which my analysis is based. The following two chapters discuss the two dimensions that are used throughout the book: Apollonian and Dionysian dimensions. These dimensions help me identify not only differences but also similarities between the human scientific disciplines. I illustrate this by analysing, for instance, the causes of health differences between groups with high and low socio-economic status.

Chapter 4 presents an assumption that is based on indications from all three disciplines: That not only dignity but also social esteem is an overriding, universal human interest. This assumption is compared with factors such as happiness, wellbeing, honour, and even glory. The subsequent two chapters have as part of their purpose to scrutinise this assumption through the lenses of the disciplines. More explicitly, these two chapters analyse the so-called blank-slate perspective to the human mind. Arguments for and against this perspective are presented. I hold that the critical points by far outcompete the favourable ones. This leads to an exploration of what might be 'written' genetically on the human slate. I bring up recent research from evolutionary science and beyond. As to my initial assumption about dignity and social esteem, it turns out to be tenable, in light of the above-mentioned research overview from evolutionary science, combined with findings from social science and behavioural economics. I connect this outcome with the concept of social rationality that is developed throughout this book.

The last three main chapters of the book investigate how the three disciplines conceive of human interests in continuity and change. I show how continuity and change are far from clear-cut since they always have to be understood in their social and economic context. Social science may have a reputation of favouring social, political, and economic change. The more conservative side of social science is often forgotten, such as the emphasis on human interests in tradition and community, which necessitates a degree of continuity. Since large parts of the world are in one way or the other market-oriented, and many influential countries are market liberal, the economic approach is frequently seen as one of continuity (of a market liberal system). This is also in line with the traditional view among economists about human interests (called preferences) as stable (Binmore, 2005). Evolutionary science, finally, emphasises how all people share basic needs (food and shelter for oneself and one's kin). Evolutionary scientists indicate the relative material equality that characterised the human origin of nomadic, hunter-gatherer society, to which we all are genetically adapted (Gat, 2000). This aside, evolutionary science conceives of interests in continuity and change as based on the chances of individuals in various social positions to adapt to or change their social environment.

The final chapter draws conclusions from the book and discusses how these conclusions may be used for developing new dynamics between the social, economic, and evolutionary sciences. In focus are challenges and opportunities for finding a balance between making these sciences an integrated part of life sciences, while maintaining critical edges of social and economic sciences intact and further sharpened.

Part I

Manifest and latent interests

Prologue

This part of the book shows how humans and society at large can be thoroughly understood only if we bring into the picture both the manifest and latent dimensions of human interests. As with all dualisms, the one of the manifest and the latent is always in intimate interaction, in the brain as well as in culture. The two dimensions are perhaps never possible to analyse and understand in complete separation. Nonetheless, their different characteristics and their complementarity are continuously subject to research in large parts of the human sciences, and certainly deserve close attention in this book.

The stereotypical image of the social, economic, and evolutionary sciences is that they are more or less fully distinguishable concerning whether they consider manifest interests of dealing with explicit problems in the most efficient way or latent interests in social bonding, distinction, competition, culture, and so forth. According to the stereotypical image, economics would be preoccupied with manifest interests in society, interests in making choices that are selected strategically so that they maximise benefits and minimise costs. Evolutionary science would be concerned mainly with latent interests, since the latent level of, for example, 'pre-cognitive' mental processes is far older and more deeply rooted than is the capacity for systematic and conscious calculations about benefits and trade-offs towards optimal solutions to manifest problems. Social science would be concerned with both sides, according to the stereotypical image. However, this part of the book illustrates how all three human sciences have a foot on both sides, and more increasingly so than ever. The rapidly growing fields of behavioural economics and neuropsychology are examples of this, where the economist focus on the latent level of humans and society is increasing. Still, the proportions remain vastly different between the human sciences as to in which side they take their main interest.

The standard social science criticism of economics remains the issue of how economics, in its eagerness to handle manifest problems with economic instruments, sometimes disregards the importance of latent interests in preserving or creating the social glue that consists of culture, habits, traditions, and moral values. Evolutionary science, unsurprisingly, keeps its main focus on latent interests, since the 'interest of evolution' as well as the interest beneath human emotions, implies a very powerful type of rationality. In our terms, this is a basis that, when the perspective of evolutionary science is added to parts of the social and economic sciences, can be understood as 'social rationality'. This rationality differs substantially from the rationality that is confined to maximising the satisfaction of *manifest* interests defined by society or by latent, yet consciously strategic ones: such as maximising economic profit or reducing environmental harm.

1 Dual systems in the human sciences

A major reason human scientists find their research fields fascinating is presumably that human life, like all life, has not only a manifest level but also a latent one. We have to look for clues at the latent level to make sense of ordinary as well as extraordinary occurrences. To anyone imagining how intelligent creatures in space would try to make sense of ordinary situations on Earth, it becomes all the clearer that human scientists need to search for explanations and logics below the surface. Just to mention one situation that an intelligent, extraterrestrial creature would find peculiar, there is the huge difference in government spending (worldwide) between car-based infrastructure compared to bicycle- and public transport-based infrastructure. This gap remains huge even though traffic congestion in daily commuting is enormously costly for society and individuals concerning health, wellbeing, monetary costs, and environmental conditions. In the event people do not find this disparity peculiar, it is most likely due to the conventionality of congestive, car-based commuting. To understand, and fully explain it, however, is challenging, particularly how causes may partly differ between regions and countries. It demands extensive studies below the surface, of latent interests and structures.

What are manifest and latent interests?

Manifest interests refer to interests that are apparent, well recognised, and (seemingly) obvious. Latent interests, reversely, are the ones underlying the manifest level. Latent interests are hidden, concealed, invisible, or, at least, less apparent than interests at the manifest level. Based on these broad descriptions, it is possible to locate a plethora of human scientific perspectives, concepts, and theories that are located mainly at the manifest or latent level, or at both of them.

When latent, often subconscious, aspects of human interests are discussed, Sigmund Freud's psychodynamic perspective might for some readers be what first come to mind, especially his basic idea of the subconscious, the 'id' (Freud, 1930). Freud was of course very clever and immensely creative. Yet, significant parts of his theories are today placed in serious doubt. Some of his notions are pseudo-scientific in Popper's sense: They are impossible to falsify, whereas to be called science, Popper's criterion for science is that falsification of its claims must be, in principle, possible (Popper, 1959/2002). Some of Freud's work on dreams and dream interpretations may not meet this criterion. Other parts of Freudian thought constitute scientific theories, since they are, in principle, falsifiable. Neuroscience and social science have recently falsified certain other Freudian notions. For example, there is Freud's catharsis theory, contending that human aggression is stored at the latent level of the unconscious. Accordingly, aggression is continuously accumulated in a hydraulic system. Strong pressure is created after a while in this system, which necessitates that people vent the system, by letting the aggression out. This is a scientific claim, not a pseudo-scientific one. It is in principle falsifiable, and it has been falsified in practice. This theory has influenced or inspired a wide range of arrangements and activities, not least aimed at reducing aggression among violent and criminal men. Repeated studies have shown that encouraging aggressive people to act out their aggression (in controlled settings) rather increases their inclination to act aggressively after such sessions. Applying Freud's catharsis theory widely is therefore highly risky. This serves as an example of an erroneous theory that concerns the latent level of humans. Other Freudian theories that refer to the latent level have turned out to be more useful, such as work on psychological defence mechanisms advanced by his daughter, Anna Freud (Freud, 1936). Certain psychological defence mechanisms have even been elevated to 'human universals' in recent decades, identified in most if not all cultures (Brown, 2004). However, Anna Freud's explanations for the main latent function of defence mechanism turn out to be at odds with more recent studies in evolutionary science (Suddendorf, 2011). Leaving these shortcomings aside, Freudian contributions can hardly be overstated, to the creative arts, to the understanding of the importance of children's wellbeing, and to a wide-ranging recognition that human interests are much more than the manifest level reveals.

It should be noted that the Freuds did by no means discover the latent level. Notions of a latent level of human interests are several centuries, perhaps millennia, old, and are not least subject of much of Eastern philosophy (Moskowitz, Skurnik, & Galinsky, 1999). Throughout the last couple of centuries, and currently more than ever, Freudian notions of the latent levels are only a part of a broad range of ideas and studies of implicit, partly hidden, and sometimes unconscious processes of life and society take place in all human sciences. In this book, Freudian ideas are mentioned only very briefly, since they would have required an entirely separate category within the human sciences, to be given reasonable justice. Instead, when discussing social science, this book pays its main attention to other perspectives in, for instance, sociology and political science, crudely categorised as 'mainstream social science'.

To take an example from social science, the classical sociologist and economist Weber identifies the formal rationalisation that had taken place in the transformation from traditional to modern society. To be sure, people have always been equipped with the potential for seeking (albeit not always finding or choosing) the most efficient means of satisfying specific interests. Prior to modernity, however, this means-end patterns of action was what Weber calls a practical rationality (Weber, 1922/1978). It refers to a vague and often unsystematic tendency to solve immediate and routine problems using the most efficient means. Importantly, this practical rationality had (and still is, since it is still highly common) a strong personal bias, geared towards pragmatic self-interest, and oriented towards personal qualities of specific people in specific positions. Formal rationalisation, in contrast, is supposedly governed by formal rules in which personal qualities of specific people in certain positions are irrelevant. In modern society, it is possible for any person to identify in daily life at the manifest level how modernity is characterised by a high degree of bureaucratisation. This way of organising political and economic life was introduced with the manifest goal of avoiding corruption and nepotism. Moreover, modernity included division of labour and competence. It also entailed a strong work ethics, as well as increased expertise, all stimulated though commodification of most formal exchanges of goods and services. Underneath this manifest level of material improvements and rational activities, Weber analyses the latent level of modernisation. In his view, the latent level includes hidden interests behind this development, as well as unintended consequences that are often unapparent or even concealed to people's everyday awareness. On this note, the distinction between manifest and latent might be used to raise the question to what extent the transition from a complete, practical rationality to a formal one has entailed a mere movement of the satisfaction of certain personal, special interests from the manifest level (of which everyone was aware) to the latent, hidden one in modern society and onwards.

The following table shows the basic relations between the manifest and latent level of agency and structure. Concepts from the three human sciences are included. I will only briefly touch upon the obvious point that agency and structure are intertwined, co-dependent, and always in motion. The relationship between agency and structure are elaborated on far more extensively in several of the references used in this book representing the three human sciences.

Agency and structure – always floating

Concerning Weber's concept of formal rationality, he takes particular interest in analysing how that type of rationality, with its extensive focus on means, exerts enormous pressure from (in my terms) the latent structural level on people's interests and priorities. The concept of 'iron cage', in Table 1.1 (Square 4), refers to how modern people are stuck in how means, such as money and work, have become ends in themselves, a state of disillusion where the human satisfaction of more profound interests is never reached (Kalberg, 1980). To identify latent functions and partially concealed side effects of the manifest traits of modernity is an endeavour that Weber shares with several other classical social thinkers. Marx's terms 'alienation' and 'false consciousnesses' are only two of several terms he has coined to elucidate negative consequences of modern, capitalist

Table 1.1 Manifest and latent interests: agency and structure

Interests	Agency	Structure
Manifest	1 Conscious and purposeful activities aimed at satisfying manifest interests	2 Infrastructure, economic system, policy, planning, norms, institutions, social conventions aimed at satisfying manifest interests (equality or inequality)
Latent	3 Underlying, human motivation; moral foundations; human biases; hidden self-interest	4 Partially informal and hidden power relations, mechanisms behind these; qui bono?; iron cage; alienation; false consciousness; anomie; natural selection; invisible hand; social dilemmas

society. Durkheim uses the term 'anomie' to refer to the normlessness and moral chaos to which modernity may give rise.

However, social scientific identification of consequences and functions at the latent level does not necessarily have to concern reprehensible and pessimistic aspects. Another classical sociological thinker, Simmel, recognises, to be sure, similar developments at the manifest level, as does Weber. Simmel analyses how these developments are dependent on cultural changes at the manifest, structural level, such as an increased liberty of association, an increased freedom of people to invest only parts of their beings in each of the various groups and associations in which they chose to be engaged. This helps to stimulate creativity and innovation, on which modernity depends, particularly in capitalism (Simmel, 1900/2004). Finally, the sociologist Merton has elaborated extensively on the terms manifest and latent (about functions in society) from a sociological perspective. He employs these levels for examining interests among various groups of professionals, by comparing, for instance, medical doctors' manifest interests in serving humanity and reducing human suffering, and the latent functions of this profession, such as high social status (Campbell, 1982; Merton, 1959). In the terminology of this book, the benign ambitions at the manifest level may be best understood as a positive side effect of the latent function of gaining high social status. In sum, social science usually perceives the manifest level as highly varied – from reprehensible to good, depending on what takes place at the latent level of power relations. Both the manifest and latent levels are, according to large parts of social science, blank slates on which society, through its dynamics of structure and agency, writes what society's norms and power relations should be. If the lower segments of society have a genuinely active role in shaping and altering society's structures, a better society is in principle possible. Different class interests and conflicts at the latent level make struggles towards 'the good society' an adversarial and often a tragic one.

In traditional economics, however, the concept of 'the invisible hand', coined by Adam Smith in the eighteenth century (Smith 1790/2013), refers to a logic and order at the latent level that makes sense of, and among some human scientists helps to legitimise, individualist preoccupation of selfish interests at the manifest level. Agencies of single individuals (see Table 1.1, Square 1) may appear petty and narrow-minded. Economists must go beyond this level, and see what consequences this narrow-mindedness has in the aggregate. By looking beyond individual self-interest, even selfishness, Smith has become famous for recognising how the economic system of market liberalism (Table 1.1, Square 2) may reach an increasingly efficient production, with increased supply of afford-able goods and services as a result. These material benefits are best understood as being located at the manifest, structural level. Underneath this level operates the benign invisible hand that creates balance and better lives for all, given that society does not distort the space for this invisible hand to operate (Table 1.1, Square 4). It is hard to avoid associating Smith's notion of 'the invisible hand' with the hand of God. Whereas daily life for separate individuals may seem ruth-less and unfair, the larger schemes of things constitute a beautiful balance, given that the invisible hand is provided with its due space to operate through its own logic. Even so, Smith is ambivalent. In parallel with his hope for a benign, invis-ible hand, he disdains corporate greed and calls for the government never to adopt policies suggested by businessmen without thorough, prior scrutiny:

> The interest of the [businessman] is always in some respects different from, and even opposite to, that of the public ... The proposal of any new law or regulation of commerce which comes from this order ... ought never to be adopted, till after having been long and carefully examined ... with the most suspicious attention. It comes from an order of men ... who have generally an interest to deceive and even oppress the public.
>
> (Smith, 1776/1843, 107)

Finally, there is evolutionary science. Aside from evolution-based schools of thought, which claim the existence of 'group selection' and not just genetic selection (Wilson, 2012), evolutionary science is routinely interpreted as an approach that sees selfishness everywhere as the main human characteristic. It is fair to say that Dawkins' book *The Selfish Gene*, first published in 1976, is one of the most misunderstood books in modern times (Dawkins, 2006). If the reader mistakes genes for humans, the ruthless selfishness of genes described in that book becomes both highly implausible and utterly disturbing to read. Some social (and religious) thinkers that are sceptical of evolutionary theory base their scepticism on the gap they see between 'selfish genes' of 'natural selection' (Table 1.1, Square 4) and the high level of cooperation and unselfish behaviour that everyone may observe in daily life (Table 1.1, Squares 1 and 2). How can the beautiful parts of social life – warmth, loyalty, self-sacrifice, and generosity – exist at the manifest level, if all there is at the latent level are evolutionary pro-cesses of natural selection, such as selfish struggles of genes and individuals? It is not necessary to enter the infected debate of whether natural selection takes place at the level of individuals or groups to give a satisfying answer to this question. Even if Dawkins (who is strongly opposed to the notion of group selection) would be correct that all life is driven and evolves based on selfish genes, this would still be fully coherent with all the emotions and 'non-selfish' interests of humans: of love, solidarity, willingness to struggle collectively towards a more equal society, and to take enormous risks for others (not just for our kin). Supporting this view, the political scientist Axelrod has convincingly shown through statistics how some generosity benefits the generous person in the long run. Importantly, however, as everyone knows, solidarity, generosity, and care for others are typically 'unconscious' strategies felt in a profound and sincere manner (Axelrod, 2006).

One of the most elucidative responses from evolutionary science to the question about the gap between ruthless evolutionary processes and the unselfishness that exists among humans and non-humans comes from the primatologist Frans De Waal, who describes this misunderstanding as the 'Beethoven error'.

> The Beethoven error is to think that, since natural selection is a cruel, piti-less process of elimination, it can only have produced cruel and pitiless creatures.... In the same way Ludwig van Beethoven is said to have pro-duced his beautiful, intricate compositions in one of the most disorderly and dirty apartments of Vienna, there is not much of a connection between the process of natural selection and its many products.
>
> (De Waal, 2009, 58–9)

Evolutionary scholars appreciate the large-scale aesthetics and symmetry of natural selection, probably similar to the beauty economists may perceive in economic processes steered towards the 'equilibrium point', the price that leads to an equal amount of supply and demand, a point shaped by the invisible hand of the market. At the same time, evolutionary scholars of today do not hesitate to point to the ruthlessness of evolutionary processes regarding the immense suffering it creates both among humans and non-humans. They fully recognise the amoral character of natural selection at the latent level, a character that may entail everything from Hell to Heaven on Earth. As it turns out, what we all correctly identify at the manifest level as deep-felt compassion and gentle support for others may serve strong interests at the latent level of those who are compassionate and gentle ones at the manifest level. This dual impact takes place although the benevolent ones are often not aware of it, let alone have calculated it. Scholars have seen through analyses of large amounts of aggregate, statistical data, how following certain patterns of cooperation and support for others is most often highly functional and beneficial also to the people collaborating with and helping others, as long as others do not cheat on us (Axelrod, 2006). This makes it possible to identify the evolutionary basis for how it is possible for nature to have developed a human inclination of helping others, and how this inclination may increase the chances of survival and reproduction of less selfish individuals. Using another evolutionary terminology, it is many times favourable to 'selfish genes' (at the latent level) that humans have the drive and manifest interest in collaborating with and helping others, given that a sufficient degree of reciprocity between people prevails.

In sum, to understand the relationship between the manifest and latent levels of human existence in society is perhaps what the human sciences are all about. However, in the remainder of this book, the scope is a narrower one. Here, the manifest level concerns manifest interests in the sense of explicit and apparent interests in reducing certain manifest problems, such as problems with the environment, health, and comfort as well as to material and financial stability or accumulation. The latent interests that are subject to investigation here are partially unconscious, hidden interests. Sometimes these latent interests are interpreted as 'biases'. It is common that they are seen as distorting our manifest, 'sound' interests in solving manifest problems in the most efficient ways. As it turns out, the latent level has a strong social component that must be understood to get a deeper understanding of how human interests, manifest and latent, may be better satisfied in society. A key argument throughout this book is that the latent level of human interests, as 'irrational' and bias-producing it may seem, incorporates the better part of what makes humanity the tremendous (some would argue too tremendous) survival machine that it has been so far.

To recognise the distinction between manifest and latent interests, not just in the general sense, but also in the latter, more specific sense, is crucial to making the human sciences as stimulating and relevant to society as they can be. Very little can be deeply understood, and very little can be changed for the better in society, unless this distinction – in many of its variations – be treated seriously in human scientific analysis and society as a whole.

This is far from easy, of course. Consequently, the human sciences pay most attention to the manifest level. At this level, actors and organisations show their explicit, project-oriented interests that they often intend to satisfy through conscious calculation, and practical or formal rationality. This can be seen in efforts towards economic optimisation or explicit problem solving, such as in reduced harm to health or environment, problem solving subject to calculations of trade-offs between alternative choices and priorities. The latent level, on the other hand, is by parts of the human sciences and the surrounding society seen as a fussy, even unscientific, area to try to understand. There are three ways in which human scientists usually treat impacts from the latent level of human agency: The first way is to treat it as weak and insignificant, at least at the aggregate level, such as in some versions of rational-choice theory (Eriksson, 2011). The second way is to treat the latent level of agency as strong, but as filled with biases and shortcomings distorting people from what this scientific perspective has in focus: the optimising of manifest interests. The second way usually entails a preoccupation with how people could be 'nudged' into avoiding the pitfalls of the latent level of human agency (Thaler, 2015). Accordingly, people should be lightly and voluntarily pushed to pursue their manifest projects in more practically and formally rational, linear, and straightforward manners. To nudge individuals and institutions to maximise their manifest interest (by helping them make the choices that satisfy such an interest to the highest extent), or to optimise (by helping them select the alternative that is most cost effective for satisfying a certain interest), are the main ways in which behavioural economics is applied.

This book asserts that even if the first way to treat the latent level is based on an incorrect understanding of human motivation, that level first may actually have its proper place in specific issues of possible effects of policies of incentives and disincentives for large groups and categories of people. On a large scale, there seem to be cases where individual variations in latent interests are evened out. Effects of certain taxation policies, environmental premiums for purchases of cars with low emissions, may be examples of this. Still, more often than not, the misunderstanding that is the basis for ignoring or downplaying interests at the latent level entails faulty predictions of human activities, as several indications show throughout this book. The second way to treat the latent level is more accurate. Humans are indeed prepared, at the latent level, with predispositions for certain ways of making decisions that may seem flawed and biased in cases of, for instance, individual and specific decision making with long-term consequences, decision making that modern life forces us to make. However, by treating the latent level as mainly biased and flawed, there is the risk that the social motivation of the latent level is downplayed. Instead, this book advances a third way for the human sciences to conceive of the latent level. This book argues for broadening the analysis in human science beyond the hyper-specific decisions of planning for their financial future or other manifest interests. Human scientific examinations also need to include how individuals and society's institution may better seek not only manifest but also latent human interests – beyond the individual, specific decisions. This requires examining latent traits not merely as biases, but as instruments of what in this book is called social rationality.

Dionysian and Apollonian dimensions

The distinction between two mental systems has been identified in groups, cultures, and whole societies. For example, the nineteenth-century philosopher Nietzsche demonstrates how the history of theatre, music, and other fine arts could be understood as an oscillation between what he called Dionysian and Apollonian ideals (Nietzsche, 1872/2010). Accordingly, the Romantic era of the nineteenth century embedded a culture embracing Dionysian traits, whereas the preceding period, classicism, along with the Enlightenment, elevated Apollonian traits as ideal. The distinction between these two gods stems from Ancient Greek mythology. Dionysus has through millennia been admired, as well as disdained, for his (or her; Dionysus is sometimes depicted as female) impulsiveness, spontaneity, quickness, drinking, orgies (albeit more meditative than erotic), partial unconsciousness, and apparent thoughtlessness. Nietzsche, although calling himself 'a disciple of Dionysus', tailors Dionysus into a character that corresponds with Nietzsche's own personality as a passionate, introverted individualist. In this book, however, it is essential to keep the dimension of the Dionysian much closer to the ancient view. In Kourvetaris' words, the ancient view of the Dionysian emphasises the role of ecstasy, wild dance, and intoxication, 'experienced always by the individuals in a group' (Kourvetaris, 1997, 231). The overriding role of the group, often by forgetting about one's individuality, is central to the ancient view of the Dionysian. His half-brother, Apollo, is an opposite character, highly conscious, controlled, self-constrained, long-term planning, slow, making well-informed decisions. Being the god of health and soundness, Apollo is apt for representing, for instance, many of our modern society's persistent efforts and hopes to improve human wellbeing and reduce environmental harm. Apollo is a visionary god (Kingsbury & Jones, 2009). Apollonian visions have been particularly vivid in Western society, especially since the Enlightenment. In focus are Apollonian interests in making life safer, more comfortable, and pleasurable, by reducing or even eliminating suffering out of material shortage (Nesse, 2005). Moreover, there is a distinctly Apollonian trait in the notion of economic rationality. This trait involves making sure that the goals such as improved wellbeing and reduced environmental harm, be reached as efficiently as possible, at all levels of society, from the individual, through organisations and corporations to entire countries, and beyond.

To be sure, the Apollonian dimension is particularly easy to associate with manifest interests. Interests in solving substantive problems are to a great extent manifest ones. Reversely, the Dionysian dimension is readily associated with the latent level. Interests in strengthening social identity, bonding, and esteem are to a great extent latent. One of the several reasons is that humans are better at convincing others that they are trustworthy and loyal to the group if they fully believe in their own trustworthiness, and signal this honesty unconsciously to the group (Trivers, 2011). Thus, I usually refer to 'manifest, Apollonian interests' when I write 'Apollonian interests', and refer 'latent, Dionysian interests', when I write 'Dionysian interests' in this book. At the same time, there are clear, latent traits of Apollonian interests, as in hidden strategies aimed at satisfying financial interests, strategies not visible to others, and sometimes not entirely understandable to the actor herself. Reversely, there are manifest traits of Dionysian interests, as in many kinds of explicit, social initiatives where the social bonding seems to be an intrinsic goal. Less common are manifest efforts towards satisfying the Dionysian interests in social esteem.

We have already seen in Table 1.1 how the social, economic, and evolutionary sciences recognise and analyse interests at the manifest as well as latent levels. For instance, the fact that economics emphasises strategic agency does not lead this discipline to downplay latent factors such as hidden strategic agency or market structures where a latent, invisible hand may operate. Again, however, to try to place an entire discipline in one of these categories turns out to be as futile as attempts to do so by placing each discipline at one of the manifest or latent levels. Table 1.2 and the rest of this book show how the perspectives of the disciplines are further understood by bringing the Dionysian and Apollonian dimensions into the picture. Here, human interests take place within four fields. Yet, the Dionysian and Apollonian dimensions are always interdependent. Their interdependence can be seen in relationships across this table. As an example, employers, market actors, or policy makers can at the manifest level make use of people's Dionysian interests (Square 1). This can be done through work retreats,

Table 1.2 Manifest and latent interests: Dionysian and Apollonian

Interests	Dionysian	Apollonian
Manifest	1 Open, conscious, purposeful, and explicit strategies for how best to satisfy Dionysian interests (e.g. in social bonding, exclusion, and esteem)	2 Open, conscious, purposeful, and explicit strategies for how best to satisfy Apollonian interests (e.g. in improved health, reduced environmental harm, increased material accumulation, and comfort)
Latent	3 Hidden, implicit or unconscious interests (e.g. in social bonding, exclusion, and esteem), often obscured by manifest, Apollonian interests and activities	4 Hidden or implicit interests and strategies for how best to satisfy Apollonian interests (e.g. in improved health, reduced environmental harm, increased material accumulation, and comfort)

Tupperware parties, or socially oriented entertainment in order to better satisfy their own or society's implicit and latent, Apollonian interest (Square 3) in increasing the productivity of employees, of making profits, or reducing environmental harm. Another example is when people and organisations focus entirely on trying to maximise or optimise the satisfaction of manifest, Apollonian interests (Square 2). This is seen in endeavours explicitly aimed at maximisation of safety, comfort, convenience, and choices, whereas the latent, Dionysian interests often override these interests when the two are in conflict. The evolutionary biologist and political scientist, Johnson, has examined how humans and cultures throughout history, and still today, are inclined to believe in myths and unsubstantiated knowledge claims (a compromise in Square 2). We do this with the latent Dionysian benefit of reducing individual selfishness and strengthening the bonding and loyalty of a community (Johnson, 2016). He shows evidence that even the sense that God is constantly watching you is part of this evolutionary adaptation to the necessity of trust and loyalty between people in a group. 'We act as if our thoughts and actions will be judged, if not by God, then by some other cosmic, carmic, or super-natural force. And again it does not have to be religious' (Johnson, 2016, 6).

The notion of an Apollonian and Dionysian dimension is consistent with the neuroscientific findings of dual mental systems (Sherman, Gawronski, & Trope, 2014). This is so despite the fact that Nietzsche is in some of his writings sceptical of Darwinian natural selection (Johnson, 2010). This scepticism seems to be based more on a misunderstanding of Darwinian principles than about any thorough disagreement. Today, it stands clear that the notions of Apollonian and Dionysian dimensions (which were initially created in Ancient Greek mythology) are fully coherent with evolutionary theory and neuroscience. The first thing to be noticed in a neuroscientific reflection is that the Dionysus–Apollo distinction is neither directly translatable to emotion versus reason nor irrationality versus rationality. In fact, as social science has long shown, and neuroscience has confirmed, emotion and reason are never entirely separated (Evans & Cruse, 2004). Consequently, the Dionysus–Apollo distinction is best understood as representing two types of logic that are mutually dependent (logics which both involve emotions, yet in different ways).

It has only been a question of time before both the Apollonian and Dionysian sides have started to be recognised by all human sciences. It is gratifying to see today that all three human sciences currently to a certain extent accommodate research that is translatable to Dionysian and Apollonian dimensions of humans and society. To what extent this entails their taking into account both dimensions for understanding human interests remains to be examined in the rest of this book. The views differ substantially across the disciplines concerning the relative weight of the systems, what they are, how they can be explained, and how they relate to human interests. There are vast differences in how the two Apollonian and Dionysian dimensions are interpreted and analysed in the respective human sciences, and what types of policy recommendations these interpretations entail. Thus, there is a strong need to sort out assumptions about human interests in the Apollonian and Dionysian sides of scholarships in all three disciplines. This analytical effort is necessary in order to identify areas where misconceptions exist, and where there is potential for active learning between the two sides and between the disciplines about human interests.

Example: Apollonian or Dionysian factors behind worse health of low socio-economic status groups?

Studies consistently show that belonging to the category of people with low socio-economic status entails an increasing risk of a broad range of health risks (Pillas *et al.*, 2014). This category of people can expect lives that are several years shorter, on average, than can people in the middle- or upper-class categories. There is scientific consensus that psychiatric diseases, rheumatoid arthritis, cardiovascular disease, gastrointestinal disorders, and pulmonary disorders, to only mention a few types of health problems, are far more prevalent among people at lower socio-economic levels. Why do so many diseases and disorders follow this socio-economic pattern? Moreover, why do so many diseases and disorders follow a clear socio-economic continuum? First of all, scientists have falsified the assumption that the general causality pattern would be one where unhealthy people end up in lower socio-economic classes. Instead, we should stick to possible factors that make people with lower socio-economic status worse off regarding health.

The Apollonian inclination in parts of all the human sciences is to search for explanations in absolute levels of access that people in different socio-economic categories have to various resources. The levels of access to resources that people with lower socio-economic status have (regardless of what people of higher status have) are what matter for their health levels meticulously.

Unsurprisingly, improvements to health among people at all socio-economic levels, whether in the developed or developing world, are to a great extent a result of improved medicine, health access, safer workplaces, reduced violence, and improved economic resources wherever such improvements have taken place. In other words, strengthening Apollonian factors have generated health improvements among entire populations.

Does this mean that Apollonian factors may also explain the differences in health among people with high and low levels of socio-economic status? Not as much as we might think. Scholars from all human sciences and social medicine have studied the role of Apollonian factors carefully. Access to health care is such a possible factor. Yet, the health difference persists also in countries where there is socialised medicine available to everyone. Clearly, access is not merely about formal access, but also about more subtle aspects such as seeking health care on time, where we can find particular socio-economic differences. At the same, the health inequality also persists in health problems where it does not matter how often the person seeks medical care, such as mild types of juvenile diabetes. Aside from access to health care, many other Apollonian factors – risk factors and protective factors – should be investigated. Several lifestyle factors are possible: whether people eat healthy food or junk food, have risky jobs, live near hazardous, toxic areas, do physical exercise or not, live in safe or unsafe neighbourhoods, and so forth. All these Apollonian factors turn out to matter. However, they only explain around one-third of the differences in health and life expectancy between people of high and low socio-economic status.

Cholesterol levels, smoking, blood pressure, and physical exercise and other lifestyle factors have in longitudinal studies of civil servants in the UK only explained one-third of the health differences between people of low and high socio-economic status (Marmot, 2005; Sapolsky, 2004; Wilkinson, 2001; Wilkinson & Pickett, 2006).

This means that we have to expand the analysis by also taking Dionysian factors into account. Human science scholars have long recognised the significance of certain types of long-term stress for bad health. Moreover, they are increasingly acknowledging how patterns of stress differ substantially between people who have low and high socio-economic status. Summarising the research literature on the relationship between stress and socio-economic level, the neurobiologist Sapolsky provides the following list of factors: (a) a sense of minimal control over the conditions that lead to stress; (b) limited outlets for frustration that the stressor causes; (c) a sense of no predictability about the intensity and duration of the stressor; (d) interpretations of the stressor as a sign that the circumstances are worsening; (e) lack of social support for reducing the stressor and the sense of pressure; (f) lack of support from family, friends, and community, for the duress that the stressors cause (Sapolsky, 2005). Some of these problematic factors are partly Apollonian, in the sense that they could be reduced through social, political, and occupational measures to improve, for instance, the working conditions for low-status jobs (by reducing the work hours, reducing monotony, making the workplace safer, etc.).

Yet, there are deeper problems here. There seems to be something intrinsically bad for people's health by a constant sense that they have lower socio-economic status than others. Even when researchers keep the work tasks and material living conditions constant (in an Apollonian sense), there are significant differences in stress, and thus in health and life expectancy, between groups of high and low socio-economic status (Marmot & Brunner, 2005). Even in countries with universal medicine, and even when taking into account lifestyle differences between different socio-economic groups, office messengers face several times higher risks of chronic heart diseases than do people doing paperwork at higher status levels, such as administrators and executives (Marmot, 2005). Moreover, this health difference persists far beyond the age of retirement, as Marmot has shown through longitudinal studies of civil servants at different levels of the hierarchy. The striking persistence of health differences between different socio-economic groups has, moreover, been seen in elegant studies that appear to constitute a perfect 'experiment'. Nuns in a convent live under identical conditions, in the Apollonian sense (routines, social interaction, food, and other material conditions). Still, substantial, stress-related health differences are found between nuns aged 70, differences where genetic factors and Apollonian factors can be ruled out. The consistent basis for these health differences turns out to be the differences in socio-economic status prior at the age (around 18–20 years old) when the women on average have become nuns. It seems as if each nun carries her socio-economic status with them throughout life. This probably takes place through the interaction of the nuns, where sociolects, cultural capital, and perhaps self-confidence, in general, are constantly signalled between the nuns all through their lives. The lower her socio-economic level before becoming a nun, the higher the risk is of stress, and in turn of worse health also decades after that (Snowdon, 2008). This finding should be compared with studies of how social and economic inequalities in childhood impact people's health in adult life (Pillas *et al.*, 2014).

The phenomenon of carrying one's status level in one's body and mind is very similar to what the sociologist Bourdieu denotes by his term 'habitus' (Bourdieu, 1990). In parallel with his investigation of this phenomenon, it is recognised and examined through a variety of research methods in parts of the other human sciences as well, yet applied to health through a variety of methods. The key point is the importance of people's relative position in the hierarchy, their Dionysian interests. The crucial role of people's Dionysian interests to their health and wellbeing has, moreover, been investigated through studies of income inequality in communities. Through 15 years of research, the social epidemiologists Pickett and Wilkinson, together with their colleagues, have found that greater income disparities between the wealthiest and poorest in a community predict lower levels of health, on average, than in communities of less inequality. Intriguingly, this result is found regardless of the absolute levels of income (above the levels where people's basic material needs are met). Even more striking is that decreased income inequality seems to predict better health not just for the poor but also for the wealthy (Pickett & Wilkinson, 2008). All these findings point towards the highly significant role of the Dionysian dimension for wellbeing and health. It raises several human scientific as well as policy-oriented questions of how society may better help to satisfy human *interests*.

Conclusions

The human sciences are united in recognising that human interests, to be fully understood, must be examined at more than one level.

The manifest level is where explicit, open interests can be identified. The latent level is where implicit, hidden, or sometimes even unconscious interests can be found. In order to identify interests at the latent level, we must think more creatively about research methods. This is done by bringing in indirect methods, large-scale analyses of aggregate behaviour patterns, and more recently brain scanning.

Both agency and structure have a manifest and a latent level. It has become a truism that agency and structure exert a mutual influence on each other in processes of social change. To fully see this in analyses, both the manifest and latent levels of agency and structure need to be elucidated. The three human sciences emphasise different parts of the four fields that the two dualisms constitute. Parts of the human sciences ignore entire fields here.

The chapter introduces still a dualism, of Dionysian and Apollonian interests. It has its basis in Greek mythology, scholarship in the humanities, and has more recently received (implicit) support from neuroscience and behaviour economics. This dualism reflects the more instinctive interests in social bonding, status, and esteem (Dionysian) and the controlled, planned, strategic, gratification-delayed traits of humans and cultures, for instance in increasing comfort, efficiency, benefits to health, environment, and to one's economy (Apollonian). The Dionysian and Apollonian dimensions do not imply a separation between emotions and reason. Instead, they follow two different logics, and emotions and reason are parts of both logics. Social rationality usually involves an interplay of the Dionysian and Apollonian dimensions.

2   The Apollonian dimension

The Apollonian dimension in economics

Positive-sum games and economic efficiency

If we begin by shedding some light on Apollonian contributions from the three disciplines, economics, again, comes most easily to mind. Economics has a strong tradition of emphasising that people are rational at the manifest level and that people make sure they are sufficiently informed to calculate how to best satisfy their manifest interests. Counter to what the other human sciences routinely claim about economics, this does not necessarily imply that the most fundamental human interest or goal is to maximise material accumulation. Rather, rationality, according to economists, concerns means, not ends. This science rests on the belief that people are usually rational, picking the most efficient means to reach the end with which they are most happy. No end, or manifest interest (often called preference), is in principle more rational than another interest. This means that economic rationality usually refers to calculating the benefits and trade-offs of alternative choices, and ending up with a suggestion of what is the *optimal* level of the good or service, above which it costs more than it benefits the individual. At the same time, since money in most current societies is one of the most efficient means towards meeting manifest interests of comfort, convenience, personal health, and increased personal choices, economics usually finds it unlikely that people would make choices that strongly go against the preference for economic wealth and accumulation. Therefore, it is nevertheless relevant here to discuss the focus on economic human interests. Particularly traditional economics has a reputation for placing an overwhelming emphasis on economically rational choice when making assumptions and drawing conclusions in their research. This sometimes includes a Homo economicus view of human interests. The term stems from Mill's description of what he calls 'economic man': '... a being who desires to possess wealth, and who is capable of judging the comparative efficacy of means for obtaining that end' (Mill, 1844, 137).

Even if we do not use this straw man to illustrate a traditional view in economics of human interests, it is fair to say that economics is founded on the following idea:

Increased economic efficiency that is obtained by individuals, companies, organisations, and states that voluntarily exchange goods and services is the way to better meet the (manifest) interests of the rich and poor alike. To be sure, Apollonian interests do not need to refer to financial interests. Still, the vision of economic efficiency is certainly Apollonian, a vision involving planning, systemacy, balance, and – as economists might hold – human wellbeing.

Before Mill makes the term 'economic man' famous, the founding father of classical economics, Smith (1776/1843), argues that increased division of labour is the key to greater economic efficiency. Again, this ideal is an Apollonian one. Smith gives the example of division of labour in pin production. When different workers are responsible for isolated parts of the production process, more pins can be produced in a shorter time by a lower number of workers than if each worker were responsible for the whole production process of a pin. As a consequence, pins can be purchased more cheaply than before. Less affluent people are also able to buy the number of pins that they need. To be sure Smith, and subsequently Marx, well recognise the immense boredom and impoverishment of the soul that this division of labour may entail for workers. Moreover, Smith argues that division of labour could entail 'the almost entire corruption and degeneracy of the great body of the people … unless government takes some pains to prevent it [i.e. corruption and degeneracy]' (Smith, 1776/1843, 327). Nonetheless, increased economic efficiency would at the end of the day favour human, manifest interests more than inefficiency. Particularly, if provided with education, something to which Smith strongly subscribes, workers could become free to move on and apply for alternative occupations, Smith argues.

What is at the heart of economic efficiency that economists hold so dear? From Smith and onwards lies the conviction that every voluntary exchange of goods and services between two or more independent actors increases the satisfaction of Apollonian interests – and indirectly, hopefully, Dionysian interests, of all parties involved. All parties get a share of the increased value that each exchange generates. Smith famously claims that if everyone acted based on her or his direct self-interest on the market, this would create a market beneficial to society as a whole. Self-interest can refer to individuals, but in some cases also to the (collective) self-interest of groups, corporations, and organisations (Tullberg, 2006). Moreover, self-interest is in many cases highly compatible with collaboration, albeit where the others serve as instruments to someone's selfish goals (Sabbagh, 2010).

The key notion is that self-interests may generate increased satisfaction of collective interests. As Smith points out, no actor – not even workers on the assembly line – would agree to offer their services (as in workers offering their time and effort to the employer) or goods, unless it satisfies their interests more than not offering these services or goods. Full economic efficiency has been fully reached once there is no alternative state of affairs in which some people in the exchange would be better off without this making anyone else worse off. The state of economic efficiency is also called Pareto-optimality. Even if economists often like to portray their human science as independent of particular values and interests of people, the concept of economic efficiency and Pareto-optimality rests on the assumption that each person always prefers an alternative that is more efficient, cheaper, or more reliable, or that in other ways improves and even maximises the satisfaction of the specific, manifest interest at stake.

Every actor, organisation, corporation, or state, according to traditional economics, has this Apollonian trait, and uses it to meet their interests. This points to the notion among economists of rationality: to respond to incentives to increase the satisfaction of one's interests. The conviction that all parties that are involved always gain from market exchange means that economists stress that market exchange, in the sense of trade, is a positive-sum game (sometimes called a non-zero-sum game). Social thinkers, at least since the fourth century philosopher and church father, St Augustine, long before Smith, assume that market exchange is a zero-sum game, where one actor's gain means another actor's loss. St Augustine maintains that 'if one does not lose, the other does not gain' (Muller, 2007, 6). Smith, and virtually all his followers, including traditional economists of today, frame market exchange completely differently: Market exchange and exchange is a positive-sum game, where all parties involved are winners. This view, in turn, is the basis for the general optimism in economics about the benefits of economic growth. To meet our manifest interests is what human interests are to a large extent about, this view contends. Through economic efficiency in free capitalism of free individuals, there is ample room for increasing these interests to a higher degree the more efficient the economy becomes.

All humans are responsive to incentives and disincentives

Accordingly, all actors have potential to increase the level to which their manifest interests are satisfied. From the perspective of positive-sum games and economic efficiency, people are not in any complete sense captives within social, economic, or cultural structures. Since no one is immune to incentives and disincentives, people are always able to do certain calculations about pros and cons of his or her actions, habits, and routines. Not even people or groups on society's margins, people such as drug addicts or criminals, are fully caught in underlying social, cultural, economic, mental, or physiological structures. Even they make conscious choices at the manifest level, actively weighing costs and benefits of their activities. For many decades, psychiatrists have tried to cure addiction – to drugs, alcohol, or the like – as a disease. However, some economists find this approach illogical. If addiction were a disease, it would be impossible just to quit it. As economists point out, however, it is very common that people quit their addiction. The scientific problem is accordingly that the human sciences do not fully understand the rationality behind addiction, how addicts satisfy their interests through rational choices. The term 'rational addiction' is used by the economist, Becker, along with his colleague Murphy. (In other studies they have also investigated what they call the rationality of crime.) They use this term 'rational addiction' for understanding how even drug addicts can be argued to do active, cost-benefit calculations of their drug use (Becker & Murphy, 1988). In that theory, cost-benefit calculations refer to calculations that go far beyond money. The calculations may refer to a broad range of human interests. Studies using this perspective have focused particularly on individuals and groups on society's margins, people who nevertheless seem to make active choices in changing their lives based on their manifest, explicit interests (Ferguson, 2000). For instance, in the Vietnam War, half of American soldiers have been reported to have used opium or heroin regularly. Still, despite problems with addiction, 90 per cent of them appear to have quit using drugs when they got back to the US. According to Heyman, a psychologist influenced by the economic theory of rational addiction, this majority of Vietnam veterans had actively responded to incentives and disincentives surrounding the use of drugs. Their Apollonian reasoning, with long-term plans and visions, and their calculations of how to make these visions materialise, seem to have dominated. Having a stable relationship, a family, a job, and a stable circle of friends were incentives that made them quit their drug use. Similarly, 75 per cent of all drug addicts living in the US, mainly students, quit when they are around 30 years old, 70 per cent without even seeking help. They have actively and consciously made their own choice, voluntarily, out of freedom and power to have an impact on their lives (Heyman, 2010). Scholars of rational addiction consequently argue that the human sciences should shift the focus from those who do not quit their addictive behaviour to the majority of addicts who subsequently quit their use of whatever they are addicted to. A more general conclusion of this strand of economic thought is that human agency is to a large extent rooted on the manifest level of conscious, rational choice, where people, groups, and organisations actively compare costs and benefits.

According to traditional economic thinking, it is often not necessary to move beneath the manifest level. Supporting or hindering factors beneath individual agency are either illusory, weak, or surmountable unless they impede free market exchange and fair competition. If not even the majority of people at society's margins (criminals, drug addicts) are captives of latent forces, then still less so are people located closer to the centre of society's statistical bell curve, the argument contends. The notion, discussed above, of 'rational addiction' examined in studies of seemingly excessive food consumption, soda drinking, alcohol or drug use, reflects a view common among economists that not even people at society's margins are complete captives (Richards, Patterson, & Tegene, 2007).

The commons and social dilemmas

As I have already mentioned, economists conceive of economic efficiency on a market of economic growth as beneficial to everyone's manifest interests. Market exchange is a positive-sum game, where each party who chooses to be involved in a market exchange increases her or his interest satisfaction. This is the root of the positive views on market exchange among economists. However, economists admit that rationality, if interpreted as people's capacity and inclination to use the most efficient means to reach their manifest interests, leads to problems in certain contexts. Whereas they conceive of the market as an arena that ideally is based on positive-sum games, they still recognise – and analyse – the many situations in modern society in which individual rationality leads to socially undesired outcomes. The economist Schelling, for instance, has studied a wide range of social problems from this perspective. Racial segregation in neighbourhoods is one such problem. Refreshingly, he does not divide the world into one of complete racists versus complete non-racists. Instead, he analyses the actual choices of where to live. Judged by their 'revealed preferences' (their actual moving patterns) most people seem to fit in neither of the two extremes. Instead, most people reveal a preference for partial segregation. Yet, few people show with their choice of housing that they accept to be part of a racial minority smaller than one-third in their neighbourhood (this proportion differs between studies and between which minorities are studied). What happens when everyone prefers a certain degree of racial diversity whereas no one prefers to be part of a minority smaller than one-third? Once the neighbourhood has reached a 'tipping point', towards such a disproportion, people of that minority start to move. A migration pattern begins between neighbourhoods, which 'mathematically' leads to what very few individuals appreciate: extreme segregation. The individual rationality of acting according to one's interest in partial segregation leads to the undesired collective outcome of a far higher degree of segregation (Schelling, 1977/2006).

Schelling has also studied environmental issues, such as traffic congestion, particularly how the individual choice of travel mode involves a tension between individual (economic) rationality and social consequences that are problematic for everyone. If we move further into the environmental domain, preservation of a natural environment usually has the character of a zero-sum game. An individual's or company's, gain from exploiting global commons – water, air, and soil, for instance – entails a loss for the rest of the population (human, non-human, and plants) today and in the future. According to the dominant view of rationality among economists, individuals and companies are doomed to try to become 'free riders', exploiting the global, regional, or local commons to a greater extent than would be sustainable if everyone did it. From an economics perspective, it can indeed be rational for individuals, at the aggregate level of multiple people, to destroy the planet, even if no one wishes that anyone else be allowed to harm the planet. Heavily influenced by game theory, which is nowadays included as a branch within economics, economists recognise this as 'the tragedy of the commons', particularly in the context of environmental pollution. The biologist Hardin coined this phrase. He bases his now famous article about this issue (Hardin, 1968) on a pamphlet from 1833 by an English economist, Forester Lloyd. The latter notes that herders who share a common land tend to lead this land to overgraze. As long as it does not cost them anything extra, single individuals, groups, companies, and states will always be motivated to exploit the commons more than others, at the expense of the larger collective. This is in line with the Apollonian manner of always searching for the most efficient means to satisfy one's manifest interests, for instance in comfort, convenience, and material prosperity. Moreover, since global commons are, at least in part, of a zero-sum character, this human drive takes place at the expense of others. All human sciences try to find ways for society of handling this problem. Economists attempt to develop ways of reorganising parts of the global commons so that they become subject to positive-sum games. The basic recipe by economists is to set, or change, the price that polluters have to pay. A price can be constant, by adding environmental taxes to the relevant practices, such as flight transportation or beef consumption. Alternatively, a region may introduce a cap and trade system. This refers to governments setting a ceiling on how much total emissions is allowed during a certain period. Each polluter, such as certain companies, is either given, or can purchase permits to pollute at a particular maximum level. If they find ways to be more energy efficient (or whatever the permits concern), they can sell parts of their permits to others, who will then be allowed to pollute more than what is allowed with one permit (Baldursson & Sturluson, 2011). According to economists, this makes actors aware of the 'opportunity cost' of continuing to pollute as usual, in extension stimulating environmentally friendly innovation. This cost is, in this case, the alternative that the actor has the strongest interest in pursuing, but has to forgo if the actor continues to pollute as usual. As an addition to taxation as well as cap and trade systems, economists analyse the possible consequences of privatising parts of the global commons as such (forests, land, and so forth), so that the owner(s), based on the same rationality, will be motivated to preserve this part. In sum, these instruments are developed and analysed by economists with the aim of managing in an economically efficient way the free rider temptations to exploit global commons.

The Apollonian dimension in evolutionary science

Evolutionary science often criticises economics for having a simplistic and even erroneous understanding of humans. For instance, through findings from studies of the brain, evolutionary science draws conclusions that differ substantially from the view of traditional economics about incentives and disincentives. Dopamine is a neurotransmitter in the brain strongly associated with how people determine value and seek reward. However, it is not the case that dopamine neurons respond to incentives and disincentives themselves. Instead, dopamine neurons respond to the difference between our expectations and reality. The fire rate of dopamine is increased when the reward is higher than people's expectations; moreover, the firing rate decreases when the reward turns out to be lower than people's expectations. Importantly, when people receive rewards or punishment (what economists often call incentives and disincentives) that are equal to what people expect, the dopamine neurons neither increase or decrease in their firing rate, and does not make people very motivated to act according to these incentives or disincentives (Berridge & Robinson, 1998). Such evolutionary scientific findings indicate that the design of incentives and disincentives is far more complicated than traditional economics has recognised (findings on which behavioural economics elaborates further).

At the same time, parts of evolutionary science have Apollonian features comparable with those of Apollonian strands of thought in economics. It would have been strange otherwise. Both economics and evolutionary science concern competition and collaboration over access to limited resources. The notion of positive-sum games, for instance, is an important one, not just in economics but also in evolutionary science about human interests. The evolution-oriented science writer Wright devotes his entire book, entitled *Nonzero* to trying to show how not only humans are motivated by positive-sum games, but how the very phenomenon of positive-sum games is the basis for all life and interaction on earth (Wright, 2001). Beginning at the molecular and cellular levels, Wright indicates – with impressive stringency – how molecules, organisms, via Homo sapiens and to global information networks have all evolved, and continue to evolve, based on cooperation where both, or all, parties have their manifest interests satisfied through the mutual benefits of cooperation and sharing. Wright even claims that there is an inherent directionality in evolution, from primitive and to more complex positive-sum games. Ultimately, all parts of the world, not least humans, groups, organisations, corporations, and states will be fully connected globally in a way that violent and aggressive acts would cost more for each potential aggressor than it would potentially benefit each potential aggressor.

Wright is a science writer, and he has collated and analysed research that to a large extent comes from the field of evolutionary game theory. Both economic game theory and evolutionary game theory are obviously interested in games: strategic interaction between players. Yet, there are two clear differences. Whereas economists suppose that people are rational in the economic sense of the term, evolutionary scientists claim not to believe so. Nor do evolutionary scientists assume that 'actors' – be it people, animals, plants, or cells – are aware of the game in question. For our purposes, it is interesting that evolutionary science does not presuppose that humans are necessarily conscious and knowledgeable of what matters from an evolutionary perspective. It is possible for people to operate in a strategic way without being aware of their own latent interests beneath these operations. In Wright's examples, a lot of positive-sum games between people as well as between lower creatures at all levels of biology, may benefit both parties yet without them being aware of it.

Reciprocal altruism as Apollonian

When discussing the Apollonian dimension of human interests, the logic of reciprocal altruism is central. To be sure, reciprocal altruism seems to operate among virtually all forms of life, including very simple organisms. At the same time, there is something reasoned, self-disciplined, and even 'cerebral', about reciprocal altruism as regards human collaborations to manage problems. From an individual's point of view of direct self-interest, several problems at stake might not be the most urgent ones. Still, it is crucial to handle several bigger issues in light of the interest of the group, the entire humanity, and many other life forms on earth.

The logic of reciprocal altruism moves beyond the latent interest in directly spreading one's genes individually or via biological relatives (or pseudo-kin), interests that I discuss in the next chapter. Instead, reciprocal altruism implies the development of trust towards collaboration for mutual benefits also among unrelated individuals, groups, states, or regions. Reciprocal altruism implies that in most social situations there is potential for cooperation mutually beneficial to the parties involved.

Ever since Trivers' groundbreaking paper (Trivers, 1971), evolutionary science has identified reciprocal altruism as a strong part of evolution. A potential for human interests in social and political change emerges by recognising – consciously or unconsciously – the possible mutual gain also between us and people other than our kin or pseudo-kin.

All people and groups are in one way or another involved in cooperation based on reciprocal altruism. However, there are a few but very significant challenges. As game theory contends, collaboration is dependent on a first risky move, as well as in establishing and maintaining mutual trust between the parties involved. The party that begins to offer help in an attempt towards collaboration is always at the risk of not having her or his favour reciprocated. To be sure it may appear as a small thing to do others a favour without getting anything back that time. However, throughout human history the favours have included extremely dangerous or important ones, such as helping out in the hunting of large animals or taking care of someone else's baby when the parent is sick. Moreover, hunter-gatherer society – to which humans are genetically adapted – entailed mainly long-term relationships where trust, as well as sensitivity to the level of trustworthiness of others, was key to survival. The logic of reciprocal altruism, which is 'programmed' into our genes, is expressed in a number of ways of doing favours and reciprocating. The simplest way is to demand instant reciprocity as soon as one party has done a favour to the other party. If the other party fails to reciprocate, the first party will, in this simple model, also defect, that is, avoiding to reciprocate. As soon as the other party defects the first party will imitate this avoidance to reciprocate. Individuals imitate each other instantly in this model of reciprocity. Slightly more complex versions include ways of punishing cheaters, ways of forgiving cheaters, and so forth. According to evolutionary scientists, these are fundamental building blocks of human society: of developing trust, while at the same time continuously punishing cheating (Antoci & Zarri, 2015).

Is there one successful way of playing the social game, of initiating and maintaining social collaboration towards social change? Crudely speaking, three strategies are possible. The first one can be called 'Quaker', and it refers to always cooperating even if the other party cheats. The second strategy is called 'doormat' and implies the strategy of defecting regardless of what the other party does to you (Fang, Kimbrough, Pace, Valluri, & Zheng, 2002). Obviously, neither of these strategies is very successful. The demand for reciprocity, although not necessarily instantly, has turned out to be most successful in order to benefit from collaboration, as has been shown through extensive statistical calculations of the outcomes of versions of the games mentioned above (Axelrod, 2006). Intriguingly, this is what The Golden Rule prescribes, first found in Egypt two millennia BC. Meanwhile, human motivation to use resources for punishing cheaters prevails universally (Bone & Raihani, 2015). The modern example is our willingness to spend extensive tax money for punishing criminals, also for several other reasons than for preventing future crimes. To the extent our willingness to punish exceed our interest in merely preventing further cheating and crime, this points to the Dionysian side of cooperation, that I analyse in the next chapter.

Given this, how about the principle 'an eye for an eye'? Although it may appear to be equal to the simplest form of tit for tat, of direct mirroring of the move of the other party, a couple of differences should be pointed out. First, the principle of 'an eye for an eye' tends to lead to retaliations that are more extensive than the first hostile act. We can see this in 'honour cultures' and in the history of family feuds. Evolutionary anthropologists argue that strict principles such as an eye for an eye, and of in other ways instant, aggressive retaliation have most often evolved in herding cultures, such as in the Middle East and among herders in North and South America. In such cultures, it has been necessary to give other groups the reputation that one never tolerates that others fail to resist the temptation of stealing one's animals. Evolutionary scholars hold that the authoritarian, patriarchal, and punishment-oriented norms are most often found in cultures with a history in herding in tough and rough places (Gilbert & Andrews, 1998).

However, in most types of societies, including hunter-gatherer society, complete and instant retaliation and punishment of the cheater have not necessarily been beneficial even to the punishing party. In hunter-gatherer society, as in agricultural and modern societies extensive punishment is risky and costly, particularly using two among the worst possible punishments: social exclusion or putting a person to death. If there is no acceptance of breaking any rules or norms of collaboration the community runs the risk of also losing the resources of the temporary, petty cheater, such as her or his competence and strength. This is one reason most cultures have developed a certain degree of tolerance of cheaters, for instance by extending the (unconscious or law-written) tit-for-tat procedure into retaliation after repeated cheating (Berger, 2011).

An Apollonian path towards peace

Why should we place evolutionary game theory in the category of Apollonian evolutionary science perspectives? This is not entirely obvious, and the issue is not clear-cut. There is an interesting view in parts of evolutionary sciences here. The view contends that games take place at an instinctive, unconscious level among primitive organisms and creatures. Some would argue that the other 'pole' of complex, human, global networks also operates at an unconscious level, in the sense that a single individual has full awareness and control. However, at least at the human micro and meso levels, evolution has, according to evolutionary scientists, equipped humans with consciousness. This includes an Apollonian ability to plan, be strategic, postpone short-term interests in favour of greater, long-term interests, and so on. People are often capable of making conscious decisions to manage and take control over their primitive impulses, and this is associated with increased activity in the prefrontal cortex of the brain (Reyna & Zayas, 2014). To examine a positive result of this human ability, the evolution-oriented psychologist Pinker has tried to show how humanity has realised the benefits of developing more and more positive-sum games, where interests of all parties are satisfied to a certain extent. According to Pinker, echoing several previous scholars, this has led to a tremendous decline in violence around the world, if we look at the statistics of lethal violence (Pinker, 2011). Although news media, due to their logic of short-term sensation seeking, have an inherent bias towards showing lethal violence and catastrophes, Pinker contends that the risk of being killed is a fraction today of what it used to be (with a steady decline since hunter-gather societies, albeit with a few exceptions). If we trust that Pinker's thesis is correct, what factors have made a decline in violence possible? Pinker, drawing upon an amazing range of often rigorously collected analyses made by other human scientists (not just evolutionary scientists but also social scientists and economists), makes long lists of explanations. At the heart of his argumentation is the following stance: Societies and cultures around the world have become increasingly civilised and enlightened. It is not far-fetched to associate this argument with a view that humans have become increasingly Apollonian; Apollo is the god of the sun, of light. Through factors such as increased trade, education, information, international travel, and cultural exchange, substantial norm changes towards highly reduced tolerance of violence have taken place, Pinker maintains. When he generalises about people and cultures of today he portrays them as more self-restrained, less impulsive, more long-term planning, cooler, with a higher ability for abstraction and for thinking in ethical terms, better at statistics, and – yes – more intelligent, compared to our ancestors. All this is a characterisation of Apollonian traits. When he ends his book by giving advice for how society may reach further decline in violence, his main recipe is the following: 'We can entertain … the possibility that more education can lead to smarter citizens (in the sense of "smart" we care about here), which can prepare the way for democracy and open economies, which can favour peace' (Pinker, 2011, 665).

Although he does not use the terms of this book, Pinker calls for a further increase in Apollonian traits. The key factor that he points out is closely connected to education, namely reason. Pinker does so by actively downplaying and problematising another factor that is often more highly embraced in society than reason: empathy. What does he have against empathy as the recipe for further reductions in violence? Here, he draws on neuroscientific studies, where it is noted that empathy may be notoriously unreliable, too biased towards (Dionysian) priorities, of friends, relatives, cute animals, beautiful nature (Molenberghs,

2013). Moreover, empathy usually entails prioritising the visible, and what is close to us in time and space. Echoing the moral philosopher Singer, Pinker holds that 'it is hard-headed reason more than soft-hearted empathy that expands the ethical circle ever outward' (Pinker, 2011, 660). This quote reveals two Apollonian traits. First, the characteristics mentioned further above, about the benefits of impulse control, conscious planning, and so forth. Second, it implies a strong belief in human progress. Through sound and sober thinking, humanity evaluates previous outcomes and learns from mistakes. Thus, there is a directionality from worse to better living conditions. Whereas a minority of evolutionary scholars go one step further, by claiming that a directionality is predestined in nature, even to the extent that it can be called teleological, directed towards an ultimate end of all life on earth (Nagel, 2012), most evolutionary scholars strongly reject this view of predestination and inevitable direction. Pinker does not make any strong, 'cosmic' claim here. He only holds a solid hope that humanity will become ever increasingly Apollonian, better at comprehending, reasoning, analogising, using statistics, and so forth. The ultimate, Apollonian lesson is that life becomes better for everyone if everyone – by learning more about human reciprocity, and by controlling his or her violent impulses – collaborates more and harms others less.

The Apollonian dimension in social science

Apollonian norms governing modernisation and capitalism

Social science as a whole has one solid foot on each side of the Apollonian and Dionysian, regarding how it understands human interests. Social science is to some extent divided between scholars who emphasise the Apollonian side and those who stress the Dionysian one. A difference between social science and the other two sciences is that social science more often implies that different societies are based on varying proportions of Apollonian and Dionysian culture and norms. The proportion in each society generates efforts of its people to adapt to that proportion in order to be accepted and do well in that society. As to analyses of modernisation, virtually all the sociological classics tell their versions of a similar story. The common theme is how some societies have moved from traditional ones. This has engendered a transition from a more Dionysian culture and norms to Apollonian ones. Concepts such as formal rationalisation (Weber), alienation (Marx), *Gesellschaft* (Tonnies), and organic solidarity (Durkheim) all encompass a version of this story. Max Weber's description of what he calls the Protestant ethics indicates how the Apollonian, Protestant culture became dominating. Protestant ethics and culture helped to trigger a transition into a more Apollonian, capitalist society that transcended Protestant areas. Thus, Protestant regions were more easily adapted to capitalist society compared to, for instance, Catholic cultures. In some of the theories of these classical social thinkers, people seem to be able to adapt their interests to a more Apollonian society, in others less so. Still, highly influenced by their times, the most common storyline among the classical sociological thinkers was of how modern society disturbs the deeply rooted, Dionysian character of human sociality. Tönnies' analysis of *Gemeinschaft* and *Gesellschaft* is an example of this argumentation (Tonnies, 1887/1988).

The issue of individual and group adaptation to increasingly Apollonian demands of society has been a prevalent social scientific theme after the classics as well. Whereas Weber had investigated the Protestant ethos, and its attunement to modern capitalism, the social anthropologist Gellner sheds light on Jews and other ethnic minorities in relation to the Apollonian character of capitalist society. At least since the Middle Ages, Jews were during long periods excluded from owning land, from the military and political power. On the other hand, Christians were excluded from conducting commerce, since it was perceived as sinful. The main reason that it was seen as sinful was the old economic understanding mentioned above derived from St Augustine: The economy is accordingly a zero-sum game. If someone gains, another person had to lose, this understanding contended.

Jews, and in some regions certain other ethnic minorities of the Diaspora, were permitted to be involved in the filthy work of commerce. As food production, and other production became more efficient on the farms, a surplus of goods was generated that needed to be sold. A category of people was needed who brought food and other products from the countryside and who brought it into the towns and sold it: This category of people consisted of merchants and traders. Although merchants were needed in order to distribute goods, Jews and other minorities were disdained for it. At the same time, they were seen as a functional part of society, albeit at the margin. They were by and large tolerated. According to Gellner (himself being a Jew), this growing class of merchant and trader minorities developed an ethos very different from the ethnic majorities in the European countries. Farmers (of the dominating ethnicity) led a simple, habitual life close to their kin in small local communities, with no expectations of moving upward on the social ladder. At the high end of the social scale, there was the nobility. Its ethos was land owning, conspicuous leisure, military force, and high expenditure. A high degree of Dionysian traits, in other words, characterised both the masses of farmers and rural workers as well as nobilities, yet in immensely different ways. Against these ways of life of the ethnic majority, the ethnic minority merchants, in many cases Jews, had to develop a contrary ethos in order to survive, an Apollonian ethos that the nobilities scorned: thrift, systematic effort, impulse control, orderliness, budgeting, forethought, and book learning (Sombard, 1913/2015). As capitalism and early industrialism started to modernise society, including a transition to more legally equal society, highly developed Apollonian ethos and skills of the merchant and trade minorities gave them a substantial advantage over both the nobilities and the lower agricultural classes. Suddenly, the Jewish and certain other minorities did far better financially, than the ethnic majority. This led to envy among the ethnic majority, an envy triggering an ethnic nationalism, including widespread anti-Semitism, with the consequences of which we are all too well aware (Gellner, 1983).

Simmel on competition

Among the classical sociologists, Simmel is probably the one who has in the most nuanced way analysed the Apollonian traits of modern society. Instead of being entirely lost, alienated, or caught in an iron cage, Simmel tries to show how people walk between groups and between identities, in order to satisfy their manifest and latent interests. He thus downplays that belonging to a certain socio-economic group and class entails social pressures that one should follow the expected paths and practices of one's social category.

One of the most interesting Simmelian thoughts about modern society (including capitalism) concerns competition. Whereas both economics and evolutionary science conceive of competition as a fundamental trait of humans, as of all organisms, social sciences are routinely much more hesitant. Social science frequently portrays competition as a phenomenon that in artificial ways have been increased exponentially in capitalist society.

Although there may be some truth to this, Simmel's view is different. He shows certain benefits of competition, benefits not explained in such detail among economists or evolutionary scholars. Competition is not only, Simmel holds, about reaching a pre-calculated end in the most efficient manner. It also has a latent implication, namely to have people approach each other, and better understand the interests of others. Competition is not just about one social class against another, or poor groups against rich groups. It is also two parties, companies or organisations competing for attracting a third party to collaborate by accepting the offers of one of the former parties. This third party could be a consumer, a voter, an organisation, or someone in any other role for whom two other parties want to compete. Competition forces people to try to understand the manifest as well as the latent interests of a third person or group. Still, this recognition does not obstruct Simmel from observing that market society makes people more Apollonian. Simmel recognises that people in a market society become more abstract, calculative, and less impulsive in their thinking (Simmel, 1900/2004).

Ever-increasing embrace of Apollo in knowledge society

The sociologist, Bell, has turned his focus to a far later development in capitalism, namely post-industrial society, relying on the 'economics of information' rather than on the 'economics of goods' (Bell, 1976/2008). He refers to the 1970s and onwards, and examines what this era demands of human drivers and interests. The demands seem to be those that Weber and Gellner had highlighted although to an even higher degree or even at a second order: self-discipline, monetary saving, long-term educational planning, ignoring or putting off one's impulses in order to prepare for a better life later, to postpone one's short-term interests. According to Bell, the demands of post-industrial society, sometimes called 'knowledge society' or 'information society' have made the Apollonian, personal character a far better candidate for success, in terms of increased or maintained high social esteem, than the Dionysian character.

Psychologists have echoed this admission of the benefits of an Apollonian character. Most famously, this has been done in a set of psychological experiments of what has been called 'the Stanford marshmallow experiment'. Children aged four were told that they were allowed to eat one marshmallow immediately, or two marshmallows if they waited for a little while the tester left the room. Around one-third of the four-year-olds managed to wait for the tester to come back (around 3 minutes). In follow-up tests, this more patient one-third of the children have turned out to do significantly better at SAT scores, in their carriers, as well as in how highly their peers rate them in terms of popularity (Mischel, Ebbesen, & Zeiss, 1972). From a social science perspective, the most important part of this result might be what it reveals about the specific society and time in which this study was done. It was conducted in the United States in the early 1970s and onwards, but it is probably possible to extrapolate the results to other liberal democracies around the world. These societies elevate the Apollonian parts of human qualities. These qualities include deferring gratification, fighting impulses, and reasoning on a more long-term basis. This corresponds to what Weber labels 'formal rationalisation'. It refers to the preoccupation of how to optimise means and procedures to reach other means. The goals, if there are any, may lie very far ahead in time. Sometimes the goals are not clear to the person at stake, and they may only be extrinsic, replaceable by other objectives. Here, it seems, we are back at the view of rationality, which bears some resemblance to the Apollonian parts of economic science. Accordingly, people and organisations always compare (and, according to economists, 'should' compare) trade-offs between various alternatives. If the trade-offs of one choice are higher than the benefits, and the opportunity costs are higher than the benefits, people are motivated – or should be motivated – to make alternative choices, the Apollonian dimension of economic science maintains.

Moving from the social scientific focus on Apollonian traits in society, and what these traits do to human interests, one perspective could serve as examples of Apollonian social science: rational choice theory, social scientific style.

Rational choice theory in social science

When discussing Apollonian social science, it becomes necessary to bring up rational choice perspectives in social science. This is a highly contested issue. Some social scientists maintain that rational choice has no place there, and that it would even be an oxymoron to try to use rational choice reasoning in social science, particularly in sociology. In a gently mocking manner, the economist Duesenberry has made a, by now classic, statement about the difference between economics and sociology: 'Economics is all about how people make choices. Sociology is all about why they don't have any choices to make' (Duesenberry, 1960, 233). This is a caricature, of course. However, there are sometimes grains of truth in caricatures. Sociology and the other social sciences focus on 'how networks, social norms, socialization processes, and so on influence how individuals act by shaping their preferences, beliefs, opportunities, and so on' (Stern

& Hedstrom, 2008, 878). Nevertheless, this focus may very well incorporate rational choice perspectives (Liebe, Preisendorfer, & Meyerhoff, 2010). Much of the Apollonian side of mainstream social science borrows some of its vocabulary from rational choice-oriented economics: free riders, collective goods, and transaction costs are examples of such terms (Stern & Hedstrom, 2008). Aside from this implicit or even non-deliberate use of rational choice terms in social science, there is the more explicit and conscious use. Not least in social sciences on environmental and health issues, the possibility of people to actively search for and follow a rational choice to fulfil their manifest interests is commonly implied. Social scientists regularly study such topics in a context of policy alternatives. Thus, many social scientists find it necessary to study questions that concern which incentives and disincentives work for motivating people and companies to reduce their environmental harm or harms to health. For instance, social scientists have examined the choice of travel mode for trips between Berlin and Paris, choices between aeroplane, car, and train. Based on the parameters of the manifest interests of speed, comfort, and cost-saving – arguably Apollonian parameters – social scientists have calculated and interpreted the degree to which these parameters are significant to people's choices of travel mode (Liebe *et al.*, 2010). Travel choices are, of course, highly relevant to issues of environment and health.

To examine ways of increasing individual responsiveness to incentives and disincentives is a focus much influenced by rational choice theory. The underlying notion is that people will always respond to incentives and disincentives if these instruments are only designed in the right way. Not just in economics, but also in Apollonian social science, this notion is typically focused on how different manifest interests can meet. An example is how economic or practical incentives can make people choose non-fossil-fuel-based transportation or a vegetarian diet.

We should immediately reject the most simplistic versions of rational choice arguments here, as well as the most ignorant criticism of more sophisticated versions of rational choice theory. Here I shed light on the most ignorant criticism. Rational choice perspectives are according to the vulgar versions of criticism treated as erroneous since rational choice perspectives are mistakenly assumed to contend that each person (i.e. all of us in every situation) calculates the expected consequences of her or his options and chooses the best of them. The second step of the simplistic criticism is to make the obvious remark that each individual is not always Apollonian in this absolute way, and by observing that individuals sometimes 'act impulsively, emotionally, or by force of habit'. Accordingly, since people have a Dionysian, latent side as well, rational choice theory must be wrong (Hechter & Kanazawa, 1997, 192). The problem of this critique, as the sociologists Blau (1997) and Whitford (2002) have noted, is that sophisticated versions of rational choice theory are intended to explain only macro-level outcomes, not each individual act in each particular situation. Thus, despite the fact that each person does not do her or his uttermost to maximise free rider benefits in every situation, there nevertheless seem to be real and severe environmental challenges at the larger scale, manifested in overfishing, dumping of hazardous waste, and so forth.

Is there any difference between rational choice-based research in economics and social science? Social scientists engaged in rational choice theory maintain that the sociological version is more empirically oriented, generating data that guide a broader narrative. Economists typically try to specify a mathematical model used for analysing societal processes. Besides, economists tend to assume that people on average collect the relevant information and shape correct beliefs, based on which they choose consciously the actions that in the best way satisfy their interests that are usually manifest, self-regarding, and exogenous. Social scientists, in contrast, even those involved in rational choice theory, focus on how people's beliefs and interests are influenced by social situations. As we shall see in the chapters on continuous and flexible interests, the social scientific perspective elucidates how human interests are highly flexible based on the social situation (Stern & Hedström, 2008). For all these differences, rational choice theories are united across disciplines by using actors (rather than social structures) as the point of departure for explaining social phenomena. Second, these actors have the ability and interest to choose between two or more alternatives of action. Finally, each rational choice theory includes a rule of decision, formulating which action the actor chooses. The action that 'best' meets a person's interests is, however, not confined to the satisfaction of her material interests as in material utility maximisation (Liebe *et al.*, 2010).

Conclusions

The Apollonian dimension of traditional economics can be seen most clearly in the following attributes. First of all, it stresses the ability and importance of focused and goal-oriented individuals to struggle towards their manifest human interests. The worries among economists about free riding and the tragedy of the commons – of individual exploitation of common resources, such as the physical environment – are based on their view that people to a large extent have Apollonian traits of calculating individual benefits. Here, the commons constitutes a structural problem. It implies a zero-sum game, since what is rational to the individual clashes with the interests of the collective to maintain a healthy environment. Second, this perspective is Apollonian to the extent to which it gives little attention to increases in economic inequality, as long as the poorest are better off by the market exchanges in question: a positive-sum game where everyone is a 'winner'. Third, the embracing of economic efficiency among economists regularly leads this discipline to recommend the commodification of parts of social life that were not previously conceived of as potential areas of market exchange. Financial arrangements are Apollonian to the extent that their proponents ignore or downplay the possible changes in social relationships into market relationships that commodifications may engender. One example is the commercialisation of kidneys. The manifest interest may seem highly valuable, such as increasing the supply of kidneys available for people with kidney problems than is the case if kidney donations are restricted to donations without financial compensation.

Parts of evolutionary science share the notion of human interests navigating between zero-sum games (of winners and losers) and positive-sum games, where everyone is better off by the exchange in question. The term 'reciprocal altruism' denotes the human inclination to help and collaborate with others, yet with the expectations of returned favours. The delay that humans often accept between doing and receiving favours necessitates social trust. Moreover, it necessitates the inclination to punish those who exploit the favours of others by not reciprocating. The motivation at all levels of society to demand a balance between favours given and received is an Apollonian tendency towards seeking balance and symmetry, at least so that 'I' or 'we' do not lose.

Social science examines Apollonian features in its endeavours of examining how a transition to modernity, globalisation, service society, knowledge society, and so forth, impacts the preconditions for the satisfaction of human interests. The increasing demand in current society of planning, strategy, delayed gratification, and of sometimes moving merely from one means to another, never reaching a deeply human end, is a development that social scientists study and partly problematise. At the same time, bureaucratisation and the reduced need for physical body power have in some cases enabled less privileged groups and women to have far higher chances in a society structured by less partial, and more Apollonian principles. However, the next chapter shows how Apollonian factors explain some, but far from all, reasons for environmental and health-related problems.

3   The Dionysian dimension

The Dionysian dimension in economic science

Dionysian critique of traditional economics

The most common criticism of traditional economics is that it is over-simplistic in its specific rational choice perspective of human drivers and interests. This criticism has been around for several decades. It is many times fussy, since it attacks different rational choice assumptions at the same time. As I have already mentioned, the most common criticism of traditional economics concerns the notion of Homo economicus. This notion contends that humans are to the core consciously planning, sufficiently knowledgeable, individualistic, egoistic, and prioritising manifest (most often material) interests. Market interaction between firms would not be possible if humans thought and acted in this way, the social and evolutionary scientists Johnson, Price, and Van Vugt (2013) contend. By definition, a firm is an organisation comprised of people, and necessitates a degree of self-sacrifice and altruism among these people in order to function. Social and evolutionary scientists are not the only ones strongly opposed to this view. Certain parts of contemporary economics are so as well. A few decades ago, the institutional economist, Sen, writes an article called 'Rational Fools'. There he states that

> The purely economic man is indeed close to being a social moron. Economic theory has been much preoccupied with this rational fool decked in the glory of his one all-purpose preference ordering. To make room for the different concepts related to his behaviour we need a more elaborate structure.
>
> (Sen, 1977, 336)

By stressing that what might be seen as economically rational may be socially foolish, and vice versa, Sen recognises the importance of Dionysian traits, and the latent interests associated with such traits. Being an institutional economist, Sen writes in a tradition where the latent interests of esteem and status are taken into account. However, the recognition of Dionysian traits has a longer history in economics. Around the turn to the twentieth century, Veblen, an (institutional) economist much read also by social scientists, develops the theory of 'conspicuous consumption' to indicate how far much of our consumption is from a satisfaction of essential, material needs only.

> In every community where goods are held in severalty it is necessary, in order to his own piece of mind, that an individual should possess as large a portion of goods as others with whom he is accustomed to class himself; and it is extremely gratifying to possess something more than others … [T]he end sought by accumulation is to rank high in comparison with the rest of the community in point of pecuniary strength.
>
> (Veblen, 1899/1967, 20)

Other economists have advanced this notion further, by examining the relationship between absolute and relative income as well as absolute and relative levels of consumption. Duesenberry (1949) indicates how people's interests are geared even more towards doing well concerning relative revenue and consumption as regarding absolute dittos. Along the same line, the economist Frank concludes the following, based on decades of studies of human wellbeing with regard to absolute and relative material standard: 'We have voluminous behavioral evidence about what people care about, and that evidence, too, clearly supports the claim that people care deeply about relative income' (Frank, 2012, 1191).

This voluminous evidence supporting the Dionysian dimension of relative income causes confusion in economics. We should remember that it goes against the basic Apollonian argument of traditional economics, which contends that people's main, or only, interest should be in becoming better off (or at least not worse off) while people should not care whether others are becoming better off to an even higher degree. Some economists, such as Stevenson and Wolfers, consequently claim to show 'that only absolute income matters to happiness' (Stevenson & Wolfers, 2008, 70). Despite such attempts, the overwhelming empirical, cross-national, longitudinal data in which subjective wellbeing has increased far less than the increases in absolute material standard provide solid empirical evidence of the key importance of the relative position to people's wellbeing. Moreover, the entire disciplines of social and evolutionary science, along with Dionysian strands of economics, point in the same direction. The satisfaction of Dionysian, often latent interests is key to human wellbeing once people have met their basic physical needs.

Yet, some confusion remains. Even among economists who accept the importance, and even principal character of Dionysian interests, the question is what this makes of human activities, which seem to compromise Apollonian interests in order to better satisfy Dionysian ones. Both traditional economics and the economics that highlights the Dionysian dimension (e.g. behavioural economics, see below) typically treat conspicuous consumption as irrational. This is problematic. First of all, the view that conspicuous consumption would be irrational seems to contradict the foundational idea of economic rationality: that economic rationality concerns means and not ends. Still, the economic science criticism of conspicuous consumption interferes with ends that economics is so concerned not to evaluate as long as they concern Apollonian interests: comfort, reasonable safety, product quality, affordability, and the pleasure that such interests may bring. Apollonian interests at the latent level (hidden for others but consciously recognised by the individual or group itself; see Table 1.2, Square 4) are also accepted as rational ends, as long as the latency does not entail fraud that runs the risk of costing more than the benefits it gives.

Let us look some more at consumption and other activities where the interests are mainly Dionysian, compromising with Apollonian interests in optimality. Luxury consumption, for instance, is often based on a Dionysian – latent or manifest – interest in distinguishing oneself from others and impressing others. The background information is typically where the whole difference lies in conspicuous consumption. In Darby and Karni's terminology, such consumption often involves 'credence goods', demanding more information than mainly looking at or experiencing the goods (Darby & Karni, 1973). It could be, for instance, that the fresh fish were caught in another part of the world a few hours ago only to be transported by plane to a restaurant here, where we may pay a fortune for it even if our local fish tastes even better. Wasteful: definitely! Immoral: plausibly! However, is it 'irrational' for the individual or group who makes such choices? According to some economists, what is irrational, and by extension economically inefficient for society, is that these types of choices move beyond the optimum, ignoring the highly reduced marginal utility that people get for the extreme cost compared with what they would be able to get for substitute goods (the opportunity cost). The concept of diminishing or reduced marginal utility is a fundamental one in economics. It elucidates how it is usually not optimal to maximise whatever manifest interest one may have. Maximising the amount of information or knowledge available is most likely sub-optimal, since it costs more (in time and resources) above a certain level of knowledge and information. After a certain point, each additional unit of information (or any other item) does not provide us with sufficient additional value to be worth demanding. Analogous arguments have been used concerning whether food consumers should be exposed to still more information on the products they buy. A particularly heated debate has taken place with regard to products labelled 'free from genetically modified organisms'. Many economists perceive this as an example of conspicuous consumption. These economists hold that such information is irrational since it does not satisfy – at least not directly – additional Apollonian interests compared with less expensive alternatives (Tool, 1988). Economists have argued that it is irrational to prefer or pay more for products labelled GMO-free, as long as GMOs have not been proven dangerous to health by the US Food and Drug Administration (Miller & Huttner, 1995). We can see a couple of problems with this reasoning. First, if people are economically rational to their core, as traditional economists argue, why not assume that some of the 'irrational' choices above are in fact rational means to getting an impressive material reputation as a person of fine taste? Such a reputation might, in turn, help the person to be welcomed into exclusive social circles that enable higher satisfaction of Apollonian interests. As to conspicuous consumption, Veblen himself never claims that conspicuous consumption is irrational in the cultural context that he examines. Instead, as the Veblen scholar Wood points out, Veblen's view is that 'the consumer maintains a modicum of decency given a certain status and role position' (Wood, 1993, 510). This moves us to additional criticism, which is a Dionysian one. To be sure, the above-mentioned 'irrationalities' may often not be economically rational in the sense of immediately optimising the satisfaction of the traditionally economic, Apollonian interests. Nevertheless, there are strong arguments that these irrationalities can satisfy other Apollonian interests (e.g. the interests of other people, animals, or 'the natural environment', in the case of paying price premiums for eco-labelled or other ethically labelled products and services), or satisfy one's Dionysian interests.

Proposition 2: as long as people and groups have sufficient information and are not subject to fraud, their apparent compromises with their Apollonian interests (in optimising their level of comfort, safety, quality of goods, and services against their costs in time and money) should not be mystified as irrational. Instead, these compromises are probably best understood regarding their social rationality.

If people do not assume – consciously or unconsciously – that seemingly excessive choices may benefit their group bonding, social position, esteem, and so forth, they can be expected not to make these choices. A social identity shared around, for example, efforts to reach a 'natural' lifestyle is common, not least in the middle and upper-middle class. This does not mean, however, that it is usually beneficial for people's Dionysian interests to go against their Apollonian ones. To the contrary, the two can be expected to go together most of the time, not least in a culture of liberal democracy. Still, when the two are in conflict, I assume in this book that people and groups prioritise the Dionysian interests most of the time. Evolutionary science explains why, and social science shows how.

Behavioural economics

Behavioural economics is particularly notable for its criticism of the Homo economicus interpretation of Apollonian traits. If traditional economics treats the latent, Dionysian traits of humans as weak and insignificant (at least at the aggregated level of populations), behavioural economics treats these traits as strong and problematic. Incorporating much knowledge of psychology, not least exemplified with the psychologist Kahneman's work in behavioural economics, identifications and analyses of human 'biases' are the main tasks of this sub-discipline. Status quo bias, myopic bias, confirmation bias, and herd behaviour are examples of biases that behavioural economists acknowledge. These phenomena stem from the latent level of human interests, partly Dionysian in character (this is particularly obvious with the term 'herd behaviour'). Through experimental and (other) statistical work, sometimes in collaboration with neuroscience, behavioural economists convincingly show how a number of latent, human biases are always operating in human decision making. Behavioural economists indicate this in debates with mainstream economists (or other actors with a mainstream, economic, Apollonian view of human interests and motivation). Perhaps this is why the storyline among behavioural economists tends to be one of negating the storyline of traditional economics: People's activities are not rooted in conscious, economically rational calculations of how to best satisfy their own manifest interests. Instead, people's rationality is distorted by latent biases, entailing irrational decision making, in the sense that the manifest interests may not be reached in an optimal way. It is intriguing to note the following: Although behavioural economics may appear to aspire to break with, and revolutionise traditional, traditional economics, their relationship seems to be one of 'opposites attract' of two different camps that nonetheless share the identity and culture of economics. It is more of a disagreement about human rationality regarding specific manifest interests than a deeper controversy over the two levels of human interests. Both sides pay their utmost attention to people's need for satisfying specific manifest interests. Although behavioural economics in many cases incorporates state-of-the-art knowledge in neuroscience, discussions about human biases still turn out to resemble discussions in computer science about 'bugs', and how to fix them, since the issues in focus often concern human action on the market and Wall Street. Kahneman and his colleagues pay their centre of attention to how people could better satisfy the specific, manifest, Apollonian interests at stake, one at a time. They use the term 'Type 1' to analyse the latent, Dionysian side of human interests, and how they could be better dealt with (Kahneman, Lovallo, & Sibony, 2011). A common message in behavioural economics for how to handle human biases is the 'patriarchal libertarianism' of nudging, to conquer, or at least help people suppress their latent level (Thaler & Sunstein, 2008). Accordingly, people should be nudged to pursue their manifest interests in more formally rational, linear, and straightforward manners. Behavioural economists do not assume that people can ever reach the status of Homo economicus. People will never be able to remove their biases. Instead, these economists provide recommendations for how individuals can work their way around their inevitable biases. Nudging takes place in at least two ways. First, it can consist of recommendations to individuals how they could rethink and recalculate their situations and interests before they make decisions. Second, nudging may refer to structural changes. Importantly, however, these structural changes are not designed with the ambition of triggering latent structural change, as in reductions of social or economic equality. Some critics have therefore commented on what behavioural economists call their endeavours: 'choice architecture', by rephrasing it into the interior decoration of choice. In his review of *Misbehaving*, a book by Thaler, one of the founders of behavioural economics, the reviewer, McMahon, writes the following: 'What he [Thaler] calls architecture, though, might be more realistically portrayed as interior design, rearranging the furniture in one room to provide a superficial cosmetic change as it leaves the overall structure and design of the building untouched' (McMahon, 2015, 1).

Behavioural economics mainly addresses how people can make optimal choices at the manifest level. These economists perceive their science as independent of any axiology (value-influence) that would have them indicate possible benefits of a revised latent structure (changes in inequality levels, power relations, and so forth). As long as this view prevails in behavioural economics, nudging can only be expected to further strengthen the latent structures and ideologies on which this view depends.

The Dionysian dimension in evolutionary science

Chapter 2, above, brings up the evolutionary concept of reciprocal altruism. This concept denotes what can be called the third layer of evolution. Reciprocal altruism refers to collaboration also between unrelated individuals and groups, for the sake of mutual benefits in positive-sum situations. For examining Dionysian traits through the lens of evolutionary science, it is important to shed light on also the first two layers of evolution: individual selection and kin selection. These two layers are more directly linked to latent, genetic interests of individuals, and could also be argued to be more 'primitive'.

Individual selection

The first layer of evolution, individual selection, is the most widely known (and misunderstood) one. On this layer, the focus is on the individual's direct, genetic interest at the latent level of passing on as many genes as possible to the next generation. To be sure, the latent interest in passing on as many genes as possible is the master principle of evolutionary theory. It runs through the other two layers as well. Still, the first layer points to the most individualistic expressions of the gene-spreading principle, where, in the satirist Butler's formulation from the nineteenth century, 'A hen is only an egg's way of making another egg' (Butler, 1877, 134). To analyse interests of separate individuals is something that social science finds relevant mainly in societies that they perceive as in one or the other way unhealthy, such as in certain hunter-gatherer societies that have failed to collaborate (Turnbull, 1987), or in advanced but overly anonymous, contemporary societies. To economic science, however, focusing on interests of separate individuals is usually the starting point. Evolutionary science, however, with genes as its fundamental unit of analysis, could be assumed to conceive of individuals as non-essential containers of genes and genetic combinations. Yet, a big proportion of the evolutionary perspective of the human sciences focuses on interests of individuals.

In some analyses, individual selection is analysed as operating as a zero-sum game: one person's gain is another one's loss. Three aspects of individual selection are particularly relevant to evolutionary analyses on human interests. The first one is the 'primitive' struggle for dominance. Examinations of hunter-gatherer society are replete with this focus. Evolutionary scientists sometimes claim that dominance was key to reproductive success in a hunter-gatherer society. The spreading of one's genes was potentially extensive for those individuals who were more well-adapted to this social and natural environment. Consequently, their offspring inherited the same drive towards domination. Here we should note the Dionysian character of individual selection. Even if it concerns individual domination, it always does so in group settings. The goal is social status and even dominance, which can be very different from what economics conceives of as fundamental: maximising utility, possibly without comparing this utility to other people's utility. Moreover, the social interest and social rationality emphasised in evolutionary science is very different from the economics focus, which, although not necessarily so, at the end of the day is very often placed on maximising *material* utility. By becoming part of the dominant segment of, for instance, a hunter-gatherer society, it is by no means obvious that an individual would enjoy more material prosperity than the lower segments.

Studies conducted from the perspective of individual selection describe social and cultural conditions as characterised by a stereotypically male competition for resources and dominance. To be sure, evolutionary anthropologists mainly analyse individual selection in the context of hunter-gatherer societies (and to some extent herding societies). Some scientists conceive of such societies in similar terms as Hobbes did in the seventeenth century of a 'natural state', namely as 'nasty, brutish and short' (Hobbes, 1651/1982, chs XIII–XIV). Evolutionary psychologists maintain that the aggressive and violent traits of individual selection are very much operating in current, advanced societies as well, such as in individual power struggles.

Another side of individual selection has been much less examined in evolutionary science, but can be much elucidated from the evolutionary perspective. Emotions of guilt and low self-esteem have long been misunderstood by social science uninformed by evolutionary lessons as the roots and causes of many types of deviant and self-destructive behaviour. However, through a more rigorous analysis it turns out that low self-esteem, as feelings of guilt, is hardly the causes of deviant, undesired behaviour, but rather an outcome of the reactions one gets from others due to one's deviant, undesired behaviour. Throughout human history, it has been vital to be receptive to signals that one is at risk of being excluded from one's social group(s). Emotions of low self-esteem seem to be – in part – such signals, responses to – often subtle – expressions of dislike and disapproval by others (Leary, Haupt, Strausser, & Chokel, 1998). Moreover, low self-esteem has been shown to be responses to expressions from others that the person has low status and esteem in their eyes (Fournier, 2009).

Kin selection

Above the layer of individual selection, there is kin selection. The fact that kin selection also is an evolutionary principle implies that it is an additional way that nature channels the latent interest among individual organisms in spreading their genes. Kin selection may explain the particular interest in changes that are particularly favourable not just to the individual, but also the person's family, relatives, and close community. The logic of kin selection is the following: If survival and spreading of genes are the main driving forces of life, this driving force ought to go beyond the individual. That a person has an interest in favouring and prioritising the wellbeing of close relatives, who share more of her or his genes than do strangers, is an obvious implication of the principle of kin selection. Kin selection implies the inclination to favour arrangements that are to the disproportionate benefit of one's family and close community.

Loyalty and almost unconditional alliance with a family or group are the credos that govern kin selection. Since kin selection far less than reciprocal altruism concerns substantive accomplishments, loyalty in kinship situations may survive a lack of competence and even a certain lack of trustworthiness of one's kin. Thus, kin selection is highly Dionysian in character. Neuroscientists associate this type of selection in particular with the socio-emotive parts of the brain in the amygdala (Yurgelun-Todd & Killgore, 2006).

The purest expressions of kin selection, such as wishing and doing the very best for one's children to help them adapt to a rapidly changing world, is a social norm in most societies (exceptions include certain temporary quasi-experiments in totalitarian societies). Still, much of the favouring of close relatives and friends in politics, and biased use of public finances, have ever since the introduction of the principles of meritocracy and bureaucracy been synonymous with corruption.

Whereas the principles and expressions of kin selection are fairly obvious in the 'pure' examples above, the phenomenon becomes most interesting in its less pure and subtler forms. Evolutionary scientists who analyse transitions towards nationalism, racism, as well as radical ideology and politics – both at the far left and right political spectra – try to explain these changes partly regarding kin selection (Bingham & Souza, 2012). The reason is that such changes typically include mantras and metaphors of 'us versus them'. This dichotomy, according to these scientists, has evolved in humans (as in all other organisms) since those with the strongest drive to support their kin, and to protect their kin against others, have had their genes also spread via relatives and to the relatives' offspring (Mateo, 2015). However, the human motivation to favour one's kin has been continually exploited, not least in totalitarian ideologies towards radical change both to the left and right. The term 'pseudo-kinship' is used by evolutionary science, alternated with the terms 'extended kinship' and 'fictive kinship'. As mentioned above, metaphors in most languages can be found that have been constructed to trigger people's pseudo-kinship, even when it is – from a genetic perspective – false: brothers in arms, the mother country, Uncle Joe (Joseph Stalin) are a few such terms (Ehrlich, 2002). In order to be willing to sacrifice their life for others (officially framed as being prepared to die for their country) the vast majority of people must first develop a sense that they are dying for their brothers or sisters. The most frightening successes in creating pseudo-kinship have triggered ethnic cleansing, religious wars, and lethal conflicts between groups of different ideologies.

The fact that kin selection is an evolutionarily rooted, universal trait has made some thinkers – rarely evolutionary scientists, however – assume that violence and warfare founded on kinship are regrettable, but necessary, ingredients in political, economic, and social change. Accordingly, there would be a latent interest in not hesitating to use violence to favour one's kin or pseudo-kin. It has often been part of the political philosophy of conservatism to claim the inevitability of human imperfection, rather than to assume that substantial and thoroughly planned political, social, and cultural change will erase these tendencies (Woods, 2002). While social liberals and leftists often call for disarmament, conservatives find it better for a group or country to increase their own strength, in order to threaten the enemies. Accordingly, there will always be antagonists and powers that inflict on one's interests. Arms race might in some cases be the best way towards peace. To be sure the conservative caution against counting on enduring peace entails substantial preparation to minimise humanitarian catastrophes in events of war and conflict, a preparation that is certainly immensely important. Still, evolutionary scientists do not fully agree about the inevitability of violence and conflict. Nor do they fully agree that the arms race might be the best way towards peace. As we know, conservatives have historically often been mistaken in their claims of what is 'part of human nature' and what is not, for instance about what would be the contents of women's 'nature' and men's 'nature' (Arnhart, 2005). In contrast with conservatives' common assumption that human nature is hardwired towards violence, extensive studies based on evolutionary science (using data from political science, history, and sociology) have shown how violence and wars have declined quite dramatically throughout history. Accordingly, there is not a fixed (or even increasing) amount of violence in the world (Pinker, 2011).

Why consciousness?

Similar to behavioural economics, evolutionary science well recognises, and investigates, how the bases for human judgement and decision making takes place without the decision makers being fully aware of these bases. Evolutionary scientists and behavioural economists often use the term 'biases' for studying this phenomenon. Evolutionary scientists usually address human biases in much broader ways than behavioural economists, by investigating issues far beyond specific – often economic – decision making, which has so far been the main subject of behavioural economics. For instance, the evolutionary biologist (and political scientist) Johnson, together with the political scientist Fowler investigates what he identifies as human over-confidence in certain conflict situations, such as wars and threats of war (Johnson & Fowler, 2011). Over-confidence is a human trait that per definition takes place without the over-confident person or group being fully conscious of it. Behavioural economics may very well rule out over-confidence as an 'irrational' since it may go against several human interests at the manifest level: economic stability, peace, and avoided harm to humans and nature (Dahl, 2015). Evolutionary scientists, however, frequently hold the position that activities and choices that appear to be 'irrational' at the manifest level may be counter-weighted by another kind of rationality at the level of latent human interests. When evolutionary scientists try to understand how violent conflicts could be avoided, they find it key to investigate why and how excessive self-confidence and other biases operate. Only once human scientists address why-questions, beyond descriptions of how people perform certain acts, can there be a chance of fully coping with the societal problems such biases may trigger (Johnson, 2015).

In their strong focus on the latent level, many evolutionary scientists go so far as to ask why nature would have made any aspects of human interests manifest – open and visible, that is – even to people themselves. For example, Trivers (2011) examines the benefits of self-deception among many organisms, including humans. The underlying claim here is that human nature has evolved directly from more primitive creatures, whose 'reflexivity' (a term dear to sociologists to describe people in current society (Beck, 1999; Giddens, 1991)) was dramatically less developed than ours (Boyd, 2006). Natural selection has made only those things conscious to people that benefit their evolutionary interests – survival, reproduction, and the upbringing of our offspring – by being made conscious to the subjects themselves. Much of a person's mental processes, regarding social status, esteem, and even the likelihood of having success with attracting a partner and having a family, genetic evolution has kept latent and unconscious to that person herself. Evolutionary science indicates that the majority of our mental processes can be best understood as 'automatic' or 'pre-cognitive'. To be sure, humans are arguably the most reflexive creatures on earth, with an ability to observe themselves and to create a picture of the rationales behind their own practices. Yet, human reflexivity, as well as conscious and strategic planning, have emerged so late in our evolution that it is not as deeply tied to our basic emotions as the latent level.

Why a manifest and a latent level?

Earlier sections of this book establish that humans can be understood at a manifest and a latent level, and through the relation between the two levels. The same holds for groups and societies. In the following sections, I go in some depth into why there exist two mental levels in the first place.

Evolutionary science provides several types of arguments that support the claim that there are two mental levels. One is that our more primitive, non-human ancestors thousands of generations ago had more primitive brains than Homo sapiens, the former with a lower level of consciousness. Nevertheless, Homo sapiens has inherited several primitive parts of their brain, whereas the parts enabling people to be conscious in a human way have evolved much more recently. Such abilities include doing long-term planning, creating strategies, and calculating, in several orders, the possible motives and interests of others. The latter capacity is called 'a theory of mind' (Baron-Cohen, 2001). Several evolutionary scientists have in various ways made discoveries and done pioneering work on dual mental systems reflecting this 'old' and 'new' brain development (Chaiken & Trope, 1999). Most renowned, however, for conducting research on the relationship between two mental systems is the already introduced psychologist Kahneman. His work applied these findings to problems in economics, hence contributing to the field of behavioural economics. The title of Kahneman's bestseller, *Thinking Fast and Slow* (Kahneman, 2011) gives a succinct summary of their differences. His term for the two mental systems is System 1 and System 2.

There is rich empirical evidence for dual mental systems, where the older system operates in a more spontaneous, intuitive, partially unconscious way. When people are asked to keep several things actively in mind, things that demand full use of their (in humans highly limited) working memory, it turns out in some types of experiments that these people still manage to perform well on additional tasks. In such experiments, it is reasonable to assume that these extra tasks have been solved at a latent, non-conscious level making use of the older System 1 (Evans & Stanovich, 2013).

The evolution-oriented, moral psychologist, Haidt (2008) describes the human mind as an elephant with a (human) rider. This is an illustrative metaphor, where the big elephant refers to the large, old evolutionary heritage of humans, the underlying, latent level. The rider steers to a certain degree at the same time as she follows the movement of the elephant. The rider represents the more recent evolutionary heritage of humans, of consciousness, planning, reflexivity, self-restraint, and so forth, processes taking place mainly at the manifest level. In addition to the apt size differences between the elephant and the rider, this metaphor indicates how the outcome, human action, is always a result of the interaction between the two systems. The rider never has a full influence of the elephant or vice versa. This seems to be a convincing image of human activities. Numerous experiments have been done on the part of human decision making where conscious, planned, controlled, planned, and slow processes play a dominating – yet not complete – role (Frankish, 2010). Moreover, many experiments have been conducted on the parts of human activities that are driven by more impulsive, automatic, and fast processes (Gilovich, Griffin, & Kahneman, 2002).

However, to my knowledge, these strands of science scholarship have rarely bridged these lessons over to analyses of culture and society as a whole, aside from discussions in behavioural economics about how society could deal with human biases surrounding decision making. To lift our perspective above the individual, and to focus on how the human sciences conceive latent and manifest dimensions of humans in societal contexts becomes key for understanding nuances in how the three human sciences perceive human interests.

The Dionysian dimension in social science

In parallel with the other human sciences, social science has an Apollonian side, as the reader could see above. Rational choice theory is also represented in parts of social science, along with other Apollonian traits. Not even rational choice theory, however, can in its social scientific version be purely Apollonian, focusing only on manifest interests of individuals. Institutions, norms, and traditions – Dionysian traits – are rarely entirely separated from social scientific analyses. When classical as well as more contemporary social scientific scholars relate to Apollonian traits of modern and contemporary society, they typically do so by criticising the coldness of such a strategy-obsessed and individualistic society. As a positive contrast, social scientists engaged in movement studies, for instance, frequently indicate that members active in social movements often do not belong to the social category whose substantive self-interest is in focus (Ahlquist & Levi, 2013). Instead, a large share of members is driven by solidarity and a sense of community (Fligstein & McAdam, 2011). At the same time, social scientists who fully embrace and romanticise traditional forms of society founded on strict religious and moral dogmas have become rare.

Dionysus even in Protestant ethics

As opposed to much of economics, social science typically entails analyses of lasting Dionysian influences on people and society. In societies where rulers try to hunt Dionysus down, the public regularly only reframes Dionysus, giving him (or her, as Dionysus is sometimes portrayed) a different shape. Weber's classic sociological analysis of the relative success of Northern European industrial and capitalist developments is ironically based on the main religious faith in that part of the world: Protestant Christianity. This is ironic since religious faith, dogmas, and faith-based communities are far closer to the Dionysian than the Apollonian part of culture and the human mind. According to much of Protestant theology, objective, visible, and practical results in a person's life prove her faith in God. Through the manifest results of a person's actions she, and even, more importantly, the persons around her, could get a glimpse of whether she had been chosen for everlasting life or death. Therefore, it became important for every person, in the early modernity that Weber analyses, to act in a way that others thought she was among the exclusive few who were predestined for being saved to an everlasting life. To show worldly success became a way of showing others that one had been selected by God to receive his special grace.

The religious doctrines of reformism told people that the best way to show this was by exercising self-control, systemacy, and to avoid impulsive and spontaneous action. Money should not be spent on useless things. Saving and treating one's work as a vocation were Calvinist ideals, according to Weber.

To be sure, this is obviously synonymous with an Apollonian ideal. Still, even though Weber overlooked much of another social thinker, Veblen's, important observation of the completely opposite tendency of conspicuous consumption, overt laziness of the leisure class, which is more obviously a Dionysian trait, through the latent interest of creating envy among others and to display one's success, Weber's analysis of the Apollonian ideal in Protestant ethics rests equally on his understanding of people's Dionysian interests in raising or at least maintaining their social status. A third classical sociologist, Simmel, echoes this claim by explicating the social nature of religion. Religion and even religious faith are according to him fundamentally about a relationship between people (Simmel, 1898, 108).

How can the observation that Apollonian preoccupation with manifest problem solving have a basis in latent, Dionysian interests teach us something about how to understand current problems, such as problems concerning environment and health? The answer is that there appears to be something in the current Western society's interpretations of environmental and health-related problems that has the same character. At the manifest level of environmental information, campaigning, and even advertising there is the message that people should better scrutinise their daily activities. Before they start to consume even more, the normative view contends, people should increase and broaden our reflections and take other people, species, countries, and generations into account. This implies a higher degree of self-control and planning, and the avoidance of following hedonistic (Dionysian) impulses. On the other hand, and similar to the Calvinistic frugality and self-control that Weber describes, people and cultures will only be motivated to move in this Apollonian direction if this also satisfies some of their Dionysian interests. These include interests in creating group bonding, social prestige, and cultural distinction from other groups. Similar to the old Protestant ethic, which goes against certain impulses of comfort and hedonism, a broader cultural change into reductions of negative environmental impact is likely to be motivated perhaps more by the potential for such reductions of satisfying certain Dionysian interests than by the potential for reducing environmental harm.

From a material to a moral critique of capitalism

Much of the social criticism of early capitalism was to be sure Apollonian in character. For instance, I here allow myself to categorise Marx as a social scientist, his criticism of capitalism and its proponents among economists is that it would not increase the satisfaction of manifest, material interests among the majority of the population who did not control the means of production. Marx advances what has been called his pauperisation thesis: Workers were accordingly destined to be increasingly poor, in the sense of having fewer and fewer of their manifest interests of material wellbeing satisfied: 'The greater the social wealth, the functioning of capital, the extent and energy of its growth ... the greater is the industrial reserve army ... The greater is official pauperism. This is the absolute general law of capitalist accumulation' (Marx, 1867/1992, 667).

Yet, this prediction turned out to be false in many places of the world. The working class has a much higher standard of living than during Marx's times (Paul, 2012, 182). If he revisited current, Western society today, Marx would probably have mistaken the working class for the bourgeoisie, if he only took standard of living into account (and ignored ownership and control over means of production). Instead, some Marxists along with a wide range of social science scholars have found it more fruitful to shift their focus from manifest to latent human interests: to moral and cultural implications of capitalism. Social and economic inequality is one such implication.

Ever since its classical thinkers, social science has analysed the social outcomes of capitalism often marked by modest state interference to reduce economic inequality. Social scientists have identified several societal problems that they associate with economic inequality: urban crime, violence, lack of environmental concern, health issues, and social isolation are only a few of these problems. The insistence and efforts examining the relationship between economic inequality and these societal problems have in many public fora gained ground. Several economists nowadays recognise this connection, even though traditional economic theory – Apollonian in character – gives little room for explaining why there would be any problem with market exchanges where both parties increase the satisfactions of their individual interests.

That there is a collective interest – among the rich and poor alike – in reduced economic inequality is a view heard in many public debates. Even if there are vast differences regarding what level of economic inequality – if any – should be seen as acceptable, a general framing of extensive economic inequality as problematic has become more widely accepted by economists, particularly those who call themselves 'liberal' (Krugman, 2007). In international politics, strategies for stimulating a growth of the category of people in conflict regions defining themselves as 'moderates', and 'middle class' in a wide sense of the word can be interpreted as a manifestation of this. An increasing proportion of people who are neither poor nor extremely rich are among many political scientists seen as the main recipe for stability and peace nationally and internationally. Still, the appropriate means to reductions of economic inequality continues to be subject to disputes between partly separate, ideological frames of the political left and right.

In addition to analyses of specific social problems that can be associated with economic inequality, parts of social sciences have tried to compare levels of health, wellbeing, and life satisfaction between countries that have different degrees of social inequality. One such study is Radcliff's comparison between countries with various sizes of government, degrees of labour organisations, and various degrees of state involvement in protecting consumers and workers using economic regulation. His conclusion is that more economically equal societies benefit the life satisfaction of its citizens. This benefit goes for both the unwealthy and wealthy ones (Radcliff, 2013).

Proposition 3: without support in finding legally and socially accepted ways of earning a stable position in mainstream society, it will be socially rational for people in exclusion to seek alternative ways of improving their position and of gaining esteem. Particularly for young men, we should expect the alternative ways to include crime, violence, addiction, and other compromises with the welfare of themselves and others.

However, economic and social inequality is not the only topic in the moral criticism that comes from the social sciences concerning capitalism. The Marxist scholar Marcuse has another angle to his criticism. According to him, technology has helped society, including those who were worse off, satisfy many of their manifest, material interests. Yet, capitalism obstructs people from leading fulfilling and truly happy lives. People are deceived by the artificial among their manifest interests. In his book entitled *One-Dimensional Man* (Marcuse, 1964/2002), he uses Freud's view of latent human interests as his guide to criticise capitalist society. Freud claims that culture and arts are positive ways of repressing latent sexual drives into something creative and rewarding. In this light, Marcuse maintains that capitalism destroys this positive sublimation by endlessly renewing people's manifest interest in new products in consumerist society. This has led to a 'repressive desublimination', and to 'the progressive brutalization and moronization of man' (Marcuse, 1968). Instead of real happiness, capitalism inevitably leads to 'euphoric unhappiness', he maintains. Using the terminology of this book, Marcuse holds that capitalism, in a totalitarian manner, does not imply any respect for the latent level of human interests; instead, capitalism merely exploits the latent level.

Two comments should be made about Marcuse's depiction of capitalist society and human interests. First, it is, to be sure, crucial to investigate to what extent society helps people satisfy not only their manifest interests but also their latent ones. Yet, it remains an empirical question to what extent people in capitalist society are more 'euphorically unhappy' or less 'genuinely happy' than people in non-capitalist societies, something that is notoriously difficult to examine in an impeccable and culturally neutral manner. Since Marcuse has beforehand decided that the consumerist aspect of capitalist society be the main evil of modern society, all he does is try to confirm this already decided standpoint. Second, it is far from obvious that Freud's version is accurate, concerning the latent level of human interests. From an evolutionary perspective informed by the sociology of consumption, latent human interests refer to interests that have been, and still are, immensely important for people's survival and reproduction: our social rationality of following our social motivation may help to satisfy fundamental interests. These include interests in gaining a good social position in one's group(s), in bonding, cooperation, in social distinction, in creating envy, and in engaging in mutual learning. From this book's perspective of social rationality, it could very well be that consumerism – a main trait of capitalism – used to be fairly efficient for meeting latent (social) interests, at least among people with a certain level of financial means. However, once many goods have become accessible to the majority of a population, and once mass media spreads information about these products and various consumption-based lifestyles, it becomes tough to meet one's latent, social interests merely by choosing certain types of consumer goods. This, if ever, might be the stage where consumerism leaves us 'euphorically unhappy', constantly noticing that we need to renew our consumption in order to reposition ourselves in relation to others, to satisfy our latent, social interests. In such a state it becomes particularly important that society and culture include other ways for stimulating people to meet their latent interests. For instance, Soper gives some guidelines and pre-scriptions in her work on 'alternative hedonism' (Soper, 2008). Soper suggests programmes for increasing people's wildlife activities, reading, writing, and so forth. In notions such as alternative hedonism, the positive side effects of reduced environmental harm and improvement to health are always mentioned.

Yet, the romantic Marxist utopia of a society where humans are purified into despising competition (one of the most problematised factors ascribed to capit-alism), a romantic view partly shared by Soper, will from an evolutionary per-spective have to be questioned. Competition for maintained or raised social status is core to latent human interests, evolutionary theory indicates. If seem-ingly excessive consumption is to be partly replaced by something else that meets latent human interests, this 'something else' will probably need to be other activities that involve social dynamics, including competition.

What gets lost with economic instruments?

In addition to Marcuse's and other Marxists' general criticism of capitalism or neoliberalism, there is another set of social scientific criticism of downsides to current developments. This set of criticism is specifically directed to what some perceive as an excessive, and too rapidly increasing, use of economic instru-ments for dealing with societal problems. Much of social scientists' criticism of economics is Dionysian. It contends that the Apollonian prescriptions of com-modification advanced by economics are getting out of hand.

For instance the social philosopher Sandel (2013), maintains that economic incentives and disincentives to be sure have their obvious and important role to play in traditional issues of economics: inflation, interest rates, and so forth. However, Sandel observes how more and more questions and problems in society are becoming subject to schemes involving economic incentives and dis-incentives. Economists with a traditional perspective of economics claim to think and work in the spirit of the eighteenth century economist Smith, argue for giving the 'invisible hand' of the market space to satisfy manifest, material inter-ests of all parties involved. However, current economics increasingly calls for measures that are anything but invisible-hand oriented, Sandel claims. He refers to the introduction of economic incentives and disincentives to manage virtually all social, environmental, and health-oriented problems. Using the economists' own language, he conceives of such measures an interference by special inter-ests, by economists.

What then would be the problem of economic incentives and disincentives for solving manifest problems: to the environment, to health, and so forth? Sandel routinely brings up two kinds of problems in each of the practical cases that he analyses. Concerning the first kind of problems, he addresses a lack of proper Apollonian understanding of human interests among some economists. Concern-ing the second kind of problems he addresses a lack of Dionysian understanding of human interests among these economists.

The first kind of problems is that economic incentives and disincentives often do not, according to Sandel, as well as several behavioural economists, help to solve the manifest problems at stake (Gneezy & Rustichini, 2000). For instance, economic incentives do not make patients better at taking their medicines. Nor do such incentives help drug addicts to reduce their drug use, or students in high school to strive towards better results. Sandel's Apollonian-oriented criticism is discussed in depth in subsequent sections of this book. In this section, however, the second, Dionysian kind of problems that Sandel addresses is more relevant, since it refers to latent human interests and the Dionysian part of humans and society. This is a problem area where social scientists have long taken a great research interest, frequently by using the term of 'commodification' (Fourcade & Healy, 2007). Their problematising argument contends that regardless of whether economic instruments may work or not, there is something morally and culturally objectable with extending the use of economic instruments to other realms than the classical ones (of managing inflation, interest rates, and so forth). In the case of financial incentives for stimulating that some students get higher grades in secondary school, such incentives distort and obscure the deeper purpose of gaining knowledge, Sandel, along with many social scientists, maintains. Similarly, the deeper sense of care for one's body and health is distorted and ignored if financial incentives and disincentives are introduced, translating health care and hygiene to economic carrots and sticks. Using economic incentives and disincentives to handle every issue puts 'shadow prices' on everything, including the relationship between spouses and between parents and children. Issues where Sandel argues that it would be highly inappropriate and demoralising to use economic incentives and disincentives include:

- a yearly quota and auctioning for people who want to immigrate to a country;
- stimulating people to donate kidneys or blood for surgery;
- offering people ahead of oneself in a line money for taking their place in a line (to hospitals, cultural events);
- allowing people to sell their right to vote to others who would vote more than once;
- allowing people to buy and sell babies.

Although Sandel uses the two latter issues (about votes and babies) in a rhetorical way (since few if any spokespersons of economic instruments have yet suggested that these should be candidates for becoming tradable items on the market), Sandel perceives a similar danger in all the issues above. Using economic incentives and disincentives in most areas of society leads to a quantification of values in a way that was not the situation in pre-market society. Everything becomes tradable, translatable to money, and nothing has priceless value in a society where economic incentives and disincentives are used for managing all issues. The Dionysian part of human interests, of traditions, habits, religion, and long-lasting group bonding, run the risk of being lost, Sandel maintains, along with many social scientists. Through introducing financial incentives and disincentives on everything, some manifest interests may, at first, be better satisfied, he admits. Yet, such instruments are often introduced while overlooking or completely ignoring the latent interests of people and in society more broadly.

How could this be commented on from the perspective of this book about human interests? Incentives and disincentives – economic and non-economic – are crucial to the interests and activities of society (regardless of Sandel's critique). Therefore, it is necessary to improve our understanding of incentives and incentives continuously if we are to increase the satisfaction of human interests. Social science, on the other hand, has long contended that it is immoral, over-simplistic, or both, to think and plan regarding incentives and disincentives towards a better society. Economics is the discipline which so far has taken incentives and disincentives most seriously. This has been a remarkable ambition, with consequences for the better and the worse in society. As traditional economics, through its notion of Homo economicus, has over-simplified and often misunderstood incentives and disincentives, behavioural economics has entered the scene, improving the understanding dramatically. Still, the preoccupation of both traditional and behavioural economics on the satisfaction of manifest, mainly Apollonian interests is too limited. All the human sciences are needed here to raise the ambition. The human scientific analysis needs to be expanded including the topic of how incentives and disincentives (planned or spontaneous) can be shaped in ways that help to satisfy the satisfaction of also latent, Dionysian interests. Ample, empirical evidence indicates that this level is likely to be more important to human wellbeing than at the manifest, Apollonian interests alone.

Using Haidt's moral foundations to analyse the dispute

To get an understanding of the underlying, genetically rooted aspects of the adversarial views of traditional economics and the fairly mainstream social scientific outlook of Sander, the concept and phenomenon of moral foundations is useful. Certain evolutionary anthropologists (Fiske, 1992), and moral psychologists (Haidt, 2008) assert that all human sociality, including cooperation within and between organisations, is rooted in a limited number of moral foundations. Similar to taste receptors on the tongue (enabling us to taste sweetness, sourness, and so on), humans are, according to Haidt, genetically equipped with receptors of morality, structured into half a dozen moral foundations. These are (1) care/harm, (2) fairness/cheating, (3) sanctity/degradation, (4) liberty/oppression, (5) authority/subversion, (6) loyalty/betrayal. A further candidate is (7) efficiency/waste (Haidt, 2012). The seventh foundation is not part of Haidt's original list, but turns out to be useful when analysing human interests through the lens of economics.

What are the moral foundations beneath the very distinct view of economists who favour an extensive expansion of the use of economic instruments for better satisfying manifest interests? And what are the moral foundations that make

Sandel (along with many other social thinkers) so sceptical to the wider spread of these instruments? As is discussed in depth in the book part on universal and culturally specific interests, the moral foundations most strongly implied by economists are the following ones. First, liberty/oppression is a moral foundation particularly close to the heart of many debates among economists. Economists stress the moral imperative of maximising the liberty of individuals to choose if they want to better satisfy their manifest interests by buying and selling (e.g. by earning money if they move back in the hospital line or by selling their kidney). Second, care/harm is often intertwined with other moral foundations in analyses of the potential of economic instruments and expanded trade. Accordingly, society should try to maximise the satisfaction of the specific, manifest interests, one at a time, in order to increase care and reduce harm in society. Harm includes environmental problems or lack of body organs for surgery, and poverty of people who are not allowed to sell what they can offer, such as their places in lines, organs, and so forth. Third, to maximise economic efficiency and reduce economic waste is always part of such debates in economics. Economic efficiency necessitates that as much as possible is society is tradable. This entails making the value of as much as possible quantifiable, calculable, directly comparable, and in principle replaceable (based on continuous calculations of trade-offs and opportunity costs). It is intriguing that Haidt has not (yet) integrated efficiency/waste into his ordinary list of moral foundations. We can only speculate here. One reason might be that economists clearly hold the view that economic efficiency is not a matter of morality, ideology, or fairness. To economists, the imperative to maximise economic efficiency is one of science. The usual reasoning among economists is that they prioritise the societal interest in finding ways for how to maximise economic efficiency. Once they have done this, it is up to politics and civil society to make judgements about morality, fairness, and so forth. The main founder of neo-classical economics, Friedman, maintains that 'positive economics is in principle independent of any particular ethical position or normative judgements' (1953, 4).

However, this dualism that economists have constructed between economic science and morality is misleading. The neo-Keynesian economist Atkinson (2009) has convincingly pointed out that economic efficiency is only worth striving for insofar as it makes people in society better off. Economists claim that efficiency has this benefit. Yet, this claim demands that we discuss and debate what makes people better off. This is a moral issue. In the terminology of this book, economists narrow down the moral issue of 'better off' into Apollonian interests. Yet, much research points to the possibility that economically efficient market exchange, where both parties are made better off in material terms, may actually make actors at a low socio-economic level engaged in the exchange worse off in non-material, Dionysian terms. If the efficient market exchange makes those at a high socio-economic level much better off whereas those at a low ditto are only made a little better off, the widening gap is a moral issue that economics implicitly accepts. But again, it is indeed a moral issue, in which economics is already implicitly engaged. Economics is not amoral.

Another sign that economics is not an amoral science is that economists frequently engage in debates about what society should do in light of trade-offs between economic efficiency and moral foundations such as sanctity (such as 'the commodification of nature' through emissions trading), and fairness (such as reductions of economic inequality). In many cases, the economic instruments may seem very promising for managing a wide range of problems. Moreover, economic historians indicate how volatile cultural notions can be of what things and activities should be allowed to be traded and not. According to this argument, if the members of a society only make an effort trying to become more open-minded about what to trade, social benefits could be extensive. In any case, efficiency/waste certainly fits the criteria of a moral foundation, particularly if we trust the claim by economists that exchange and trade has taken place since the dawn of humanity.

How about the social science, if we allow Sandel to be one of its spokespersons (although the views on economic instruments vary extensively in social science)? Sandel implies that an especially important moral foundation relating to Dionysian human interests concerns the honouring of sanctity and minimising degradation of values, norms, traditions, and other factors constituting latent human and societal interests. Another moral foundation concerns the importance of maximising fairness, where equal treatment of those with little material means is seen as crucial, and economic inequality is reduced. To be clear, fairness is a very broad moral foundation. Some conservatives would hold that it would be unfair to reduce economic inequality (if such reductions became mandatory).

Intriguingly, another moral foundation, of increasing care and reducing harm, appears to be a moral foundation downplayed by Sandel in some of his cases. To him, it seems more important that people donate one of their kidneys for the 'right' reason – compassion, empathy, or the like, than that the sufficient number of kidneys be available for kidney transplants (if this manifest interest requires the introduction of financial incentives and disincentives). Traditional economics, in contrast, has the ambition of being fully focused on 'a good result'; to optimise the satisfaction of the specific, manifest interest at stake. To try to reach a good result and at the same time also improve the values and morality among people and in a culture is to ask for too much, according to many traditional economists. (Economic) rationality demands a specific focus on one manifest interest at a time.

Leftists and conservative thinkers united

Another interesting aspect of Sandel's criticism, which breathes a lot of leftist views on the downsides with advanced capitalism, is that this criticism is very close to the cultural conservative opposition of certain commodification. Cultural conservatives and some leftists are partly united here. Both want to preserve something that there is a risk of losing, namely Dionysian components which keep society together: moral values, stable social bonds, local connection, perhaps what Tonnies refers to in his analysis of what he calls *Gemeinschaft* (community).

This Dionysian criticism transcends to the physical environment. A similar polarity can be seen about several environmental problems. Economists with a particularly high hope for economic instruments are ready to challenge the sanctity argument of the pricelessness of global, regional, and local commons. If privatising parts of these commons makes owners care more for these areas than if they remained commons, there should be a liberty to privatise the commons, this argument contends. What matters is the manifest interest, that here includes the interest of everyone, in a preserved environment. Sandel and others, by conceiving the satisfaction of latent interests as immensely important as well, favour the treatment of parts of the physical environment as sacred, priceless, as intrinsically valuable to preserve. This goes hand in hand with an interpretation of the fairness principle that everyone, rich or poor, should have equal right to spend time in these parts of the physical environment, and to gain the enriching experiences that this brings.

Much of this tension between a perspective where the Apollonian characteristics are angled towards economic efficiency, and the more Dionysian, culturally oriented perspective implies a concern for human dignity. The former camp conceives of human dignity as one where everyone has the liberty to turn most of the issues he or she faces into market exchange, thus satisfying what they perceive as their interest and what they perceive as care. The latter camp conceives of human dignity as one where the sanctity of certain moral and cultural values must be preserved, particularly for the benefit of those of lesser means and for keeping society together, which makes all of us better off. This may sometimes necessitate that society choose the first, best instruments towards reducing manifest problems. Yet, implications for latent interests must always be taken into account, since this is where Dionysian aspects of dignity are located.

What happens to dignity if certain groups give up their votes for money is a rhetorical question sometimes heard as a critique of policy suggestions of commodification made by economists. Giving up their votes for money would reduce poor adults into only partial citizens, compared to people who can have a political impact on society and be full citizens. On the other hand, human dignity can never be restricted to latent, Dionysian aspects only, separated from manifest, Apollonian ones.

Failures to understand latent interests

A final angle in which Dionysian social science has criticised views strongly emphasising the Apollonian dimension of human interests concerns societal progress. Apollonian approaches of all human sciences imply a belief in, or, at least, a hope for, progress. Increased trade, education, technological advancement, scientific discoveries, and increased positive-sum games, presuppose more extensive, social interaction and co-dependency. This way, people of various ideologies, cultures, and religions will hopefully be motivated to unite and cooperate even more extensively, through virtuous circles, in solving and reducing societal problems, such as violence, as well as problems to health and environment. Once the globe has reached a certain level, intensity, and complexity of mutually beneficial cooperation, not least through market liberalism, there will from an Apollonian perspective be no reason left for violence and destructive activities. Such activities will only make the adverse party – whether an individual, organisation or country, worse off. They will themselves cause a reduced satisfaction of their own manifest interests, such as stability, material welfare, and reduced harm to health and environment.

Example: Dionysian consistency beneath Apollonian inconsistency

In communication about health and sustainability, the typical logic is that information and warnings about the substantive problem at stake should by the content of their message motivate people and organisations to change their behaviour. The assumption behind this action is what in cognitive social psychology is called the A-B-C-model (Affect, Behaviour, and Cognition) (Eagly & Chaiken, 1993). A plethora of studies of attitudes and attitude change – often without comparing them with their relationship to people's behaviour – have for several decades been carried out in the widest range of the human sciences (Konisky, Milyo, & Richardson, 2008). Such studies suggest that identifications of what attitudes people and organisations hold may 'obviously' say a lot about practices of these people and organisations. Applied to sustainability and health, 'CAB' would be a better name. Informing about, for instance, environmental problems associated with car use or with using meat as a main food ingredient makes people and organisations learn about these problem connections (Cognition). This would give car users or carnivores unpleasant emotions (Affect). In turn, this would strengthen people's inclination to change their practices (Behaviour), thus removing the cognitive-emotive tension (Frewer, Kole, Van de Kroon, & de Lauwere, 2005). Although important dependence exists between the cognitive, affective, and behavioural in certain parts of our daily lives, it is striking how often this pattern does not seem to hold, particularly concerning sustainability issues (Shove, 2010). Statistics of daily practices with a negative impact on environment and other sustainability dimensions are changing in a positive manner in some areas (e.g. peak car), but not in others, such as flights and meat (EUROSTAT, 2014).

This so-called 'value-action gap' (sometimes called 'the attitude-behaviour gap') is a common puzzle in social science (Whitmarsh, Seyfang, & O'Neill, 2011). It is also discussed and analysed at least indirectly in the economic and evolutionary sciences. Why do people and organisations so often differ in what they say (their opinions, attitudes, values) compared to what they do (their 'act of hand', choices of practices, modes of travel, food habits, financial priorities)? The gap prevails despite the following facts:

- people's knowledge is in many places high about health and sustainability issues;
- their stated concerns are many times very high;
- people's awareness is often high of connections between sustainability problems and daily life;

- they often assume that their own changes in daily practices would make a substantial difference.

Why, then, does not the increased sustainability- and health-oriented awareness lead to clearer reductions of environmental and other harms to sustainability?

In economics, explanations include the claim that attitudes are meaningless and worthless if people and organisations do not match their attitudes with 'revealed preferences'. The latter is people's overt behaviour (economic or other) that confirms that they mean what they state (Van Kempen, Muradian, Sandoval, & Castaneda, 2009). For example, unless people choose fair trade coffee (which usually costs more than conventional coffee), their stated preferences about being concerned with unfair trade are meaningless (Sauer & Fischer, 2010). Verbal concern without 'revealed preferences' – such as sacrifices of money or time – should never be treated as truly reflecting manifest interest.

Social science (aside from psychology and cognitive social psychology) is typically critical to studies of the relationship between attitudes and behaviour altogether. The most common criticism by social scientists contends that such studies put an excessive emphasis on the choice and power of single individuals to acquire better knowledge (about health, environment, and so forth), which in turn gives them full freedom to change their practices and make the world a better place. Instead, social science maintains, people live through social structures and institutions. Actors and structure (the latter including the political and market realms) need to be in a relationship of mutual impact, for comprehensive change to take place (Spaargaren, 2011). Manifest, explicit attitudes and behaviour are usually in focus in social science. The importance of 'structures', 'institutions', 'situations', and other social science buzzwords are identified as fundamentally important. Such social scientific identifications rarely go beyond descriptions of practical and normative constraints to free human agency. Why structures and institutions matter, beyond the practical constraints that they may entail, is rarely analysed by social scientists.

Evolutionary science, finally, has not yet come very far regarding critically analysing the attitude-behaviour gap. Some evolution-based studies of attitudes and behaviour involve the search for neuroscientific explanations as to why attitudes and behaviour seem to go together in the cases where they go together. How social context matters for bridging the attitude-behaviour gap in certain cases, is one such issue (McCall, Tipper, Blascovich, & Grafton, 2012). Still, the main point to take home from neuroscientific studies in this area is their criticism of surveys and interviews carried out in social and economic science. Although such methods may be valuable for identifying explicit attitudes and values, they usually miss a far more important part of human interests: what neuropsychologists call implicit attitudes (Walla, Koller, & Meier, 2014). According to scholars in this discipline, people who hold the examined, implicit attitudes, are not conscious of them. Implicit attitudes are located at the latent level of the human mind. Particularly in socially sensitive questions, such as one's ethical priorities – which environmental issues may embed – implicit attitudes are better predictors of behaviour than are explicit ones, neuropsychologists maintain. This means that implicit attitudes are highly dependent on the culture and social context in which people live (Stanley, Phelps, & Banaji, 2008). An intriguing issue is how human scientists should conceive of the 'new' component of implicit attitudes, in relation to acts of hand (behaviour/revealed preferences) and word acts (explicit attitudes/stated preferences). It seems that the social context in many cases constitutes limits to people's environmental concern (limits, such as poor public transportation, absence of recycling facilities in the neighbourhood, few protein-rich, vegetarian dishes in some restaurants). Does this mean that learning about people's implicit attitudes would be even more revealing than studying people's revealed preferences (behaviour and practices)? If the neuropsychologists are correct, implicit attitudes point towards the propensity for people to act given that the (infra) structure and social context be modified. Studying revealed preferences, on the other hand, only shows what people are ready to do here and now.

Our claim is that a satisfactory explanation of the apparent gap between attitudes and behaviour needs focuses more on latent human interests. The neuropsychological focus on implicit attitudes points to some extent in this direction. To move further into understanding the role of latent human interests, it is useful to distinguish between 'Apollonian and Dionysian trust'. Apollonian trust refers to a trust in the soundness, relevance, and accuracy of authoritative information, in this case, governmental information on environmental harm and what could be done about it. Here, people in many countries score very high. However, what is often overlooked is the deficit in Dionysian trust. As mentioned above, Dionysus is fundamentally group oriented, impulsive, and instinctive. Holding a Dionysian trust refers to trusting, often spontaneously, that changing our practices, in this case, those that cause environmental harm, would benefit our social bonds, status, and collaboration with the people whom we find it valuable to collaborate and socialise. The importance of Dionysian trust is not least visible through the immense power of horizontal influence, which evolutionary (Mesoudi, 2011) and social science (Bentley, Earls, & O'Brien, 2011) have identified.

However, Dionysian trust (in social benefits of imitating and influencing others at a horizontal level) is of little value if an Apollonian trust does not accompany this trust. In this example, Apollonian trust refers to the trust in the validity and importance of the information and knowledge claims from the government, NGOs, and scientists about effective ways for reducing environmental and health-related harm. The necessity of Apollonian trust is obvious not least in present-day society. The disconnectedness of daily routines and their environmental, as well as social, consequences, make people highly dependent on expert systems that help them see such connections. Still, this does not mean that the other type of trust, the Dionysian, would be 'irrational'. Counter to being 'irrational', Dionysian trust should be seen as a part of social rationality. It is socially rational to act on the Dionysian trust that allowing oneself to be influenced by other people's practices, for instance, reduced use of energy and reduced car use, may be beneficial for one's social position, among one's neighbours, peers, friends, colleagues, and beyond. This means that positive, environmental consequences – from local to global – to be sure may be extensive by such horizontal influence. From the perspective of social rationality these positive, environmental consequences will be 'only' positive means or side effects. This is arguably how successful sustainable development efforts need to be planned and designed.

Conclusions

Human scientists, who have been aware of the often overriding position of Dionysian interests of actors and organisations who make decisions, are quick to criticise traditional economics for missing or downplaying the Dionysian force.

A way in which behavioural economists and socially oriented economists claim to prove the overriding character of Dionysian interests is by indicating, through ample evidence, how people's relative income level matters more for their well-being than their absolute income level (once they are at the level of meeting their basic material needs). Along these lines, the recognition of 'conspicuous consumption' is a way in which alternative economics (along with social science) indicate the importance of Dionysian interests. Of course, traditional economics acknowledges people's interests in social bonds, esteem, distinctions, and so forth. Yet, these economists usually find the Apollonian inclination of 'optimising' the satisfactions, also these interests, through partly conscious calculations of trade-offs, costs, benefits, opportunity costs, and diminishing marginal utility, overriding.

Evolutionary science emphasises the Dionysian through the concepts of individual selection and kin selection. These scientists perceive Dionysian interests as taking place predominantly at the latent level. Evolution has kept many traits from lower animals in humans, to the extent that these traits have had adaptive value in the ancestral environment where the evolution of Homo sapiens has mainly taken place. The role of the unconscious, and of self-deception, is a human trait that has most often than not served us well throughout history. The fact that people often over-estimate their abilities, likeability, honesty, and so forth entails a signalling to others that they are capable and trustworthy. This leads to inclusions of these people in the group, which increases their chances of reproductive success. This chapter gives an example of how the common gap between what people say about their environmental concern and what they do in terms of environmental harm can be explained along similar lines.

Social science shows the latent, Dionysian interests beneath even an Apollonian, societal change, such as the increasing influence of Protestant ethics. Moreover, by expanding the Marxist, Apollonian critique of the low material conditions of workers, into a moral one about the degeneration of human life of capitalism, weakened bonds with people, and an increased marketisation of human relationships, social science stresses the key role of the satisfaction of Dionysian interests to human wellbeing. This chapter investigates differences between the human sciences in how they implicitly interpret the moral psychologist Haidt's seven moral foundations when they reason around various Apollonian and Dionysian priorities. It furthermore highlights how the leftist and conservative sides of social science are in several cases united in their Dionysian concerns, placing themselves in opposition to Apollonian concerns stressed by capitalist thinkers, mainly in economics.

Part II

Universal and culturally specific interests

Prologue

The second part of this book analyses what is probably the most infected and misconceived theme across the human sciences: culturally specific and universal interests. The theme has been touched upon already in the previous chapter. This was unavoidable, since manifest and latent interests cannot be entirely separated from questions about what types of human interests are universal and culturally specific, respectively. It is even relevant to ask whether or not the two pairs of concepts belong together in a symmetrical way. Do manifest interests (in substantive 'projects' and goals towards which people explicitly strive) overlap with culturally specific interests (in actively relating to specific cultural norms, conventions, and expectations)? Do latent interests (what underlying, hidden interests and goals people strive towards, sometimes subconsciously) overlap with universal interests (in satisfying deeply human, often genetically based interests and motivations)? To a substantial extent this pairing is accurate, I would hold. Still, the human sciences have different views on this. My ambition of providing an integrative understanding of human interests presupposes that I give a more nuanced picture than a presumption of symmetry between the two conceptual pairs.

Concerning universal and cultural specific interests, I maintain that social science scholars, in fear of becoming 'biologistic', are overly categorical in avoiding or downplaying universal interests. At the same time, evolutionary science scholars frequently too narrowly interpret cultural specificities in the Western, liberal democratic world as universal interests. Lately, for instance, scholars of evolutionary science have elevated fairness to a universal interest, an interest that all or most humans across cultures may understand and care about. Despite the principle validity of this claim, there is a particular need for social and economic sciences that may analyse how infamously plastic framings of fairness and reciprocity can be. This plasticity includes normative adaptations to unequal social orders. Social scientists note that by impregnating false beliefs into the oppressed and other less privileged groups, these groups have throughout history been misled into setting their reference points at a rock bottom level. False beliefs may be a result of being led to compare one's conditions with those of other unprivileged and oppressed groups), even believing that their ruler is 'reasonably fair', as in not being violent and sadistic (Rosen, 2013). 'Fairness' may sometimes perversely denote that rulers follow laws and contracts, albeit within an inherently unequal social structure. In addition to the problems of such false beliefs, the differentiation of views across segments of oppressed people concerning how they view their ruler in terms of fairness is one reason of many reasons why it is often difficult for oppressed and unprivileged groups to unite and mobilise into protest action (Eltis, Bradley, & Cartledge, 2011).

The term 'universal interests' demands an initial explanation. In the way it is used and developed in this book, it derives from the term 'human universals'. The evolutionary anthropologists Boyd and Silk define human universals as 'mechanisms of human behaviour held in common among people all over the world' (Boyd and Silk 2006, 590). I claim that if a trait is a human universal, as defined above, there are important human interests associated with this universal, interests at the manifest and/or latent level.

The term human universals has been developed as a criticism of an emphasis on cultural particulars – how peoples differ from each other – and as a criticism of a de-emphasis of how peoples resemble each other beneath the manifest level of different cultural expressions across peoples (Brown, 1991). In particular, evolutionary and cognitive anthropologists have conducted comprehensive, cross-cultural, ethnographic studies aimed at identifying human universals at several degrees. They distinguish between 'absolute universals' (found everywhere) and 'near universals' (found in most – possibly all – cultures). Whereas it is difficult to show empirically that they exist in all cultures, the term 'near universals' is often used instead, to signify traits found in most cultures. There are additional degrees of universality, including 'statistical universals', denoting traits that are significantly more prevalent across cultures than chance would be able to explain (Brown, 2004).

Since studies of human universals are often conducted by scholars with an evolutionary perspective, one would perhaps assume that they define human universals as fully genetically based traits. However, this is not the case. Scholars bring up some (near) universal traits that do not have a direct, genetic basis: to use fire for cooking, for instance, seems to be a (near) human universal. It has emerged and evolved culturally; in some cultures the use of fire for cooking has been discovered independently, and in others this innovation has been shared culturally. The cognitive and social capacities for teaching, learning, and cultural transmission have been necessary for this, and it has genetically adaptive value to do so, by reducing the risk of food-related deceases. Still, making and using fire is not based on our genes.

Furthermore, there are elements of the *human condition* that are universal. For example, humans in all cultures are aware that they will die, at least that this life will come to an end. People in all cultures are aware that they are vulnerable, at least physically. Physiological elements of the human condition are obviously rooted in genetics and biology (making us vulnerable and mortal). At the same time, it is reasonable to conceive of the human, universal awareness of this as moving beyond genes, similar to people's awareness of specific, cultural conditions and expectations of the society in which they find themselves.

As to a definition of culture, it suffices to give a simple one here. A useful definition is provided by the anthropologist Edward Tylor in his book *Primitive Culture* (Tylor, 1873/2010, 1): 'that complex whole that includes knowledge, art, morals, law, custom, and any other capacity and habit acquired by man as a member of a society'. Key to this definition is that culture is acquired, learnt. Although parts of Tylor's list of culture bear resemblance with Brown's list of universals, Tylor implicitly refers to culture as the specific content of the (universal) forms of morals, law, custom, habits, and so forth, content that differs vastly between cultures.

Before the rest of the theme examines how the human sciences conceive of culturally specific and universal interests, as well as how they are intertwined, the following section begins with a categorical assumption: that there is indeed an overriding, universal human interest on which all human sciences ought to be able to agree. Subsequent chapters of this theme scrutinise this assumption concerning how the three human sciences conceive of universality and cultural specificity of interests.

4 Glory, honour, or at least esteem

Is there such thing as a human interest that is not only universal but also an over-riding, universal interest, aside from the interests in meeting our most basic material and emotional needs? If there is such an interest, what would it be? The three human sciences rarely examine this topic in a systematic way. Should it not be a critical issue in intra- and interdisciplinary debates? After all, a fundamental aim of the human sciences is to produce knowledge and policy recommendations that do not deviate from the most important human interests.

Projects in liberal democracy

To begin an attempt at identifying an overriding human interest, we need to take one step back and put the matter in the cultural perspective of liberal democracy. From that point of view, it seems out of fashion to ask such a question, aside from basic needs and the long list rights stated in The Universal Declaration of Human Rights (2013). Why? Because at least in a liberal democracy (here defined as the culture encompassing all mainstream Western political ideologies, from social democratic to conservative ones), the issue sounds awkward and irrelevant, unless it is part of a religious discussion. Instead, people's goals are usually discussed regarding individual 'projects' (Bauman, 1993). In the culture of liberal democracy, people, particularly in the middle class, label as their main interests all kinds of projects that give their efforts meaning. People and society treat manifest, individual projects as finite goals when they plan them and are in the midst of them. In our role as citizen-consumers, a project can be directed towards accumulating money and goods, perhaps with the accompanied goal of not harming the environment too much in the process. In our roles as employer or employees, the project may be part of efforts of doing as well as possible in a company, public agency, or other types of organisation. Our project can be to excel in sports or computer games, to reduce environmental harm, to be the fastest car driver, to do voluntary work through philanthropy, to create pieces of fine art, or just to eat well and enjoy ourselves. As the examples here reveal, projects need not be isolated to projects of an individual only. Many projects are, of course, group-based, collective, and can take place on any societal level. As the sociologist Simmel shows already in the early 1900s, each can be involved in several different projects. She can enter different roles, and associate with entirely different groups of people in the various projects (Simmel, 1903). This mobility is core to the individualism of liberal democracy.

What is liberal about this is that any project, from a porn business to activities in Medicins Sans Frontiers, is treated as in principle valuable, as long as individuals or groups claim that it is valuable to them. Another necessary condition is that the dominant societal understanding, the dominant framing, of the project is that it does not entail apparent negative liberties. This term refers to activities that are negative in the sense that they reduce other people's liberties (Berlin, 1958). In the most shallow sense, even parts of the porn industry and other sex industries might go free from accusations of not honouring their workers' negative liberties. The content of a business, and what type of individual project, one is engaged in as employer or employee, is placed beyond evaluation. Each individual should mind her own business. The magazine *The Economist* illustrates this in a report about the sex industry: 'Some prostitutes do indeed suffer from trafficking, exploitation or violence; their abusers ought to end up in jail for their crimes. But for many, both male and female, sex work is just that: work' (The Economist, 2014).

As long as people can claim that their projects do not involve negative interference, in a direct and measurable way, with other individuals' projects all projects should be treated with the same respect (albeit with room for cultural and aesthetic remarks about vulgarity, and so forth), the culture of liberal democracy proclaims. The phrase 'De gustibus non est disputandum' is the main norm embraced in liberal democracy: 'In matters of taste, there can be no disputes'. What in other cultures are treated as matters of ethics, can in a liberal democracy be turned into issues of taste – aesthetics – as long as the matters are not illegal, and do not formally violate the principle of negative freedom. It is not a coincident that the quote above is produced by *The Economist*. The most common perspective in economics about human interests is that it is up to the individual herself to judge whether a certain project increases the satisfaction of her interests. No outside party should violate her right to decide on her projects. This norm is foundational both for economics and for liberal democracy.

The capacity and inclination of people to create their manifest goals and projects, and to have their projects provide them with meaning – in people's roles as citizens, consumers, employers, or employees, defines what makes these people modern humans in a liberal democratic society (Berman, 1983). This resonates with views emphasising the role of manifest interests, views presented in the previous part of this book.

Happiness and wellbeing

At the same time, the issue of an overriding human goal is indeed touched upon also in liberal democracies, albeit indirectly. Minimisation of risks and harm, and maximisation of safety, comfort, convenience, and choices are the usual means for trying to reach a state that is the closest as we most often get to as an overriding human goal in liberal democracy: happiness (Bok, 2010; Nesse, 2005). Human scientists continuously conduct comprehensive studies comparing answers to these questions across countries, cultures, across socio-economic groups, age groups, and so forth (Blanchflower & Oswald, 2011).

To be sure, much criticism has been brought forth. There are intricate challenges involved in trying to compare answers to the seemingly straightforward happiness question across, for instance, cultures of people speaking different languages. Moreover, even if those challenges could be handled and minimised, a more profound challenge is how to assess whether happiness really is the best measuring stick for evaluating and comparing the quality of life and societal success (Ott, 2010). It is far from obvious that a constant state of happiness (as in smiling and laughing all the time) is what people wish. Therefore, the term happiness has in much of the research been replaced with the term 'wellbeing'. Even so, some social and economic thinkers, particularly those with a libertarian view, maintain that happiness – or subjective wellbeing – is none of the government's business. Governments should only make sure justice and negative liberty be provided. Individuals should take care of the rest, through their projects. It should be entirely up to individuals to seek their happiness and even wellbeing. This view can be traced, in parts, to the libertarian, nineteenth century political thinker Constant, who claims the following: 'Let [Government officials] confine themselves to being just. We shall assume the responsibility of being happy for ourselves' (Constant, 1816/1988, 326).

Traditional economics implies a similar view, but uses other arguments: It claims that hedonic experiences of happiness cannot be rigorously measured. More fundamentally, traditional economics maintains that rational agents per definition optimise their hedonic experiences through the choices they make. Therefore, traditional economists hold that the human sciences get all the relevant information about what makes people happy by examining their manifest choices, their so-called revealed preferences (Kahneman, Wakker, & Sarin, 1997). In this book, however, I do not leave the issue of happiness and wellbeing so easily. Since the topic of this book is to learn more about human interests, some effort should be made examining what factors that converge with happiness and wellbeing repeatedly in studies across cultures and over time. As it turns out, there is one factor – or set of factors – that always comes up in surveys asking about people's happiness. The same factor always comes up concerning people's assessments about their wider 'quality of life': social relationships and social bonds. Respondents state and rank this factor more clearly and less ambiguously than they rank, for instance, the significance of their financial situation for their quality of life. (This presupposes that they perceive that they have their basic material needs and human rights met.) People's social relationships, affiliations, and sense of community are among psychologists elevated to conditions that are directly and deeply satisfying (of 'intrinsic value'). Psychologists distinguish such conditions from people's financial success (when above a minimum level), and various manifest projects, which psychologists often categorise as issues of 'extrinsic value'. This distinct ranking order should be kept in mind as we continue to search for universal, overriding interests. The psychologist Kasser indicates, on the basis of decades of psychological data, how people with their value focus on the accumulation of material possessions and wealth are subject to greater risk of depression, anxiety, and problems with intimacy. This pattern has been found regardless of income, age, or culture, once people have their very basic material needs satisfied (Kasser, 2001).

To avoid becoming entirely absorbed by the culture of liberal democracy, it is refreshing to move a few steps back in the history of ideas. Usually, when social scientists search for valuable ideas in history, they search for material that can help to improve the ethics of contemporary society. How should people lead their lives as more respectful individuals, company owners, politicians, or in some other function? Virtues, such as temperance and frugality, exemplify long-lost terms, absent in modern liberal democracy. Such terms might indeed be useful and refreshing to introduce to discussions of how people in current society should shape their means, whatever ends they are seeking, for instance in direct attempts at reducing environmental and social harm (Gruen, Jamieson, & Schlottmann, 2013).

Machiavelli

However, human scientists have made fewer efforts to trace historical ideas about what might constitute overriding human interests, if we leave aside goals such as the utilitarian objective of minimising pain and maximising pleasure, or of maximising the meeting of 'preferences' in the world. The writings of the political sixteenth century thinker, Machiavelli, are routinely criticised – in parts reasonably so – for prescribing to leaders the use of brutality and dishonesty as supplementary, political means. More interesting to our book is that he, contrary to many thinkers of today, is not afraid to discuss overriding, human interests. In his famous book, *The Prince*, he is to be sure mainly focused on rulers, but elsewhere he discusses other segments of society as well. He uses two terms to define the goal of princes: honour and glory (Zmora, 2007). Machiavelli is of the notorious opinion that the purpose, honour, glory, along with political and social stability, may to a large extent sanctify the means. This is one reason why Machiavelli is sometimes called the first modern man. He introduces the novel idea that the ruler should not primarily strive selfishly towards being loved – by his people or by God (and by pleasing God come to Heaven). Instead, the ruler should be preoccupied with his ultimate, human and earthly (societal) interests: honour, glory, intertwined with political and social stability. Importantly, however, Machiavelli clarifies that power should not, and could not, serve as a sufficient end. Power obtained through excessive use of brutality (as the lion) and slyness (as the fox), leads only to power and empire, yet without glory. Without glory, power is a failure, he holds (Machiavelli, 1532/2003).

Can we learn anything from this when trying to understand human interests of today? Machiavelli's claim about the insufficiency of power arguably overlaps with the issue of financial wealth in our liberal democracy. If there is only material wealth there is a failure, or, at least, an absence of honour and glory, also in the views of some of us culturally adapted to liberal democracy. A successful businessperson in the porn industry runs a higher risk of lacking honour and glory than does a successful person in Medicins Sans Frontiers. Although liberal democracy rarely allows for terms such as 'a lack of honour and glory' (at least not outside of sports arenas), the sense is probably there among the vast majority of people as among most people in all cultures. Why? Because honour, glory, social esteem or whatever one calls it are parts of what is universally appreciated. It might be an overriding, universal interest in the sense that all people are in various ways fundamentally motivated by these factors. The set of factors of honour, glory, and esteem takes place in, and between, all strata of human societies. Obviously, most of us might not have a chance or an interested in becoming a Machiavellian ruler or any ruler. But what I in this book call social rationality, is reflected in the immense importance the vast majority of people in all cultures give not just to intimate social relationships, but also to the above-mentioned set of factors.

When people in liberal democratic cultures use terms such as honour, they usually refer either to the past or Southern cultures (Fischer, Manstead, & Mosquera, 1999). For instance, 'honour-related crime' has become the term for the horrendous crimes committed, usually on women by their family members, in small parts of non-Western cultures. In the literature on intercultural communication addressed to Westerners, mandatory sections include recommendations for how to avoid offending the honour of people in these non-Western cultures. However, discussions comparing Western senses of honour with senses of honour in, for instance, Arabic, Indian, or Japanese cultures are rare. People in the West assume that honour is irrelevant to them. They assume that we just want to be treated 'nicely'. However, concern with honour, including its closely related terms, esteem, status, recognition, and so forth, is a human universal – albeit with cultural differences about what constitutes a violation of a person's or group's honour (Cohen, Nisbett, Bowdle, & Schwarz, 1996) – the Western assumption above is mainly a sign of cultural blindness.

Even if many people and groups do not seem to care about raising their social status and esteem, much of contemporary psychosocial ills are tied to a sense that one is not sufficiently recognised and esteemed, something that in turn typically entails a reduced self-esteem (Leary & Allen, 2011). Intriguingly, such psychosocial ills are unyielding also among groups and in countries where there is material security, with few worries about not being able to get one's basic material needs met (Luthar & Becker, 2002).

Dignity and esteem

To be sure, it is tempting to use strong terms such as glory and honour to denote an overriding human interest. However, in a world with such immense economic and social inequality, it seems awkward to use such grandiose terms. How about the most modest term that denotes human interests in their social position and bonding? This term is 'dignity'. It is stated in Article One of The Declaration of

Universal Human Rights: 'All human beings are born free and equal in dignity and rights. They are endowed with reason and conscience and should act towards one another in a spirit of brotherhood.'

The reason that I find it necessary to look also beyond dignity in this book is that dignity is frequently used in calls for satisfying the very basic physical and emotional needs of humans and animals. Moreover, the overriding human interest in dignity appears all too obvious and uncontroversial for being the main focus of a book about human interests. At the same time, it is over-simplistic to confine dignity to a stage reached as soon as the most basic human, physical, and emotional needs are met. The founding father of classical economics, Smith, who is also a moral philosopher, makes this point clear in the eighteenth century. He argues that the meeting of basic, physical needs is *not* sufficient for dignity. An additional prerequisite for dignity is the capacity to participate in community life. This, in turn, presupposes, what Smith formulates as 'The ability to appear in public without shame' (Sen, 1999, 73). Being an economist with a sociological sensitivity, Smith recognises that dignity also necessitates that a person can afford the basic material standard of her specific society. The *relative* material standard matters, which is a point that ought to be recognised more often in economic science. He gives the example of leather shoes. 'Custom ... has rendered leather shoes a necessary of life in England. The poorest person of either sex would be ashamed to appear in public without them' (Smith, 1776/1843, 368).

Consequently, Smith argues that wages must necessarily be raised, and taxes adjusted, so that everyone can afford such items that, to be sure, are not physical necessities for survival but are nevertheless culturally necessary in order to be able to participate in community life: 'Under necessaries, therefore, I comprehend not only those things which nature, but those things which the established rules of decency have rendered necessary to the lowest rank of people' (Smith, 1776/1843, 368). The institutional economist, Sen (1999), uses Smith's notions about human dignity as a basis for his 'capability approach' to poverty and development.

Although I fully agree with Smith as well as Sen above, I would like to move beyond and 'above' dignity in the search for an overriding, universal interest that people can be expected to struggle constantly to increase or at least maintain. At this higher level, esteem becomes relevant. However, even if esteem is perhaps located at a higher level of ambition than dignity, esteem might still seem watered down and unprovocative to the reader. Of course, people want to maintain and raise their social esteem! To give this claim some extra edge, it is useful to reverse the matter. What are not overriding, universal interests? There are two types of human interests that must be overridable if social esteem is an overriding, universal interest. The first one is the interest in finding optimal solutions to substantive problems (to health, the environment, economy, to social justice, and so forth). The second one is the human interest in truth finding, or at finding the best possible knowledge.

Again, my argument does not contend that these interests are not immensely important, subject to passionate and often life-saving efforts in society. What it does contend is instead shown in our following proposition:

Proposition 4: if actions, measures, and procedures towards finding optimised solutions, or towards finding the best possible knowledge, are in conflict with people's latent interests in preserving or raising their social esteem both in the short and long run, their social rationality is likely to exert an immense (often unconscious) pressure on the individual, group, or organisation – universally – to compromise the former (manifest) interest rather than the latter (latent) one.

To make this proposition slightly more sophisticated, I should introduce the notion of a hierarchical system of goals and ends. According to this model, a goal is at the same time a means to a higher goal (Pervin, 1989). For instance, it is possible to have an interest in postponing the award of social esteem at a lower level, by first engaging more intensely in a manifest, problem-solving project that in the longer term may lead to social esteem at a higher level. An example would be politicians who choose to deal with a nation's extensive environmental harm in ways that in the short run might be highly unpopular: through penalty fees for fossil-fuel-based modes of travel and goods transportation, meat tax, removals of previously subsidised employee benefits that involve pollution, and so forth. In the short run, this may reduce the esteem and popularity of these politicians. However, in the long run, such impossible decisions may create stability, employment, and reduced environmental harms that help increase the esteem of these politicians far more, perhaps even making them end up in the history books with the highest esteem. Importantly, we should not expect people to be fully aware of their means-end chains. Nor should we expect people to plan strategically according to such chains, or to recalculate constantly how to best meet interests higher in the hierarchy. Social rationality entails to a large extent processes at the latent, unconscious level.

If the thesis about the overriding, universal interest in social esteem holds, which the three human science disciplines are to scrutinise, it becomes crucial to take this thesis into serious account in all kinds of policy making. A broad strategy for doing this would be to make sure that efforts towards finding the solutions to substantive, manifest problems, and for improving knowledge in general, are organised in ways that they converge with, and even move via, the overriding human interest in social esteem. Moreover, the social rationality with its constant orientation towards preserving or strengthening self-esteem raises the need for social and political checks and balances for all kinds of processes of knowledge acquisition and policy making. Extensive research in cognitive science and psychology has recently provided the following main finding which have been developed into 'The argumentative theory': The latent function of people's argumentation is not to improve knowledge quality or to find the best solution. Instead, the latent function of an individual's or group's argumentation is to convince others that the former are right, and to have the others support this person or group, thereby strengthening our social esteem. Evolution has equipped people with a powerful confirmation bias, which means that they tend to strongly believe in the argument that they advance, often by deceiving themselves. Most people do this from time to time, since it is more convincing to others that they are correct if they send implicit signals to others that the persons themselves are truly convinced that they are correct. From the perspective of problem solving in a wide range of areas, this constitutes a huge challenge. Luckily, this has made cognitive science and other related fields embrace the well-established social scientific ideal of deliberation and deliberative democracy (Mercier & Landemore, 2012). The reason is that the only chance of handling the distorting confirmation bias of single individuals in processes of problem solving is to have several people meet and carve off each other's confirmation bias, thereby moving towards far better problem solving and solutions than even the most knowledgeable and talented individuals can manage on their own (Mercier, 2013).

Proposition 5: the socially rational function of argumentation and debate is not primarily problem solving or truth finding, but to convince and persuade others, and make others support and ally with the persuader. Argumentation often involves self-deception of the one who tries to convince the others. In addition to the well-documented benefits of deliberative processes for recognising people's interests (in several positions), deliberative processes serve the purpose of evening out (often unconscious) confirmation biases among individuals.

Conclusions

This chapter searches for a universal, overriding interest. The culture of liberal democracy is highly project-oriented, where the interest in focus is often the manifest one of completing one's personal or group-oriented projects successfully. Overriding, universal interests are mainly discussed regarding happiness (or wellbeing), although strands of liberalism conceive of such interests as entirely private affairs, as long as the government provides justice and secures the negative freedom of its people.

Although every mentally healthy human scientist is, in principle, highly in favour of people's happiness and wellbeing, the challenge is to highlight their universal, overriding basis. Machiavelli helps me advance the thesis that social esteem could be such a basis (although he uses more grandiose terms). Also, dignity turns out to be a meaningful concept to couple with esteem. Dignity is more than the meeting of material needs necessary to survival. Since humans are social to their core, driven by social rationality, people need to reach the material standard of their culture to participate fully in that culture and community life.

The thesis that social esteem and dignity are overriding, universal interests is not as watered down as it may first appear. It implies, first, that personal and societal interests in solving manifest problems – to health, environment, economy – can be expected to be compromised as soon as these interests are in conflict with the Dionysian, often latent, interests in maintaining or strengthening people's social esteem. Second, it implies that truth seeking, and efforts at improving information and knowledge, can also be expected to be compromised (often unconsciously) when improvements in information and knowledge would entail reduced social esteem of the people or groups involved. In both cases, it could very well be more socially rational to prioritise social esteem. In sum, if the thesis is correct, it has immense relevance for how society should find better ways for how to handle environmental and health problems.

5   The blank slate and its critics

As it turns out, this second part of the book has proceeded too quickly. It has done so by starting with the propositions that there are genetically rooted human universals, and perhaps even one overriding, universal interest. To give the mainstreams of human sciences justice, neither of these propositions should be made at the outset. The human sciences are not in full agreement that there exist universal human interests, aside from the most basic physical needs. To examine differences, misconceptions, and similarities on this matter, the following two extensive sectors examine how the three sciences understand it. Are we blank slates on which society and culture does all the writing? If we are not blank slates, what is prepared genetically on the slates, and how? Here we should note the distinction between needs and drives. Strictly speaking, people may have needs without drives (e.g. when they need medicine or dietary supplements without having a drive for taking these substances). Reversely, they may have a drive without a need (e.g. the drive, however strong, towards having sex is not a need in any essential sense: they would not, as individuals, die without it). In various social contexts, the relation between needs and drive becomes more complicated. As a rule, it is more appropriate to use the term of drives (non-essential for the survival of the individual) than of needs, when referring to socially and culturally based motivations.

Blank slate subscribers

Among the human sciences, mainstream social science is the one that has a reputation for promoting an absence of human universal traits, and in consequence an absence of ditto interests. There are notable exceptions. The sociologist Parsons, for example, has developed his general theory of action in close connection to modern evolutionary biology. This has made him recognise cultural patterns that he argues exists, or will exist, universally during certain stages of cultural development (Parsons, 1966). However, this is far from mainstream in contemporary social science. Nor is it obvious that Parsons enters the issue that is the focus of this book: concerning a genetic basis for human universals.

To be sure, many social scientists conduct their daily research without discussing these matters. If they were asked, a big proportion would probably call themselves agnostics about human universality. Their pragmatic position would be that universal human traits are irrelevant for them to discuss, that this issue is beyond their scientific scope. Some of them would extend this view by holding that it is beyond any social scientist's scope; whether some human interests are culturally specific or universal is better suited for metaphysical than social scientific debate. I have many times come across social science colleagues who maintain that social science should not become involved in scientific queries that concern eventual, biological, genetic roots of certain universal interests. Although I argue that it is impossible for human scientists to leave this issue aside, and that 'agnosticism' necessarily entails various homemade views on human interests, it is still important to note that far from all human science departments can be assumed to reflect actively on these matters.

Yet, in important parts of mainstream social science, there is a clear stance that humans are not equipped with any genetic predispositions, at least not predispositions that can help understand interaction in the social domain. The contention is that there is no such thing as a human essence. Instead, each newborn baby is a tabula rasa, a blank slate, with no genetically prepared intellectual or mental capacities. The culture and people around each newborn teach and govern all that is to be written on her blank slate, including what will become her interests.

An early approach holding this blank slate outlook of human nature is the psychological approach of behaviourism. It was established before the Second World War, and became the dominant psychological approach during several decades of the twentieth century. It contends that the right stimuli – in human laboratories, in schools, or more widely in culture – could be provided to people in order to produce whatever human response the stimulus-givers find desirable. The following famous quote by one of the founders of behaviourism, Watson, is self-explanatory:

> Give me a dozen healthy infants, well-formed, and my own specified world to bring them up in and I'll guarantee to take any one at random and train him to become any type of specialist I might select – doctor, lawyer, artist, merchant-chief, and, yes, even beggarman and thief, regardless of his talents, penchants, tendencies, abilities, vocations, and race of his ancestors. *I am going beyond my facts and I admit it* [my emphasis], but so have the advocates of the contrary and they have been doing it for many thousands of years.
>
> (Watson, 1930, 82)

Although Watson creates the basis for successful therapy methods that are still used today for treating specific phobias, such as problematic levels of fear of spiders, snakes, and heights, he was certainly correct in his quote that he was going beyond his facts when presenting his stimulus-response method as limitless.

But also at the very opposite side of the white laboratory coats of behaviourists, we may find the tabula rasa view of human nature. For instance, a main principle of the philosophy of existentialism, often used in social scientific theory development, is that humans have no essence. One of its leading thinkers, Sartre, maintains that 'existence precedes essence', something that for him entails that we as humans are 'condemned to be free', with no inherent drives, instincts, motivations, or the like (Sartre, 1945/2007). It should here be added that there are several versions of existentialism, and that there have recently been attempts, despite this seeming inconsistency with evolutionary thought on human nature, at combining existentialism and evolutionary theory (Barash, 2000).

The blank slate approach can be found, moreover, in what could be called ontological, or strong social constructionism, in parts of cultural theory and post-structuralist thought. Ontological, social constructionism refers to strands of thoughts maintaining, for instance, that everything human is constructed from scratch by our social surroundings. This includes gender, intelligence, aggression, compassion, competition, status struggles, and so forth. The point in ontological, social constructionism is not the obvious one that all human scientists would agree on, namely that gender, intelligence, aggression, and so forth, are always shaped and expressed in a social context making genes and social environment closely intertwined. Instead, ontological social constructionism maintains that there are no built-in limits or inclinations in humans. Everything is social and nothing is genetic or biological. The human slate is blank.

Why the human slate is not blank

To be sure, the blank slate view is correct in one respect: Social and cultural inputs are necessary for human development, and are often instrumental components for developing not just culturally specific but also universal interests. On the other hand, social and cultural inputs are not sufficient components for explaining human universals, including universal interests. The human slate is definitely not blank. To insist that it is blank is not just scientifically problematic. As I try to show below, the insistence on a blank human slate is also highly problematic in its practical applications, undermining relevant handling of social and political problems, not least to the environment and health.

What is scientifically problematic with the blank slate view? Scholars from human scientific disciplines, including parts of sociology, have written about this topic, providing overwhelming evidence – as well as theoretical reasoning – of the untenability of the blank slate view (Freese, Li, & Wade, 2003; Komter, 2010; Lopreato & Crippen, 2002; Turner & Boyns, 2001). Pinker (2002) has been the loudest critical voice in the wider intellectual and public debates here (the interested reader is recommended to read his thorough examination). The space of this book only allows for a few brief examples of what, for our purposes, is most problematic with blank slate views.

First of all, they overlook rich evidence and explanations for the ease, and universality, of a number of human traits and capacities from very early age, such as language acquisition (Pinker, 2009) and moral reasoning (Haidt, 2012). If these traits and capabilities were to have been entirely learnt, with no inherent, genetic preparation, they would not have been found in all peoples universally, and would not be learnt so rapidly or easily. Or actually, they would not be learnt at all. The blank slate approach ignores the evolutionary principle that the human brain is biologically prepared in a biased way. The existence of such helps to explain why people are immensely good at learning to do some types of things – such as (intuitively) understanding language grammar and moral principles in our culture – and astonishingly bad at learning other things, such as learning to weight our own arguments and standpoints neutrally against those advanced by others. People can learn what they can learn because of relatively specific preparedness and predispositions in the brain. Some neuroscientists argue that these predispositions are shaped as mental modules that have been naturally selected. Those people who mutated genetically in a way that gave them the readiness and inscriptions on their slates that turned out to be most adaptive to the social and physical environment in which Homo sapiens has found itself the most – hunter-gatherer society – were more likely to survive and reproduce (Cummins & Cummins, 1999). These people were the ones who managed to spread their genes on to descendants among whom some live today.

This means that humans cannot learn everything or in every possible way. Nor can humans completely rearrange, change, or learn to alter all their interests, particularly not their latent ones. The current, human ability to learn is genetically restricted to types of learning that nature selected for, particularly among our extended period as hunter-gatherers. Please note, however, that this recognition of genetic preparedness is fully compatible with the necessity of social and cultural learning and stimuli towards cultural adaptation. My latter note is not a glued-on reservation to please (us) social scientists. It is a fact tightly integrated in what is today consensus in brain science. For instance, the phenomenon of neuroplasticity (entailing, among other things, the substantial flexibility of the brain to adapt to specific, cultural conditions) is a well-established theme in neuroscience (Ansari, 2012). Importantly, the scientific programmes of neurofeminism and neuroculture aim to scrutinise scientific and popular attempts at steering interpretations of this plasticity in ill-founded directions based on power relations, gendered biases, and so forth (Schmitz & Hoppner, 2014).

Second, several universal human traits are shared with other high primates. If humans were blank slates, these traits (that are innate in other high primates) must somehow, and for some reason, have been removed right before the dawn of Homo sapiens, only to appear again in human cultures universally (including isolated cultures), yet with no genetic connection: the traits would have to be entirely learnt that second time. Aside from the utter implausibility of this development, there is no explanation of how, and why, nature and culture would have evolved in this way (De Waal, 2009). Examples of traits include the universal phenomenon that men commit a far higher share of violent crimes than do women. Moreover, the universal trait of men being interested in (potentially aggressively) controlling women, can be found among other high primates as well as humans. That gender-biased upbringing and social learning – albeit problematic in several ways – would be the only basis for the aggressive, controlling behaviour of men on women that has frequently taken place everywhere since the beginning of humankind, is not a tenable position, as the evolutionary psychologist Anne Campbell, among many others, points out (Campbell, 2012). A genetic, sex-based, preparedness must operate here. It is easy to see that this would have had a strong, evolutionary advantage for some men, particularly when they scored low in other competences, increasing their chances of reproduction. The blank slate approach ignores that there are a few, naturally selected differences between men and women (such as types of aggression and modes of controlling the other sex). To be sure, gender scholars often – very correctly – point out the universality of male aggression and an interest to control women (McKie, 2006). Their claims and analyses are strengthened to the extent that they incorporate the genetic factor here, something that would not mean any resignation or acceptance of sex-based oppression or harassment. Extensive differences in levels of gender inequality between cultures are clear signs that a genetic preparedness for male oppression of women can to a high degree be fought successfully through social policies, cultural learning, and so forth.

Third, there are numerous studies showing that there is genetically based variation between individuals, both physically and mentally. For instance, scholars examining personality traits strongly hold that variations in personality traits have a highly significant, genetic basis (Keyes, Kendler, Myers, & Martin, 2014). In other words, there is not just a cultural variation, but also a genetically based, individual variation. Twins raised apart in different cultures share far more traits and interests than what we find if we sample randomly and compare two non-related persons across cultures. Intelligence levels and personality are two features where such twin studies show significant similarity (Segal & Cortez, 2014; Wallace *et al.*, 2010). This suggests that their shared behaviour and interests have a genetic basis. Blank slate approaches ignore these evolutionary principles of individual variation and genetic heredity.

More generally, no blank slate view has been able to tell a convincing, grand story of why Homo sapiens has evolved on this earth, and why we are still dancing on it. Nor are blank slate views able to explain several other fundamental questions. Why do striking similarities exist in cultures and interests that have never met? And reversely, why is there substantial variation between people in terms of abilities and interests within one and the same culture? How come there are a number of conditions that all human scientists perceive as social and political problems – extreme, social and economic inequality, social exclusion, environmental harm, and so forth? How could human scientists explain such problems if they were to exclude the possibility of a mismatch or discrepancy between universal, genetically prepared interests and various cultural conditions (Ward & Durrant, 2011)?

Consequences of blank slate subscriptions

Above, I briefly touch upon the scientific problems with the view that there are no genetically based universal traits or interests, aside from the basic needs of food and shelter. But does it really matter whether human scientists believe that humans are blank slates or not? Is the issue not mere intellectual hair-splitting? It does matter, and it is not mere hair-splitting. A human scientist's position on this matter has vast implications for her formulations of research problems, analysis, and the recommendations she gives to the rest of society for how various social issues should be managed.

At the same time, I try to be open-minded in our book. It might be valuable to ask the following: Are there any positive social and political implications of the blank slate view, even if it is scientifically incorrect? Behaviourism, existentialism, and ontological social constructionism – despite their immense differences – have in common that they indeed have done society certain favours in certain phases of recent history. They helped society unveil bottom-quality science claims about essences of, for instance race and class, for human abilities and potential, something that was highly unusual in the youth of these perspectives. These blank slate perspectives brought about certain benefits during parts of the twentieth century by emphasising that humanity in its core is one. Particularly before the late 1960s, when gender differences, for instance, were obscenely over-emphasised, and when a racial basis for the human character was still discussed, of course without any solid data (Helms, Jernigan, & Mascher, 2005), the blank slate perspectives certainly made significant cultural and political contributions. I hold that approaches about human interests should not be judged *only* on the basis of whether they seem to be factually correct or false. Again, to help cure phobias and to raise public awareness of early illusions about race, class, gender, and so forth are no small benefits. These good deeds are similar to Freudian theories mentioned in the previous chapter, theories which, regardless of their scientific quality, have helped raise awareness about the importance of treating children with dignity. Moreover, particularly existentialism and Freudian theories remain useful by stimulating fine arts and other types of creative efforts.

Still, we can no longer disregard the shared characteristics of several Freudian notions and of blank slate notions about human interests. They are, in several respects either unfalsifiable (pseudoscientific) or false. In the case of the blank slate notion, it has turned out to be false (Pinker, 2002). The false view that humans are blank slates, that cultural influence is all there is, and that there are thus no universal interests aside from the most basic physical needs, has had negative consequences that by far exceed academia (Barkow, 2005; Machalek & Martin, 2004). By ignoring basic human motivation and the predispositions, human science founded on a blank slate approach tends to hamper open scientific discourse about human interests, and it does disservices in policy recommendations aimed at social welfare, human wellbeing, and at reducing environmental harm.

A point that I introduce above is that the blank slate approach would allow for few if any arguments why political or social efforts should ever be made to alter society in any way. If humans are entirely shaped by culture, with no inherent, universal interests as a species, it is hard to see why any social or cultural issues could be problematic. If humans were blank slates they would be complete products of the society and culture in which they were raised. Consequently, humans would be fully adapted to their own society. For instance, in capitalist societies all human scientists might have to accept economic scientists' possible claim that each individual has become culturally shaped into adopting fully and deeply the interests of Homo economicus. Still, this consequence of blank slate reasoning is never heard among blank slate proponents. Instead, capitalism, neoliberalism, totalitarianism (left-wing or right-wing), *Gesellschaft*, urban anonymity, and so forth are only a few of the social systems and conditions that blank slate thinkers blame for social problems. But in a world of humans with blank slates, a world where social and cultural learning is everything, it is very difficult, perhaps impossible, to see how any condition could be socially problematic, as long as the physical essentials are provided.

Relativising (i.e. downplaying) universal interests

The view that humans – as blank slates – are adaptable to most social systems or cultural conditions, appears to still prevail among certain groups of human scientists. It can be seen in the tendency of relativising (read: downplaying) universally human interests. Cultural relativism is a prominent concept in this context. It has several versions (Zechenter, 1997). The descriptive version mainly claims that cultures differ a lot from each other, and that it is often difficult to translate or directly compare practices and meanings across cultures. This version is fully compatible with the non-blank slate position that cultural specificities are always shaped and expressed through a close intertwining of genetic preparedness in humans and the cultural environment. Consequently, the descriptive, cultural relativism is compatible with a recognition of certain universal human interests, also beyond basic, physical needs. However, there are stronger versions of cultural relativism that seem to presuppose a blank slate perspective. So-called normative, cultural relativism maintains that there can be no transcultural standards for assessing any human interests, aside from basic needs (Quintelier & Fessler, 2012). The most extreme form, called epistemic, cultural relativism, holds that humans are shaped entirely by their culture. According to this form, there exist no cross-cultural, unifying traits, and in consequence no universal interests (Spiro, 1986). The normative and epistemic versions are, as far as I can see, impossible to reconcile with recognition of universal, deeply rooted human interests.

Most obvious examples of normative, or even epistemic types of cultural relativism are found in human scientific debates about totalitarian regimes. Some argue that a culture where babies are not allowed to see their mother's face (covered by a niqab or burka) during breast feeding deprives both the child and mother of universal interests, resulting in emotional complications throughout life. Others see such statements as signs of a 'new religious intolerance' (Nussbaum, 2012). In liberal democracy, urban planning and social structure that entail a normalisation of loneliness and social isolation, not least among the elderly or unemployed, are examples of where universal, human interests have in practice not been taken into account, resulting in health problems and general suffering (Cacioppo, Cacioppo, & Boomsma, 2014). By the lack of political action to cope with these conditions, they have in some cases been normalised, instead of being recognised as failures of a government and culture in meeting universal, human interests.

A further example of cultural relativist reasoning, which would be in line with a blank slate view, concern certain comparisons in so-called ecological footprints between the Global South and Global North. Ecological footprints, in the climate debate specified as carbon footprints, refer to the emissions of harmful pollution of the average citizen in a country, class, region, gender, and so forth, as the result of their lifestyles. The fact that ecological footprint sizes are highly different in the Global South and Global North has been discussed, problematised, and interpreted in various ways in the human sciences. Intriguingly, some human scientists argue or imply that the vast cultural differences in ecological footprints between cultures are useless to compare since people lead such different ways of life in the Global North and Global South. This view contends that people in the North and the South, as well as in cities and in the countryside, are imbedded in highly different physical, cultural, and social structures (McManus & Haughton, 2006). As a consequence, the people within the respective categories must, and should, have highly different ways of meeting their human interests. This view is, for instance, implied in the issues raised in transportation study in developing countries, issues such as 'why people in India wish to own a car' (Verma, 2014). Such basic questions are rarely asked in studies that focus on the United States or European countries, since it is already part of their culture, even where public transportation is available. Implied in such questions is sometimes that the manifest interests of people in the Global North necessitate higher material resource use than in the Global South. The question involves a confusion of people's manifest interests (in continuing to pursue their usual, manifest goals in a business-as-usual manner) and people's more fundamental, latent interests (in establishing and maintaining social bonds, collaboration, identity-based expression, and exchanges of skills). The latter do not need to presuppose, for instance, the current, extensive resource use of the Global North.

Universalising culturally particular interests

The second inclination is to reverse the above-mentioned relativisation of universal interests. To treat culturally particular interests and practices as if they were universal is the second inclination. To be sure, several cultures turn out to have a large number of practices and interests in common. However, this is not necessarily an indication that they exist in most cultures. Nor does this necessarily entail that the practices and interests are genetically hardwired. Yet, the second inclination typically involves the (premature) conclusion that the (prematurely assumed) universals must even reflect genetically rooted human universality.

An example of the second inclination concerns the meat-based food diet. This diet, although subject to endless variation between traditions, is something that many cultures and societies frame as normal, natural, and obvious. Based on the very term hunter-gatherer, denoting the human origin, it is easy to erroneously conclude that meat-based diets are an absolute universal, and therefore of inevitable interest of humankind. Moreover, the term hunter-gatherer is often mistakenly interpreted as reflecting a gender division, not just of food-collecting practices, but also of interests, or even basic needs. Such premature interpretation may imply that men are in more need of meat than are women. This interpretation is tied to the perspective found in parts of Western culture portraying vegetarian or vegan diets as only suitable for women or effeminate men (Rothgerber, 2013).

A further example of where culturally particular interests are universalised is when 'the Western way of life' is universalised as everyone's interest. This view contends that the Global South is determined to go through the same process of 'development', making similar environmental and social mistakes as the North has done. Automobile dependence is likely to rise in the South if people can only afford to become automobile dependent. People in the South are, moreover, destined to replace their traditional, in parts healthy food with the fast food and junk food culture of the North, particularly in the United States. The reason for this material determinism would according to this view be an assumed, hedonistic appeal of Western lifestyles to people universally, combined with an assumed, universal interest in the material and economic accumulation that this way of life promises. All this constitutes the basis of what some social and political analysts perceive as the inevitable and seemingly endless success of the cultural diffusion of the Global Northern way of life.

Following Global Northern patterns of material accumulation and excessive resource use are, to be sure, highly tempting to people and cultures around the world. Unless marketing techniques are unrestricted, a full movement towards cultural homogenisation is probably not inevitable, from the perspective of social rationality. Mass consumerism, excessive transportation, and unsustainable, unhealthy food practices to be sure have hedonistic components. However, the strength of social and cultural norms as well as of legal institutions may in the best cases help people and cultures use universal, latent social interests as goals and reduced harms to health and environment as positive side effects.

In the topic of how to understand and handle instances where culturally particular interests are universalised we need to recognise 'the naturalistic fallacy'. This refers to interpreting certain interests and practices that dominate over others as the most 'natural' ones (Moore, 1903). The naturalness fallacy can be found everywhere in society. In issues about food and agriculture, non-governmental organisations, policy makers, and industries have sometimes made the claim that food produced through genetic modification but without artificial pesticides should be permitted to be labelled 'natural' or 'organic' (Klintman, 2002). In discussions and marketing, the fallacy appears where the terms hunter-gatherer diet or 'Palaeolithic diet' are framed as the natural diet and therefore as the best one, regardless of culture and lifestyle of the person who are to adopt this diet (Jagger, 2013).

There are two main problems with the naturalist fallacy. The first one is that it contends that what is found to be 'natural' (e.g. a mode of food production or a behaviour rooted partially in a genetically rooted human universal) is, therefore, good, favourable, 'as things should be', or completely unavoidable. This is wrong, because there is, logically speaking, no necessary connection between 'is' and 'ought' (Wilson, Dietrich, & Clark, 2003). The claim is that organic food production is not sufficient for promoting such production. If it turns out that organic food production is unsustainable – for the environment or human health – society should seek other ways of producing food. If it turns out that the disproportionate level of violence performed by men can be partially explained by genetic or biological factors, this means neither that such violence is unavoidable or that society should in any way accept it as natural. The second problem is that claims of 'naturalness' are most often social constructions of people or groups with a strategic interest in promoting what they maintain to be natural. The human sciences need to unveil continuously situations where cultural norms and interests are framed as universally valid and as a basis for ethics and policies. The most urgent need seems to lie in opening up a wider discussion across human scientific disciplines where the naturalistic fallacy is addressed and misunderstandings removed. All serious parts of evolutionary science are well aware of this fallacy. Increased interaction and collaboration across the human sciences would make this recognition apparent.

Economics: universalising culturally specific interests?

So far this book part has examined views on universality mainly from social science. This is where we can be most certain to find claims of a human blank slate. Views from evolutionary science have been used to criticise the notion of a blank human slate.

How about economic science? What views are represented there concerning whether humans are blank or genetically prepared in naturally selected ways? This question needs to be answered in a few steps. First, economics shares some ideas with behaviourism, the latter being the classic example of a blank slate approach. The idea that people are driven by extrinsic incentives and disincentives (mainly material ones) bears similarities with the behaviourist notion that behaviours of humans (as of all creatures) can be either weakened or strengthened by means of punishment or reinforcement. To be sure, it is important to note that incentives and disincentives are relatively recent focal points in economics. These opposites are first introduced to economics in the popular magazine *Readers' Digest* in August 1943, by the General Motors CEO Charles E. Wilson, urging all industries of military equipment in the United States to pay more to workers if they increase their productivity. He calls this 'incentive pay' (Sandel, 2013). To the extent that incentives and disincentives are initiated by the State or other institutions, these instruments might intriguingly puzzle us as being the very opposite of Smith's notion of the invisible hand of the market. In economic assertions that emphasise human responsiveness to extrinsic incentives and disincentives, assertions that at the same time downplay or ignore the significance of intrinsic incentives and disincentives (e.g. specific, biologically predisposed motivations), consequently, rest on a blank slate approach to human interests.

However, other aspects speak against the claim that economics would be a blank slate science. For instance, there are certain concepts as well as historical aspirations that the traditional economics shares with evolutionary science (aims of highlighting universal interests). Concepts and metaphors that have travelled in both directions include the struggle for survival, variation, niches, and competition for resources (Witt, 2006). Actors in focus in traditional economics can be anything from individuals to business and large institutions. The economist par excellence, Friedman, even speaks in terms of 'natural selection' at the level of businesses:

> [W]henever it does not [maximise money returns], the business will tend to lose resources and can be kept in existence only by the addition of resources from outside. The process of 'natural selection' thus helps to validate the hypothesis or rather, given natural selection, acceptance of the hypothesis can be based on the judgement that it summarizes appropriately the condition for survival.
>
> (Friedman, 1953, 35)

However, this use in economics of concepts from evolutionary theory does not imply that traditional economics shares evolutionary scientists' basic, ontological, understandings of the world (Witt, 2006). The preoccupation of traditional economics in individual selfishness does only in a fragmented way correspond with evolutionary theory (the latter which necessitates a substantial degree of unselfishness among individuals). Nor does the economic notion of fully self-interested individuals work for explaining the cooperation within firms, between individuals who often act against their direct, individual self-interests (Johnson *et al.*, 2013). In sum, traditional economics recognises a few human traits, handpicked from Apollonian, evolutionary science. Economics holds that humans, and the organisations in which they participate, are not founded on blank slates, but on particular predispositions, such as competition, development of niches, and so forth. This is supported by the aspirations often stated in traditional economics, of framing this discipline as a foundational discipline of human decision making and action. Albeit in contrast also to Apollonian, evolutionary science, traditional economics understands economic behaviour of maximising (often, but not always, material) utility as a universal, inherently human rationality. When traditional economists do cross-cultural comparisons, their underlying assumption is that non-Western (as well as ancient) societies differ from modern capitalist ones, not in terms of their kind of economic exchange and rationality but only in degree (Cook, 1966). This perspective conceives of strategic calculation towards utility maximisation as a culture-independent and as a genetically evolved, universal interest in maximising utility using a minimal amount of resources and efforts. On that account, traditional economics holds that scarce ends and strategic choices between alternative means constitute a universal condition and a universal, human propensity. Markets, trade, and exchange can be found in many types of cultures, including prehistoric ones, ages before modern capitalism, the argument contends. Some economists move one step further by maintaining that 'society is embedded in the economy, not the other way around' (Wilk & Cliggett, 2007, 12).

While most of these aspects of economics point to a conclusion that economics holds a non-blank slate view of humans, evolutionary scientists are sceptical of what exactly traditional economics assumes is genetically prepared on the human slate. Evolutionary scientists maintain that traditional economics commits a fallacy opposite of those committed by some blank slate human scientists. Blank slaters run the risk of relativising interests that may very well be universal as was seen in what I call 'the first tendency', above. Traditional economics, on the other hand, follows 'the second tendency', by trying to universalise interests, reasoning, and decision making that are specifically adapted to liberal, democratic, capitalist societies. What are these critical arguments contending that economics tries to universalise culturally specific interests? First of all, there are strong signs that the interest in utility maximisation, at least in the sense of material utility or accumulation, has not been a universal human interest in hunter-gatherer societies, taking place in 99.6 per cent of human history, and to which we are genetically adapted (Gat, 2000). Instead, humans have been naturally selected for nomadic life in materially fairly egalitarian social lives. To selfishly accumulate goods would have been non-adaptive, for both practical and social reasons, to those cultures and environments. When referring to hunter-gather society, the sociologist Runciman maintains that 'investment in material possessions serves no useful purpose unless they are portable or can be safely left at sites to which the band intends to return' (Runciman, 2005, 136).

In their edited book entitled *Ancestral Landscapes in Human Evolution*, the evolutionary psychologists Narvaez and colleagues describe the general, material condition of hunter-gatherer societies in this way:

> At each campsite to which they move, families build, from natural materials, small, temporary huts, the construction of which usually takes just a few hours. Because the band moves frequently, material goods beyond what a person can easily carry are burdens, so there is very little accumulation of property ... They share food and material goods.
>
> (Narvaez, Valentino, Fuentes, McKenna, & Gray, 2014, 6–7)

Still, if the descriptions above are correct, could they not be a sign that interest in material accumulation, although not an absolute universal, is a conditional, if-then universal? If it is practically possible, then there is perhaps a universal interest in individual accumulation of goods. However, several historical studies indicate that even when it has been practically possible, utility maximisation as in individual material utility or accumulation has come and gone throughout human history (since the dawn of agricultural societies and onwards). For instance, during medieval times, material accumulation was considered a deadly sin, activities in which only socially excluded and marginalised groups (e.g. Jews) were permitted to engage, such as banking, arguably beneficial to society as a whole (Gellner, 1983).

Instead, utility maximisation, in the sense of material utility and accumulation, should be understood as a culturally specific interest. In cultures and societies where such utility maximisation is elevated into a norm or ideal, people and organisations can be assumed to direct their interests to practices with chances of generating such results. However, from the social rationality approach of this book, as well as from evolutionary and much of social scientific thought, material utility maximisation remains overridden by social interests and motivations. The anthropologist Cronk makes this logic clear: 'achievement of success as it is locally defined [as wisdom, skills, material wealth or something else] is a good predictor of both an individual's status' and of his[/her] reproductive success' (Cronk, 2005, 177).

One of the most well-known scholars supporting a similar view is the economic anthropologist Polanyi. He makes the very distinction of 'formalist economics' (with the universalising aspirations mentioned above) and 'substantivist economics' to which he subscribes (Polanyi, 1944). Substantivist economics, represented by institutionalism, maintains that human and organisational interests with regards to material livelihood must be studied and understood in the specific historical and institutional context separately. Accordingly, traditional economics has evolved in a specific cultural context, and cannot be the basis for claims of human universality (Wilk & Cliggett, 2007).

More recently, there have been cross-cultural, scientific findings supporting the view that individual utility maximisation, as traditional economics understands it, is not a genetically hardwired human trait. For example, the anthropologist Henrich and his colleagues have compared how people in a large number of cultures have played 'the ultimatum game', a simple game elucidating whether people act mainly out of individual utility maximisation as their main interest, or out of interest in punishing other players whom they find unfair. Substantial differences between countries have been found here, differences that can be explained by specific cultural differences (Henrich *et al.*, 2010). A general result that speaks against that people would be fundamentally utility maximisers in a material sense (in any culture) is the following: The vast majority of people in all cultures chose to punish a counterpart whom they perceived as too unfair. The counterpart had a number of monetary units. He or she was asked by the experiment leader to suggest on how many of the units they were ready to give the other person. If the latter person found that he or she were given a number of units that seemed unreasonably low, he or she would reject the offer, and neither would get any money. A utility-maximising person would accept the offer of any number of units above zero. However, the vast majority of people preferred not to get any money at all if they perceived their counterpart as 'too greedy' (Chuah, Hoffmann, Jones, & Williams, 2007). Instead, people were socially rational. By preferring to punish those who had been 'too greedy', people had through their monetary sacrifice contributed to strengthening a culture of equality. In real-life situations, those who were greedy in an earlier interaction would probably learn from the negative reaction of the counterpart, something that would by extension improve the norm of fairness and equality in the community.

Proposition 6: accepting mere 'economic efficiency' of a market exchange or policy change (so that everyone becomes better off, albeit to a different extent) may in some cases go against the social rationality of those, in particular, whose manifest interests are not satisfied to the same extent as those of others. Reactions out of resentment may arise, unless the inequality is reduced.

Furthermore, recent studies in neuroeconomics, which include functional magnetic resonance imaging (fMRI), have provided additional evidence that runs counter to the formalist economic notion of universal interest in economic rationality. People, when playing variations of the ultimatum game as mentioned earlier, and who reach an agreement where both get a fairly equal share of the resource at stake, have higher activities in their brain regions associated with rewards (ventral striatum) than do people who gain far more in the game than their opponents. If maximising utility were carved in genetically on the human slate, those who gained the most resources (the outstanding winners) would be those with the highest activities in these parts of the brain (Ruff & Fehr, 2014). Finally, the field of behavioural economics has during the last two decades produced rich amounts of data, mainly from economic experiments along with theory development founded more on evolutionary theory than on traditional economics. The focus in behavioural economics on human biases clearly denotes the view that the human slate is genetically prepared and predisposed in ways that have been naturally selected throughout evolution, making the slate far from blank (Camerer, Loewenstein, & Rabin, 2011).

In sum, mainstream economics has several traits indicating that it would hold a non-blank slate of human interests. There is a rather specific focus on humans as economically rational to their core, universally interested in material exchange, resource management, and maximisation of (often material) utility. Despite the criticism above of which interests economists define as universal, this science passes as a non-blank slate approach.

The blank slate: a hypothesis about political consequences?

If we look at social science, despite blank slate notions among some social scientists, it is also fairly easy to identify signs that would make large parts of social science a non-blank slate approach. For instance, Apollonian views in social science seem to imply a built-in human rationality, an inherent interest in social learning, in optimising and maximising social interests, an innate sense of reciprocity, and so forth. Furthermore, in parts of social science with a Dionysian character, the emphasis on the human core as a social, group-bonding species with a high receptivity and motivation for social influence implies that the human slate cannot be blank, but must be genetically prepared for this social receptivity.

Yet, in an extensive survey study of sociologists in the United States, results still point in the direction of a blank slate approach, at least before analysing the results more thoroughly. In 2012, Horowitz and colleagues did a comprehensive survey of 543 sociology professors specialising in theory. Their reason for selecting sociologists specialising in theory was that these could be expected to have faced issues of the relationship between culture and genetics. These sociologists were sampled among members of the American Sociological Association (Horowitz, Yaworsky, & Kickham, 2014). The authors were able to collect 155 surveys that were usable (response rate: 29 per cent). Interestingly, the authors note a broad range of response rates concerning whether a certain, specified human phenomena can be explained, at least in part, by evolutionary/genetic factors. A clear pattern can be seen here. The respondents show far more willingness to consider evolutionary explanations of less politically sensitive phenomena than of highly sensitive ones. For instance, 59.8 per cent of these sociologists accept evolutionary explanations for the human taste for fats and sugars. Fear of snakes and spiders also get a relatively high percentage, 49.4. Only 32.3 per cent of the respondents find it plausible to use evolutionary explanations, at least in part, for the fact that most violent crimes are committed by men worldwide. An even lower percentage of respondents, 22.7 per cent, find evolutionary factors as plausibly significant parts of the puzzle of explaining veiling and segregation of women in certain societies.

To be sure, some of these figures can probably be attributed to knowledge deficits to a certain extent. The low level of responses accepting evolutionary explanations also in less political issues indicates a knowledge deficit in the basic of human evolutionary thought. That almost 40 per cent of the respondents deny evolutionary factors concerning human tastes for fat and sugar ought to raise strong concerns about mere knowledge deficits. Also, it is not far-fetched to speculate that there is an underlying fear that wide societal diffusion of biological and genetic perspectives may entail that there will be a reduced demand for social scientific research. Furthermore, in light of the claims in this book about the fundamental human interest in social bonding and a shared sense of identity, we could entertain the following speculation: Denying evolutionary factors even behind less political topics, such as our tastes for fat and sugar, reflects this latent interest in maintaining a shared social science identity distinguished from the other human sciences.

However, both worries about reduced demand for social sciences, and about a dissolving of a common social science identity should genetic preparedness on the human slate be fully accepted, are probably ill-founded, if these worries even exist. As is shown in preceding sections, the intertwining of genetic and social influences necessitates an even more extensive – and arguably more fascinating – social science than would be the case should substantial parts of social science continue to ignore genetic components. How society, its institutions and norms are socially constructed, is only one among several social scientific areas that are likely to remain highly important. Perhaps it will become even more so once there is a broader recognition in the human sciences of the genetic preparedness on the human slate. One of the founders of evolutionary psychology, Barkow, makes the following reassuring claim to social science.

> The nonradical social constructionism typical of the social sciences is not only compatible with evolutionary psychology, it is required by it ... A culture-bearing species, one that like ours depends primarily on socially transmitted information pools for adaptation to local conditions, must also evolve mechanisms permitting and even requiring social construction.
>
> (Barkow, 2005, 25–6)

A major reservation that Barkow gives is implied in his vague term 'nonradical'. By radical he refers to what I earlier in this book call 'ontological social constructionism' (which he – and I – think should be avoided), and with non-radical he refers to what can be called epistemic social constructionism. The former connotes a blank slate perspective of humans. The latter, however, is represented by broad perspectives where social science studies the cultural multitude of how humans, groups, organisations, and societies construct situations and human conditions socially, as problematic, irrelevant, beneficial, and so forth. Epistemic social constructionism is indeed fully compatible with an acknowledgement of a genetically prepared human slate. It is a core human feature to create meaning by constructing our impressions socially. Many aspects of society that people experience as 'objective' and 'absolute' are in fact socially constructed, relative, culturally dependent, and so on. How this is done, and why, remains a key area of study where social science has expertise. We would argue that social science is better equipped to study social constructions than are those evolution-oriented schools with a natural scientific basis. The reason is that social science is trained in investigating differences across cultures, whereas evolutionary science is trained at investigating similarities, generally speaking.

Moving back to the survey of how American sociologists conceive of genetic and biological explanations: In addition to the serious scepticism of genetic explanations among these scholars on average, the wide range of responses, clearly founded on the range of political sensitivity between issues, deserves to be analysed in more detail. A far-reaching yet plausible interpretation would be that the blank slate approach of parts of social science is not a scientific approach about what, if anything, human brains and minds are equipped with. Rather, the blank slate approach is better understood as a theory, or hypothesis, about political consequences. The approach appears to rest on assumptions about what ethical, normative, and political conclusions society would draw if partial, genetic, and biological explanations were accepted for morally sensitive issues.

More concretely, knowledge deficits among social scientists are most likely not the primary reason most respondents find it implausible that any evolutionary factor could help explain the universally higher level of male than female violence. Nor do knowledge deficits among social scientists help explain why the largest share of the respondents refuse to recognise any genetic influence on 'the widely observed tendency for men to try to control women's bodies as property' such as veiling, virginity cults, and so forth (Horowitz *et al.*, 2014, 496). Instead, both quantitative and qualitative data from these studies point to the respondents' underlying hypotheses about political consequences by introducing partially genetic explanations. Respondents who are sceptical about evolutionary explanations in these studies have associated such explanations with political resignation, or even of political acceptance of the phenomena at stake. A few of the respondents expressed these concerns openly, such as in this quote.

> By emphasizing hard wiring due to evolution, there is an implicit acceptance of the behaviour as if there is nothing or very little that can be done to alter the behaviour or as if any such attempts are doomed and misguided. There is no incentive to consider the possibility of altering social environments to reduce the likelihood of fighting, or bullying, or raping, or veiling/segregating women, etc.
>
> (In Horowitz *et al.*, 2014, 499)

Another quote makes this hypothesis about political consequences even more clear: 'The cultural determinist view offers more progressive possibilities alive to issues of social justice, while the biological determinist view undermines human agency and is most often enlisted to justify hierarchy' (Horowitz *et al.*, 2014, 499). It thus seems that the epistemic issue of whether men and women are blank slates, or whether they have slightly different genetic preparations on their slates, is not where the issue lies, according to these sociologists conducting this study. It could even be that respondents – if pressed about the epistemic issue – would admit that genetic factors may be involved in the violence and control of women.

In sum, the responses reflect mainly political concerns as well as misunderstandings about the relationship between scientific findings and ideological, political and cultural implications.

Conclusions

If the human sciences are to develop a knowledge exchange about human interests, this will necessitate an agreement on at least one point: Humans are not blank slates on which culture can write whatever its most influential actors wish, in the expectation that people's interests will be adapted accordingly. Social science, along with certain social movements, has certainly made significant contributions in modern history based on a blank slate perspective. Thus, primitive perspectives of genetic determinism and social Darwinism could be replaced by a sound recognition that people in various categories are far more similar than they are different. However, once these primitive perspectives have been falsi-fied, the insistence in parts of the social sciences on a blank slate has turned out to be highly counter-productive for increasing the understanding of human inter-ests and how to reduce the number of societal problems. Few societal problems can be fully understood if human scientists ignore that humans have evolved genetically to adapt to our ancestral environment. Much of current health prob-lems are stress-related, by being rooted in a mismatch between the ancestral life-styles to which we are genetically adapted. This claim does not contradict the human scientific claim that social learning is central to adaptation. To the con-trary, as is shown in the next chapter, humans are genetically prepared for genetic learning, since those in early human history who were active, social learners have always been better at adapting to their specific culture, in turn increasing their chances of survival and reproduction.

Traditional economics, although it bears some similarity with behaviourism (a blank slate theory) by assuming that external incentives and disincentives can move people in any direction, still recognises that humans are no blank slates. However, this does not mean that traditional economics is correct in what it assumes is written on the human slate. There are convincing signs that this dis-cipline universalises interests that are more prevalent in specific cultures. The claim in economics that utility maximisation (concerning each specific, Apollon-ian issue at stake) is written on the human slate genetically (and thus universally) has been contradicted by a number of cross-cultural studies by economic anthro-pologists and others. Instead, the interest in the achievement of success as it is locally defined, turns out to override the interest in utility maximisation. This can be seen in the far higher ability and motivation humans have to seek socially rational ways to act and interact with others, rather than to calculate optimal ways towards utility maximisation. The human brain is notoriously bad at the latter. This points towards the evolutionary claim that natural selection has not prioritised this ability or interest.

6 Understanding the prepared slate

If we from now on maintain the position that the human slate is not blank, what then has natural selection written on it? This question refers to an enormously vast and challenging area of research, which would be impossible to give due justice to in this chapter. Instead, the objective of this chapter is to give a few hints at what it could mean that humans have universal interests founded on genetically evolved preparedness. As the reader shall see, these hints point not only to the fact that humans are not blank slates, but also to the fact that genetic preparedness rarely means that genes would be independent on social conditions for human traits and interests to 'materialise' in human behaviour and activities.

For human traits and interests to be expressed in activities, such as social interaction, stimuli from the social environment are needed. Below follow a few examples. They are divided into gene-environmental interplay at the level of our entire species, and at the level of individual variation.

Interplay as a species

The first example of the nature-nurture interplay refers to the position along a spectrum that evolution has given Homo sapiens. This spectrum, the neuroendo-crinologist, Sapolsky, among others, describes as ranging from 'tournament species' on one side to 'pair-bonding species' on the other (Sapolsky, 2013).

Among tournament species, there is constant and fiercely aggressive competition between males for status, and for mating with a maximum number of females. Most males never get to mate, whereas a few males get to mate with a high number of females. Tournament species are highly polygamous, where down to 5 per cent of the males account for 95 per cent of the mating. Responsibility for taking care of the offspring is almost entirely the task of the female, whereas the male can be expected to be absent for lengthy periods of time. Tournament species are characterised by a major difference in size, shape, and appearance of males and females (a high degree of sexual dimorphism). Males are far bigger, sometimes twice as big, as the females. Examples of tournament species include mountain gorillas, baboons, lions, grouse, and elephant seals.

The existence of pair-bonding species reflects an opposite 'strategy' of evolution for the competition and spreading of genes. Among pair-bonding species, there is a very low degree of competition between males for status and mating, particularly once a female and male have become a pair. The female and male stay together throughout life as highly faithful companions. Both are responsible for taking care of the offspring. In some cases, the male takes a bigger responsibility than the female for their offspring, which can lead to the female seeking a new mate (a phenomenon called cuckoldry). The male and female look very similar in shape and size (a low degree of sexual dimorphism). Examples of pair-bonding species include gibbons, swans, black-backed jackals, and – of course – turtle doves (Cohas & Allaine, 2009).

The obvious question is where humans should be placed along the continuum between tournament species and pair-bonding species. The direct answer must be: somewhere in the middle. There are (at least) two ways of assessing this from the perspective of the entire history of Homo sapiens. The first way is to examine DNA, comparing the proportion of women and men who have passed on DNA since the dawn of Homo sapiens, around 70,000 years ago. As it turns out, the ratio is around 25 women for 15 men. In other words, we seem to have around 67 per cent more foremothers than forefathers (Lippold et al., 2014). A second way is to compare the bodies of women and men, regarding relative size, shape, and so forth: our degree of sexual dimorphism, that is. Studies show a relatively low degree of sexual dimorphism, compared to most anthropoids and primates (Rigby & Kulathinal, 2015; van Hooff, 2011). In sum, humans seem to end up between the two extremes, yet a bit closer to pair-bonding species than to tournament species.

To finish the assessment here, however, would be a cardinal error. Alternatively, it would entail the risk of committing up to three mistakes. The first two mistakes are quite common in uninformed attempts at incorporating genetics and biology into understandings of social life.

The first mistake is to exaggerate the human proximity to the extreme side of tournament species. A ridiculous (and highly unscientific) understanding of Homo sapiens is that we are a tournament species at heart. This view contends that the inevitable destiny is that males are to their core driven to compete fiercely and violently for women, who are in turn the passive sex, the trophy of male competition. The philosopher, Hobbes, although developing far more sophisticated arguments than this one, is regularly associated with this view of aggression being deterministically written on the human slate. Hobbes pictures humans in their 'natural condition of mankind' a condition in which life is 'solitary, poor, nasty, brutish, and short' (Hobbes, 1651/1982, chs XIII–XIV). In this natural condition, there is 'a war of all against all'. Hobbes' solution is a strong State and an (unwritten) social contract between people ensuring that humans (aggressive to their core) be protected against each other.

The second mistake is to exaggerate the human proximity to the other extreme, namely to pair-bonding species. This view contends that humans are essentially peaceful, non-competitive, uninterested in stressful comparisons and status struggles against others. Another philosopher, Rousseau, is frequently associated with this thinking, along with notions of 'the noble savage'. The enemy of this peaceful species is usually various social and political systems, such as systems for private ownership, capitalism, and a state interference with people's lives. Rousseau famously points out that

> The first man, who, after enclosed a piece of ground, took it into his head to say, 'This is mine', and found people simple enough to believe him, was the true founder of civil society. How many crimes, how many wars, how many murders, how many misfortunes and horrors, would that man have saved the human species, who pulling up the stakes or filling up the ditches should have cried to his fellows: 'Be sure not to listen to this imposter; you are lost, if you forget that the fruits of the earth belong equally to us all, and the earth itself to nobody!'
>
> (Rousseau, 1755/2004, 27)

Rousseau believes that the human slate is virtuous, but that society corrupts us.

Recent human sciences indicate that neither Hobbes' nor Rousseau's view about the human slate is accurate. By drawing a picture of a war of all against all, Hobbes fails to take into account human genetic preparedness for cooperation, social bonds, and alliances. These are universal interests found in all societies throughout the entire human history. Reversely, by drawing a picture of the free, uncivilised individual and group as free from competition, status struggles, from thinking about how we look in the eyes of others, and so forth, Rousseau fails to take into account human genetic preparedness for these very processes (Leary & Allen, 2011). In fact, no visionary attempts at creating a community where no social status dynamics and competition – formal or informal – seem to have existed. Throughout the centuries, many political ideas, as well as personal practices, have been suggested to remove our human propensity to compare ourselves to others, and to compete for social status. Mindfulness meditation is one such practice. The professor of psychology specialising in mindfulness meditation, Siegel, admits, with a stroke of self-irony, what typically takes place during the big mindfulness conferences. The most experienced mindfulness teachers often end up around the dinner table all engaged in intense discussions where they – implicitly – compare and compete about who has reached the highest competence for avoiding comparing themselves with others (Siegel, 2010).

Keeping in mind roughly where on the spectrum humanity is genetically located between a tournament and pair-bonding species is, to be sure, highly valuable to avoid mistakes of trying to place humanity at either of the two extremes. However, if we attempt to identify a fixed point where humanity is located on this continuum, we would fail to give due justice to the close intertwining of nature and nurture. All serious human science needs to recognise, and accept, that what is often called nature and nurture is almost never clearly separable. How the intertwining and co-dependence may work becomes understandable at the basic level if one looks at two rather distinct cultural developments. As the main part of humanity moved away from the long period of hunter-gatherer ways of life to what is called the Neolithic period some 12,000 years ago, two distinct strategies for securing food supply were pastoral (herding) cultures and horticultural cultures, growing crops (Bowles, Smith, & Mulder, 2010). Both these novel ways of life made it possible to produce a surplus of food. This surplus, in turn, made it possible to have more children than in a hunter-gatherer society. More children entailed a demand for even more food supply. Two classical ways have been particularly common for ensuring and increasing food production, ways that are still tried today. The first way is to use one's land more efficiently (by raising cattle more efficiently, for example). The second way is to acquire more land. Horticulturalists began to fight over irrigated land, and moral rules were established ensuring private land properties. Since it is far harder to steal land than to steal cattle, horticultural societies have been able to survive and reproduce relatively peacefully.

The pastoral way of life was another matter. Pastoralists were far more mobile than horticulturalists since cattle can be moved around. Moreover, pastoralists were not as in demand of high-quality and irrigated land as were horticulturalists. The former many times settled in the dryer and rougher places, including the mountains. When needed, they would move the animals to watersheds. Pastoralists early on invented ways to raise their cattle more efficiently, through, for instance, selective breeding. As their populations grew, and pastoralists became better at raising their animals more efficiently, the animal herds grew. At this point, pastoralists began to use horses to control the herds. Still, the risk grew much higher that this large-scale herding would entail the temptation of other pastoralists to steal one's cattle. This risk has prevailed in the pastoral way of life ever since. To avoid high levels of tension and aggression along the borders between pastoralists, alliances were developed based on systems and rules for reciprocity. Current cultural expressions, such as festivities, gift exchanges, and other rituals often have their roots in this pastoral need for alliances and reciprocity. Still, cultural analyses of societies founded on pastoralist ways of life indicate that these have been, and sometimes still are, more aggressive and violent compared to horticultural societies, and compared to, for instance, rainforest societies (Kaplan, Hooper & Gurven, 2009). In movies and fiction, cattlemen are usually portrayed as closer to using violence than are people who make a living in other ways. Some truth seems to lie in this stereotypical image. Key reasons include the constant threat of having one's cattle stolen, along with the limited types of resources, and food available in pastoral societies. They were fully dependent on very few types of animals for their existence. Some anthropologists indicate that monotheistic, patriarchy-oriented, highly authoritarian religions and cultures were developed in pastoral societies to serve the function of protecting the pastoralist through absolute divine rules and strict punishment should someone break the rules. They maintain that this can be seen especially clearly in pastoral societies in desert areas (Johnson & Earle, 1987; Linquist, 2015). Throughout history, these cultures have had particularly strict rules making sure that the men exert control over women. In contrast, horticultural and forest societies have more often developed polytheistic religions, where people worship both male and female gods for the weather and climate to become more beneficial for fertility and harvest. In rainforests, for instance, there can be thousands of various edible plants. According to some human scientists, this multiplicity may have been a stronger ground for tolerance and pluralism than in societies relying on only one or a few sources of food supply, even regardless of the amount of food available. This example shows how humans, located between a tournament species (highly aggressive) and pair-bonding species (highly peaceful), by being fundamentally dependent on the natural and social environment may, in entire cultures, slide quite far in one or the other direction on the continuum. The main point of these examples is that differences genes may have little or nothing to do with the fact these pastoralist cultures have been more aggressive than horticultural cultures. Instead, it is mainly the pastoralists living conditions that have had to lead to more aggressive cultures that include stricter rules, norms, and punishments. In the same way, human scientists may analyse how human adaptation to various modern cultures and subcultures demand a sometimes extensive sliding on this continuum, for better or for worse.

Interplay in individual variation

In addition to what evolution has written on our slate as a species, evolution always entails genetic variation among individuals of a species, humans included. An individual variation includes, for instance, to what extent an individual's personality is characterised by what makes up the acronym OCEAN: Openness to experience, Conscientiousness, Extraversion, Agreeableness, and Neuroticism (Cobb-Clark & Schurer, 2012). Moreover, individual variation exists concerning IQ level, and where on (or outside of) the autism spectrum a person lies, along with the genetic preparedness for a broad range of other mental disorders (Manuck & McCaffery, 2014; Uher, Alemany, & VanWinkel, 2014). Having said this, the main message from evolutionary science is that the environment has an enormous influence on whether the individual's genes will be switched on or not. This is true both when the issue is the risk of certain mental disorder, and the genetic potential for having a specific, useful ability.

The environment is anything from the influence of toxins, diet, or hormones on the genes, reprogramming them (phenomena within the research area of epigenetics), and to the influence of the social environment (social norms, interaction between people, and so forth). In this book, I focus on the latter. This subject is gigantic. Here are only three, among several, forms of interplay between genes (of individuals) and social environment. These three forms are called gene-environment correlations.

The first way is called passive gene-environment correlation (Knafo *et al.*, 2013). If, for instance, both parents have high education and IQ, they might perhaps also have many books in their home. On top of this, they might be knowledgeable about nutrition. In sum, this will enable these parents to provide their child with the opportunity to read books and to eat nutritious food that helps the child's brain develop optimally. Without the child having to take any independent action, she finds herself in a positive circular loop towards high IQ and education.

The second way is called 'active gene-environment correlation' (TenEyck & Barnes, 2015). It refers to the fact that children show individual differences in their inherent tendencies to seek certain types of social environments and experiences. Studies have shown how children with parents abusing various substances (partly based on a genetic tendency for sensation seeking and low inhibitory control) run a higher risk than others to seek similar kinds of sensations through abuse of substances. If they turn out to initiate a substance abuse, this, in turn, increases other sensation seeking and reduces an already low inhibitory control. The peers the person associates with are likely to reinforce further this circular loop.

The third type of interplay is called 'evocative gene-environment correlation' (Burt, 2009). Subtle signals from a child that reflect moderate degrees of certain personality traits may be reinforced by parents within whom the same traits are part of their personality. If a child says that she is too shy to go to a party, it is not uncommon that a shy parent emphasises strongly with the child in her shyness, suggesting that the child can stay at home instead. This further enforces the circular loop of shyness.

All these three types of gene-environment interplay indicate how a genotype that prepares for certain tendencies, for instance towards delinquency or shyness, may trigger positive feedback loops that make the traits increasingly strong the older the person gets.

In sum, what is prepared on our blank human slates as a species or individually is, as a rule, highly dependent on the social environment to become expressed in feelings, emotions, interests, and activities individually or culturally.

Gender-based interests?

What would a substantiated non-blank slate approach say about universal interests that differ between the sexes? Is it possible to identify genetically based universal interests among women that differ from those of men? If so, why? This is an area of heated debate. Unfortunately, discussions mainly take place separately within single human scientific disciplines, with only occasional dialogues across. The topic of gene-environment interplay entailing universal differences between the sexes is a comprehensive topic. In this section, the ambition is to introduce the mainstream evolutionary perspective, followed by recent comments and criticism from feminist evolutionary scholars. As the reader shall see, these observations raise several critical issues that the social and economic sciences are well equipped to examine, if taking into account evolutionary science.

First, it is relevant to ask a fundamental question of theoretical biology and evolutionary genetics: Why is there more than one sex, most often two, in the majority of species? This issue is probably – and understandably – a frequently asked one during periods of war, and high levels of violence when particularly the male side of the population bears marked similarity with an extreme tournament species. Why there are sexes, and why they are two, is are valid and significant questions in biology and genetics. It is well known that few species reproduce by cloning. Less well known is that several species, particularly during earlier times of evolution, consisted of only one sex. This meant that every individual could mate with everyone else (Czaran & Hoekstra, 2004). Scientists indicate that in-breeding is often a huge evolutionary disadvantage in one-sex reproduction. As to asexual reproduction (cloning), the lack or variation of individuals becomes problematic. Individual genetic variation is necessary for increasing the chances that some offspring are not lost to parasites, predators, pathogens, or tough environmental conditions. Moreover, reproduction involving two sexes enables mutations to be repaired to a higher degree than is possible in the other forms of reproduction (Dimijian, 2005).

In light of these advantages of two sexes, and given the moderate sexual dimorphic asymmetry (here: physical differences) between women and men, why would there possibly be any universal, genetically based, differences between the two sexes? After all, both women and men ought to be driven by the same types of social rationality and motivation discussed earlier: social esteem, bonding, cooperation, companionship, developing skills and competencies, providing wellbeing for their children, and so forth. This is certainly true when people are asked, and when we look at the world roughly. In line with this, all human sciences – including evolutionary science – are in agreement that traits of women and men are far more similar than different. Individual differences in personality traits, behavioural traits, manifest interests, and so forth, are, concerning several features, more extensive than are these differences between the sexes. Moreover, such differences between women and men typically vary along a continuum rather than being all-or-nothing traits (Carothers & Reis, 2013).

At the same time, the issue of sex differences in universal interests deserves some additional attention. In his seminal paper from the early 1970s, the evolutionary biologist Trivers (1972) presents what he calls 'the parental investment theory'. This theory is an elucidative example of how evolutionary science and economics share certain concepts. Terms such as investment, cost, resources, potential, and so forth, bring one's thoughts to economic rationality. The use of such terms is, however, not far-fetched for examining the evolutionary basis for possible differences in interest between women and men. Parental investment consists of the resources, energy, and time that a parent has to allocate to a child. This, in turn, influences (reduces) the parents' remaining resources to invest in the child's sibling. Trivers examines the differences in resources that evolution 'demands' from women and men. There are indeed several fundamental and obvious differences. Women have to invest disproportionately in each child. First, there are the reproductive costs that are physiologically obligatory (Frederick, Reynolds, & Fisher, 2013). For men, there is always a possibility for a cost that is minuscule (a few minutes). This is never the case for women. Instead, they face 40 weeks of pregnancy, which includes an increase in caloric needs by around 10 per cent. After pregnancy and a (risky) child delivery follows a lactation period, which in hunter-gatherer society (to which humans are genetically adapted) could be expected to last around 2.5 years (Kaplan, 2000), increasing the caloric needs by 26 per cent (Dufour & Sauther, 2002). In addition to this resource intensity for women, their physiological potential for reproduction is highly limited in time and in the number of children she can have during her life, compared with the potential for men. According to Trivers, these (indisputable) sex differences must entail differences in interests and behaviours between women and men. Given the immense, latent force of evolution, making all humans of today the result of ancestors motivated (at least at the latent level) to reproduce and spread their genes in a successful way, the above-mentioned physiological, reproductive differences between women and men ought to be reflected in different interests and behaviours. It would accordingly be impossible for women and men to expose identical interests and behaviours, since their physiological conditions for spreading their genes and increasing the survival of their offspring look so different. A final factor to bring up here is the fact that women, as a rule, have material certainty, since they have carried the baby. The fact that they know that they are the mothers, whereas men cannot know for sure that they are the fathers, has accordingly implications for how men and women relate to parental investment. Please note that Trivers does not assume that any of this takes place at the manifest level. In fact, he emphasises the importance of unconscious, latent processes through which evolution operates (von Hippel & Trivers, 2011). He also notes that it often takes statistical measures to see how these differences in parental investing materialise in different behaviours and interests between women and men.

What are the differences in interests and behaviours, according to Trivers? In brief, he expects women to be choosier than men. As for men, he expects them to put much energy on competing with other men to impress women, through physical fitness, various skills and talents, and through constantly trying to reach a high status in the workplace. The image becomes a stereotypical one where women are selective and coy, whereas men are eager, always struggling for the attention of women. Gender scholars typically interpret this as an image of the active man and the passive woman, an image that they hold stems largely from the fact that most of the scientists who have produced this narrative are men. Still, although gender scholars are correct by stating that it is a stereotypical narrative formulated by men, it is not obvious who is the active or the passive one here. After all, the woman is here perceived as the one with the final power to make the active choice, according to this theory.

Aside from this issue of perspectives, what do empirical data say? Indeed, some types of cross-cultural studies seem to make Trivers right in his assumption that the differences in physiological conditions appear to entail differences in behaviours and interests. Studies in up to 37 different countries (on several continents) indicate some significant sex differences regarding, for instance, what factors are most important in a mate (Buss, 1989).

It should be noted that cultural differences turned out to be more influential than the respondents' sex concerning several questions (Buss, 1989; Stone, Shackelford & Buss, 2007). Moreover, evolutionary scholars with a feminist perspective have examined conditions under which women are anything but coy and choosy (Judson, 2002). Although critical studies admit that females clearly are selective when they seek out mating opportunities, several scholars are sceptical to the image of male competition and female choice (Gowaty, 2013). The parental investment theory says little about what happens to the manifestations of possible, latent differences in women and men in more egalitarian societies. As we have seen above concerning the sliding scale of humans between tournament and pair-bonding species, it can be expected that modern phenomena such as contraception, more women and men in the workforce, and so forth could be expected to narrow further the differences in gender-based interests. Cultural processes towards a civilisation and feminisation of several societies ought to have a rather far-reaching impact not just for how people answer questionnaires about gender issues, but could, in the long run, entail the deeper strengthening of self-control thus avoiding destructive, aggressive behaviour (Pinker, 2011).

The male dominance in destructive behaviour

Based on what has been mentioned above, how about the potential for reducing the male-dominated destructive behaviour? Again, there are worries among social scientists that acceptance of the claim (which evolutionary scholars perceive as a fact) that violent aggression is genetically prepared in men far more than in women, would lead to resignation or even to the legitimation of violent aggression. However, in the examples above about cultural differences in levels of aggression, along with the vast differences in violent aggression across different parts of the world, are convincing signs that politics, norms, and cultural factors may have enormous effects regarding reductions in violence. For instance, the prevalence of partner violence in a 12-month period is around ten times lower, around 4 per cent, in highly developed countries, such as Denmark, than in the low-income, developing countries, such as Ethiopia, where it is around 40 per cent (Heise & Kotsadam, 2015). Furthermore, the prevailing tendency towards reductions in violence over time, which Pinker (2011) argues has taken place for millennia, has everything to do with culture, environment, and learning and very little – if anything – with changes in genetic traits. Still, in all cultures, throughout human history, including the tendencies of reduced violence mentioned here, men are hugely overrepresented as actors of violence. It would be severely risky if the human sciences ignore this, a risk that Barkow succinctly elucidates through the title of his article 'Biology Is Destiny Only if We Ignore it' (Barkow, 2003). Here is an example of what can happen when human scientists do not take basic findings in biology and evolutionary psychology into account when they construct theories and provide policy recommendations that relate to social and psychological issues:

Example: the public delusion that low self-esteem is a root of most social problems

In the late 1980s and early 1990s, it became 'common wisdom' that low self-esteem is the cause of an immense range of social problems, including violent crime. This 'wisdom' came partly from studies indicating that people involved in deviant behaviour frequently have a lower self-esteem than others. The prominent sociologist Smelser stated, in the preface to an extensive report on this matter, that 'many, if not most, of the major problems plaguing society have roots in the low self-esteem of many of the people who make up society' (Smelser, Preface in Mecca, Smelser, & Vasconcellos, 1989, 1). Smelser was backed up by dozens of high-profile experts. Perhaps this is why he made this huge claim even though he also had to admit that that 'one of the disappointing aspects of every chapter in this volume ... is how low the associations between self-esteem and its [presumed] consequences are in research to date' (Mecca *et al.*, 1989, 15).

The theory that low self-esteem is the leading cause of significant social problems influenced school programmes as well as the formation of a Task Force to Promote Self-esteem broadly in California, by the California legislator. However, since the theory was at odds with basic lessons in evolutionary theory and personality, the theory got it wrong in several ways. If anything, low self-esteem is rather a result of deviant behaviour than the cause of deviant behaviour. Even if unpleasant, the potential for a lowered self-esteem is in our human interests. There is an important evolutionary function of low self-esteem, namely that it helps people check their 'socio-meter', their level of acceptance by others in their social group, and to become more agreeable to make sure they remain part of the group bonding. This has been crucial throughout ancient history to prevent people from social exclusion. At the same time, things are different for highly violent people. In-depth studies in sociology that are more in line with evolutionary theory, have dared to question the unwarranted assumption that violent aggressors are the weak ones, the victims. For instance, Diane Scully has shown that the self-esteem problem behind, for example, violent rape, is rather far too high self-esteem than too low (Scully, 1990). To stimulate further raises in self-esteem among highly violent people is bound to be devastating, as it only promotes their grandiose self-images and triggers even more violence, particularly in group-oriented programmes to promote self-esteem.

However, the human sciences should not just be concerned with sex differences in violence alone. There are also other issues that people in most realms of society argue are highly problematic, issues where men are over-represented. Environmental harm in daily life is such an issue, not least in the sector of travelling and transportation (Scheiner & Holz Rau, 2012). Moreover, at a more subtle level, the hope for an increased feminisation of society that Pinker expresses above, definitely points to critical issues where all the human sciences need to become more engaged to provide the knowledge basis for a pacified, more human society. This is an old idea, a cliché, in fact, with roots in conservatism. A typically conservative view has been that women civilise society; they tame the manly beast. Clichés are not necessarily wrong. The benefits of feminist development are shown by ample data from several sciences.

The higher genetic variation of men than of women

It hardly needs mentioning that a crucial task for the human sciences and all societies will remain one of further examining and developing ways of strengthening the rights and interests of women, a gender equality to the benefit of everyone. Still, parts of the human sciences often interpret this vital task in incomplete ways. A possibly significant reason is that social science and society as a whole ignore a fundamental, genetic factor.

There is a significantly higher individual variation among boys and men than between girls and women. For this section, sexual dimorphism (differences between the sexes) is reflected in the significantly higher probability of boys and men being on the spectra of the common mental disorders ADHD, the autism spectrum, and bipolar disorders. So far, human sciences and the public debate on gender inequality typically frame the problem as one where men, as one homogeneous category, have a tendency to control, and play an unfair game against women, as one homogeneous group. Men, no doubt, try to exercise such control both as agents and as primary influencers of social structure. The particularly high genetic variation of men entails that we can expect that one share of boys and men as a category, just like women, both show up at the top of the ladder of high achievements and prestige. The problem that scholars of gender studies and other social and economic sciences indicate is how men, as a category, continue to play their usual unfair game through their old boys' clubs and male-based, informal networks. In effect, such homosocial cultures exclude many equally competent women from high positions and from exerting equal influence. Moreover, gender studies and the other human sciences are highly plausible in their expectations that activities at these high positions entail a degree of arrogance that becomes more prominent the larger the social, political, and economic inequality between groups in society. Here, elite male culture seems to play a key role, given that men are disproportionately represented in the influential positions of politics, business, academia, and beyond.

However, this is only one among several gender-based problems. What is far less understood and discussed is the 'lower end' of social exclusion, delinquency, and criminality among groups of low social status. Here, boys and men are also over-represented, to highly significant degrees. This has partially a genetic cause. X-chromosomes contain far more genes and are much larger than Y-chromosomes. Genes in one of the X-chromosomes in a pair have a higher likelihood of being sufficiently protected against genetic vulnerability if the other chromosome is also an X-chromosome, as among species with XX-pairs (girls and women). Among boys and men, however, Y-chromosomes cannot sufficiently protect against genetic vulnerability found in the X-chromosome. Genetic vulnerability (through the risk of errors and irregularities) in the

X-chromosome cannot be sufficiently protected by their Y-chromosome, since the latter is much smaller and contains fewer genes. This helps explain why boys and men are over-represented among people with the disorders as mentioned earlier, increasing the risks of mental deviance, delinquency, violent crimes, including the marginal and socially excluded groups. Feedback loops between (a) male culture that rebels against norms about education, (b) boys' significantly lower scores in school, and (c) a higher proportion of violence and crime, may partly be explained by this difference in individual genetic variation between males and females. A key lesson from the human sciences, such as sociology and evolutionary psychology – also supported by primatology about baboons and gorillas – is the following: A society with many low-status males that are excluded from the peaceful cooperation and social bonds is the first recipe for social unrest (Geary, 2010; Sapolsky, 2013). All societies aimed at becoming good ones ought to handle this challenge (in addition to increasing the status of women of course). On this note, it is important to ask what happens to the (lower) percentage of girls and women who have the disorders mentioned above? They have turned out to suffer even more than boys and men with the same disorders, regarding the reactions from peer and society, in turn leading to a high degree of social exclusion. The reason that girls and women with these disorders face particular challenges is, for instance, that these females appear to others as deviating more from the stiff, cultural norms about how girls and women should behave than do men with ADHD in their deviating from cultural norms about males. This turns out to be still another challenge of gender inequality that needs to be managed far more actively by the human sciences and by society.

In sum, a far wider knowledge pool and range of strategies are required to shed a full light on challenges related to gender-based inequalities, and what opportunities are at hand for better meeting the interests of all.

Foundations prepared on the slate

Universality as form; cultural specificity as content?

There are several metaphors for what human scientists assume is prepared genetically on the universal human slate. 'Grammar' is such an image. In fact, much of the idea of a universal, genetically based grammar was initially developed in the field of linguistics, which makes the grammar metaphor especially suitable. Chomsky and his many followers in linguistics note, like the rest of us, that learning one or several languages comes extremely naturally to humans, particularly when we are children. When no language has been available to children (as for groups of children who have grown up in extreme social isolation), they have still effortlessly invented their own language. According to Chomsky and several of his colleagues, languages follow the similar logic, a 'universal grammar'. This can be seen even in cases where people within the cultures using the respective languages have never been in contact with each other (Chomsky, 2007). Consequently, whereas languages vary extensively between, and within, cultures, there is still a universal, linguistic, latent grammar that is genetically prepared.

Another area where scholars have tried to discover genetically based universals is emotions. Ekman has spent decades comparing the facial expressions of peoples in various regions of the world. By having research subjects in different cultures select pictures of facial expressions based on the emotional states of people in the photos, and by asking people across cultures to show a number of emotional states with their own faces, he has discovered a high degree of similarity between all the cultures that he studied. The basic emotions that he argues are possible to discern by examining facial expressions are the following ones: sadness, happiness, disgust, anger, surprise, and fear. Moreover, Ekman gives a long list of emotions that he claims are universal and genetically rooted, although this extensive list of emotions is not discernible by examining facial expressions (Ekman, 2007).

Others use the term of 'schemas' to describe the preparations on the human slate that they analyse. This term is used in studies of cognitive development. The developmental psychologist, Piaget, uses the image of universal, 'cognitive schemas'. He argues that they are innate since these schemas help humans adapt to needs for organising and making sense of pieces of information at particular stages of their development as children. If a child is given the opportunity to interact with her environmental and social surroundings, the interplay with her cognitive schemas will lead to the child's active construction and understanding of the world. Piaget expands his analyses to the moral domain, by stipulating and examining how children in different ages reason morally (Piaget, 1932/1997).

The moral psychologist Kolberg uses Piaget's work on moral development as a starting point, and extends it theoretically and empirically. By telling children of various ages stories that include moral dilemmas that he asks them to discuss and resolve, Kohlberg has defined three levels (in six stages) of moral development (Kohlberg, 1981). The first he calls 'the pre-conventional level'. It is initiated in infancy and preschool. Characteristic of this level is that right and wrong is fully defined by whether one's action leads to punishments or rewards. The second level he labels 'the conventional level'. It starts during school age. Here, the child emphasises the importance of following rules, and of doing what is approved by others, particularly by authorities. The third, 'post-conventional level', starts in adolescence and continues throughout adulthood. This level refers to an understanding of morality as based on a social contract aimed at mutual benefits, a contract that also transcends expectations of returned favours. At this highest level, the person recognises that what is morally right and legally right are not always the same thing (Crane, 2010).

A different way of categorising genetically based forms of morality is to try to identify and explain a specific number of moral foundations. In a previous chapter Haidt's six moral foundations (or seven, including 'waste/efficiency') were mentioned. They deserve to be mentioned again: (1) care/harm, (2) fairness/cheating, (3) sanctity/degradation, (4) liberty/oppression, (5) authority/subversion, (6) loyalty/betrayal. A further candidate is (7) waste/efficiency (Haidt, 2012). Moreover, he has tried to explain why specific moral foundations have evolved genetically throughout the long history of Homo sapiens. Since moral foundations can be traced to our genes, they exist in all human societies. Still, this gives room for tremendous variation as to the cultural content of the moral foundations of various groups and societies.

When made with a high level of scientific rigour, several efforts of identifying genetically rooted, universal grammar, schemas, and foundations have been well received in significant parts of the wider scientific community. Identifications of universals may help to clarify what the human mind and its interests are not: entirely social learning-based or arbitrary. Moreover, such identifications of universals can be practically useful in the human sciences. In studies of environmental problems, for instance, the six or seven moral foundations identified by Haidt can be used. They may help us examine whether manifestations of all moral foundations have been subject to analysis or whether manifestations of some moral foundations are absent in, for example, analyses of whether society responds, or fails to respond adequately to environmental harm done by people, organisations, or states.

Example: moral foundations in environmental, social science

In the field of social science on environmental policies, the following can be noted: (1) The care/harm foundation is regularly in focus concerning environmental pollution by corporations. A fundamental question implied in such studies is whether corporations may ever truly care about reducing environmental and health harm (Holzer, 2010). (2) The fairness/cheating foundation has been examined in studies of greenwashing, and of how to deal with false environmental claims (Boström *et al.*, 2015). (3) The sanctity/degradation foundation has been subject to analyses of marketing and regulation of goods and production processes of cultural controversy. Such products and processes include genetically modified organisms, claims of 'natural products', and whether it is environmentally protective, morally degrading, or both, to put a price on parts of the natural environment (Klintman, 2006). (4) Liberty/oppression has been in focus in studies of which subsidies and economic penalties are, or should be, used to reduce negative environmental impacts of producers and consumers (Kock, Santalo, & Diestre, 2012). (5) Authority/subversion has been studied in analyses of environmental expertise (Lidskog, Mol, & Oosterveer, 2015). Moreover, they have been studied in environmental policy making concerning which combinations and sequences of hard and soft regulations are the most efficient ones, for reducing environmental harm rooted production and consumption (Sarkar, 2008; Tamm Hallstrom & Boström, 2010). However, the sixth moral foundation, loyalty/betrayal, has so far been largely overlooked or ignored in environmental, social science. Perhaps along with sanctity/degradation, loyalty and authority/subversion are foundations that may at a first, simple glance seem more relevant to non-Western societies, to religious groups, or pre-modern societies than to contemporary, market liberal ones. By being human universals, loyalty/betrayal and authority can be expected to be found, and to have a substantial impact, also in organisations of a market liberal society, even in corporate decision making.

At the same time as constructions of universal foundations can be useful, and seem to reflect essential mental modules, it is necessary to make room for nuances and reservations. First, it is not clear whether the universal foundations mentioned above are discrete, that is, clearly distinguishable from each other. Some scholars argue that universal foundations are plastic. Second, it is tough, if at all doable, to draw fixed borderlines between universal foundations and culture-based content. The human sciences can be expected to continue their movement back and forth across their stipulated lines, between what they perceive as universal foundations (forms) and cultural variations (contents). There is a constant and dynamic interplay between universal foundations and culturally specific conditions. This interplay entails that such lines between the universal and culturally specific may need to be drawn differently in various cultures during different times. Third, we should not forget that people and communities, even the human sciences, also operate at the latent level of social rationality, striving towards esteem in parallel with their manifest objective of acquiring knowledge. The content of social rationality differs across the human sciences. Evolutionary scientists and neuroscientists have so far been given the highest prestige by bringing home from their fMRI-scan laboratory studies compelling indications that the scientist or group has discovered a human universal or a new finding of universal validity. All the examples so far in this chapter are findings developed with aspirations of universality. Reversely, among cultural anthropologists, for instance, what gives the highest prestige is to bring home from one's ethnographic field strong indications of having discovered traits that are unique to a particular culture. Classical examples of anthropological claims of cultural uniqueness include the ambitious ethnographic studies conducted by Briggs, a cultural anthropologist. After having spent extensive time periods with Utku people among the Inuits, she draws the conclusion that adult Utku members are '[n]ever in anger', as her book is entitled (Briggs, 1971). The Utku word for 'anger' rather translates into 'childishness'. Only children, along with a few adult eccentrics, are angry. According to Briggs, it is not simply that they repress their anger. Instead, children learn throughout their upbringing that it is futile ever to be angry. The harsh environmental climate places absolute limits to what people can do in their lives that a Stoic-like resignation becomes the most proper mind-set and life philosophy. The Utku culture of resignation has, according to Briggs, removed anger – this basic emotion – entirely from the emotional repertoire of Utku adults. Another example is ethnographic studies aspiring to have identified one uniquely Japanese emotion: *amae*. This emotion, although impossible to translate accurately into English, cultural anthropologists and ditto psychologists have translated roughly as follows: Amae is an emotion of interdependence between people, an emotion of indulgence that is nevertheless perceived by both parties as positive (Niiya, Ellsworth, & Yamaguchi, 2006).

The claim beneath identifications of cultural uniqueness is that the unique traits, and in consequence culturally particular interests, are not just a unique combination of basic, universal, emotion. Instead, they are culturally particular emotions, impossible to derive from universal ones (Solomon, 2008). Several questions need to be addressed here. Is it that certain emotions are untranslatable between cultures because there does not happen to be a specific name for them? Alternatively, is it that humans universally may sense the entire repertoire of emotions, although some emotions are more easily recognised and experienced in certain cultures, and less so in others, making some emotions inaccessible in certain cultures?

Although claims about universality or cultural uniqueness should not be ruled out beforehand, they should be systematically scrutinised by all the human sciences. Such scrutiny needs to take place both of the 'internal factors' of how they were discovered (the quality of the scientific procedure, methodology, rigour), and of 'external factors' (social aspects, such as which types of results are associated with particular prestige.) Sociology of science and knowledge has a particularly strong history of examining the external factors, and will continuously be needed here. Nevertheless, cross-checking between the human sciences will be needed in order to decipher integration and intertwining of universal foundations and cultural specificities, as bases for human interests.

Heuristics and framings

We have seen how evolution has prepared the human slate with a repertoire, for instance of basic emotions and moral reasoning. Most of these genetically prepared traits are dependent on the social environment to develop. Moreover, these traits are highly plastic, enabling people to adapt to the cultural and social environment where they find themselves. This section discusses other ways in which the human slate seems to be genetically prepared. In the same way as people have a universal interest in, for instance, being able to engage in moral reasoning and decision making, they have an interest in making sense of the social and physical world in efficient ways to be socially included, without being exploited by others. To better understand how people and groups make sense of what sometimes seems to be the chaotic, arbitrary, and unpredictable reality, the research area of mental 'heuristics' and 'framings' turns out to be particularly apt for mutual learning and cooperation between the human sciences. Strands of thought within all three human sciences take a great interest in this area, and the respective findings of each human science appear more or less compatible across these sciences. Still, there are, crudely put, two complementary dimensions in which heuristics and framings – as described above – are understood in the human sciences. These ways can be described by use of the distinction between Dionysian and the Apollonian dimensions of human sense making.

The Dionysian dimension of heuristics and framing

To refresh our memory, the Dionysian dimension takes place beneath fully conscious, strategic, and planned mental processes. This dimension is closely tied to what Kahneman calls System 1 thinking, and to what Chaiken and Trope (1999) label 'old' brain development. The Dionysian dimension refers to spontaneous, fast, and energy-efficient mental processes for making sense of the world. To understand why this old dimension is still highly influential in humans, we have to realise that the potential stimuli from the world are virtually endless. The key to survival and reproductive success is to be able to sort out the stimuli that are essential for this success, and to be spared irrelevant stimuli. This principle of adaptation is most clear by examining how evolution has equipped various species with the sensory abilities. Dogs have a more sensitive nose than have humans; bats can identify higher sound frequencies than can humans. It is reasonable to assume that these and other human sensory limits have been of adaptive value throughout our history. A reason is that a main evolutionary challenge is how to minimise the amount of energy that the brain uses. The human brain costs as much as 20 per cent of our metabolic rate (energy intake) when we are resting, compared to around 9 per cent for other primates (Fonseca-Azevedo & Herculano-Houzel, 2012). Despite the fact that the sophisticated human brain has been the primary reason for human evolutionary success, the size and energy use of the human brain has continuously been an evolutionary challenge. There are strong reasons the human brain must be economical, with computational limitations. The reasons include the vulnerability throughout history due to a great need for protein- and energy-rich foods, birth risks (for mother and infant) associated with large head measures of infants, and the record-long period in which children are dependent on their parents (compared to other species). Moreover, it has been adaptive in most environments to be able to make certain decisions quickly.

Uncompromised brain computations every time people are to act, to calculate consciously every possible interpretation and outcome, would make them too slow to avoid dangers and to seize opportunities. Therefore, humans are genetically equipped with various types of heuristics – shortcuts, simplifications, and rules of thumb – through which we make sense of the world and make decisions (Gilovich *et al.*, 2002).

All three human sciences recognise human heuristics, albeit in different ways and by attaching different normative positions to them. So far in this chapter, the description of heuristics uses the outlook of evolutionary science. This outlook emphasises the adaptive value of human heuristics. At the same time, evolutionary psychology, for example, recognises several mismatches that these genetically evolved heuristics may constitute in modern life.

Economic science does not have one coherent view on heuristics. Traditional economics downplays or ignores human heuristics. This is intriguing. Traditional economics assumes that the individual is selective and economical in her use of (limited) resources for optimising the satisfaction of her utility. This economics ignores the following fact: To do such complete, strategic calculations, making use of all available information before we make any decision would require far more energy by the brain than the 20 per cent humans use. Furthermore, the brain size would possibly need to be larger than it is. Constant, conscious, strategic decision making where all information is weighed would be extremely uneconomical, and would be at odds with basic lessons from evolutionary science. Also, traditional economics overlooks how evolution has maintained many traits of our more primitive ancestors (before Homo sapiens). The traits that have been adaptive, such as several unconscious, innate traits at the latent level, have remained in the evolution from non-human to human genes (De Waal, 2005).

Acknowledging this misconception has been the basis of a branch of economic sciences that I mention in a previous chapter about the Dionysian critique of traditional economics: behavioural economics, often in close dialogue with other scholars of decision making. One of the ideas in behavioural economics and decision theory is that people do not make decisions through 'precise' calculations. Instead, people use various types of comparisons, reference points, and so forth. Accordingly, people use what is called 'bounded rationality'. It is constituted by two limiting factors. I mention the first factor above: the limited computability in the brain. The second factor concerns the specific structure of rules and regularities in the particular problem area or situation in which people are to make specific decisions (Gigerenzer, 2015).

Behavioural economists and other decision-making scholars with an evolutionary understanding of heuristics and their biases have in common that they recognise that these simplifying tools have evolved as adaptations to our ancestors' needs and interests in the hunter-gatherer society. Thus, these scholars emphasise that heuristics are best suited for dealing with rather concrete, short-term, real-world problems. Such problems were predominant in the hunter-gatherer society. In a pivotal paper, Tversky and Kahneman (1974) introduced the following three key heuristics (the reasoning about evolutionary adaptation is my own):

Representativeness heuristics is the human propensity to judge the likelihood of a certain event by how much it resembles a very common case. This heuristics leads people to overlook other, vital factors, such as chance. An example uses the fictitious character of Janet. She works in a bank, is a former student of the humanities, active in environmental organisations fighting for environmental justice. To the question of what Janet is, people usually answer that it is more likely that she is 'a feminist bank teller' than 'a bank teller', even if this is logically impossible. In previous as well as modern societies, the representative heuristics is highly useful for making decisions and drawing conclusions about regular events, such as if someone is a bank teller (in the modern world) or chief, child, pregnant woman, community member, or non-community member.

Availability heuristics is perhaps the most well-known human propensity to simplify reality. Humans make use of the stories and anecdotes that are most easily available when they are to judge the likelihood of an event to occur. Sensational anecdotes of airplane crashes, terrorist attacks, and rare but frightening diseases may all represent real events. However, humans are more likely to exaggerate the likelihood of such occurrences than of less sensational, but more likely ones, such as car accidents, falling accidents in the home, and so forth. Throughout evolution, it has been highly adaptive to learn from other people's narratives and anecdotes. The noble art of statistics is only a few centuries old.

Before its existence, stories and direct experiences were all people had. What may today be interpreted as 'irrational fears' founded on sensational news coverage has throughout human history been highly adaptive (unless the fears have entailed complete passivity). Ignoring a frightening story once could be enough for not surviving and reproducing.

Anchoring heuristics, finally, is the tendency for people to make use of reference points that they perceive, frequently persuaded by others, as 'the normal' from which one should not deviate too much. Thus, sales persons many times inform customers of a 'recommended price', which is typically very high. Customers are likely to be satisfied if they can buy the product in question at a price modestly lower than the recommended price. In green marketing and policy making, reference points are frequently developed for how much pollution is permitted in certain types of production, and as thresholds for what levels of hazardous chemicals are permitted. Although such reference points are usually based more on negotiations between various groups of stakeholders than on any 'hard science', they have the function of creating public trust and comfort, as long as products and pollution levels do not deviate substantially from these anchored, socially constructed levels (Boström & Klintman, 2011). From an evolutionary perspective, the anchoring heuristics may have been of adaptive value by community members recognising social norms (honouring 'normality'). These are based, in turn, on reference points for various activities. Our anchoring heuristics equips us with a social perceptivity.

Tversky, Kahneman, and other scholars of behavioural economics have, since the paper mentioned above was published, identified and analysed additional heuristics, as well as a higher number of biases that are prepared on the human slate (Gilovich *et al.*, 2002). Their main claim is that these have been of adaptive value to our ancestors. However, given the empirical field where behavioural economists are most active – financial and economic decision making – it is not strange that they perceive these heuristics and biases as mistakes, errors – irrational, that is. Optimising one's plans for health insurance, pension funds, and loans for going to college is certainly not the strongest human skills. Some genetically carved human biases stand in the way of such long-term decision making. If interpreted more broadly, such heuristics and biases, I would hold, still in modern society provide people with a social potential that would hardly be possible without them. The representativeness heuristics enable people to use 'common sense', which includes a degree of stereotyping of that help to strengthen bonds between people. Availability heuristics strengthen people's social bonds by preparing them with an interest in other people's experiences and viewpoints. Anchoring heuristics, finally, make people recognise and care about cultural norms, by being sensitive to when they or other people deviate from their culture's reference points. Consequently, even if these heuristics sometimes make us make sub-optimal decisions at the manifest, Apollonian level, such as in specific economic cases, it is reasonable to assume that there are other instances where it is more socially rational to stay fairly close to these heuristics rather than to try to become entirely liberated from them. At the same time, the human slate does not only prepare for social bonding, but also for exclusion. The Dionysian dimension of several heuristics and biases includes preparing people for stereotyping, which in certain situations entails prejudice of other groups. This, along with the importance of not committing the naturalistic fallacy, of drawing conclusions that heuristics are natural and therefore good, are two factors that raise the following important issue: That all the human sciences need to continue examining the constant human and organisational inclination of making judgements in a sweeping and sometimes even dehumanising manner.

The Apollonian dimension of heuristics and framing

One way of using heuristics is to develop and communicate frames. The principle is here, as always when heuristics are concerned, that the multifaceted reality must be narrowed down, limited, illustrated, formulated, and sometimes dramatised so that others can make sense of it. What the term framing means is revealed by its name. People and groups frame the parts and interpretations of reality that they find meaningful, and sometimes also that they find strategic. Sociology of everyday life has identified the strong influence that cultural framings have on what problems people in a culture recognise, and on what measures are prescribed for handling these issues (Goffman, 1974/1986). Behaviour economics, and research influenced by this economic sub-field, has provided significant contributions to knowledge about framing (Stoker, 2014), as have studies in communication (Shaw & Giles, 2009) and policy analysis (Holzer, 2007; Schön & Rein, 1994).

The basis for the existence and power of framing processes is what was described above with the Dionysian dimension in human perception and decision making. When examining framings, the interest of the analyst often lies in the strategic, Apollonian dimension: How groups and organisations can plan, develop, and alter how various issues are framed, to meet whoever's interests are at stake. The whole field of 'nudging' revolves around making use of the human need for simplified framings of reality. For instance, when the issue concerns the free choice of donating one's organs after one's death, there are vast differences between countries. Countries with an opt-out policy (where people must inform the agency actively if they do not wish to donate) have a much higher percentage of people donating than countries with an opt-in policy, where people must inform the agency actively if they wish to donate (Shepherd, O'Carroll, & Ferguson, 2014). This is another issue where the difference is simply one of how the issue is framed. Although there is something commonsensical here, it points at the same time in an intriguing way to the power of narrative and language, which are areas where social science and humanities have the longest and strongest traditions. It is not merely that language and verbal formulations dress fixed human interest in words. More fundamentally, language and words may dramatically influence and alter human thoughts and interests.

Social science fully recognises this potential of language and symbols. Still, these sciences often highlight the strategic dimension of framings, in public debate and policy making. How does this work? From the social scientific perspective of strategy and resource mobilisation of, for instance, social movements, framings are anything but innocent, mental processes only. Instead, reference points, symbols, language, and rhetorical patterns, can sometimes be strategic tools through which certain potentially powerful groups – business leaders, and non-governmental organisations – influence public debate and policy making (Benford & Snow, 2000). Simplified problem framings that get a strong 'cultural resonance' are powerful tools for influencing political decision making (Gamson, 1992).

When heuristics are analysed as framings, the dynamics and process-orientation become visible. In their policy analyses, the social scientists Schön and Rein (1994) examine two types of framings. The first type is what they call disagreements. These are disputes that take place within a common frame. For instance, a government and an environmental movement may differ in their views of what exact limit levels for car emissions should be stipulated by the government below which the government will provide a 'green subsidy' for automobiles that emit lower levels. All parties involved may agree that less environmentally unfriendly automobiles should be subject to 'green subsidies'. The dispute merely concerns levels and degrees. According to Schön and Rein, disagreements can often be resolved by looking at the facts (here about financial costs and environmental benefits of various emission levels). The second type of framing is controversies. They take place in separate frames. There is little or no agreement about what is the issue at stake, and what should be done about it. If, for example, the government suggests a certain level of fossil-fuel emissions below which cars should be subject to 'green subsidies' whereas influential environmental organisations only accept that non-fossil-fuel-driven vehicles be subject to subsidies, the dispute has more of the character of controversy. They can rarely be resolved by new and better facts. Controversies concern something deeper: values, and in some cases ideological differences. The sociologist Frödin (2015) makes a similar point by claiming that social scientists, for instance in the World Social Science Report of 2013, entitled *Changing Global Environment*, assume that controversies (about complex policy paths and societal phenomena) can be resolved in the same way that disagreements can. Committing the 'knowledge-action fallacy', assuming that improved knowledge itself may provide adequate solutions, is one manifestation of the juxtaposition between controversies and disagreements.

There are indeed ways of resolving controversies. So-called 'reframings' may lead to resolutions. It is not necessary that both parties – or any party – becomes fully satisfied by the resolution created through reframing. However, reframing can, at least, lead to decision making. For example, reframing has taken place concerning smoking policy. Should smoking be permitted in public, indoor spaces? This was long a controversy, not least in Western countries. Whereas both sides had to admit the health risks of smoking, several ideological and cultural issues constituted disputes between divergent framings, one in favour and the other against permitting smoking in indoor public spaces. Both sides tried to reframe the issue into one that gained cultural and legal resonance: The individual's right to smoke, the individual's right not to inhale smoke, asthmatic people's right to avoid inhaling smoke, each person's responsibility to go to non-smoking areas if they did not want to inhale smoke, and so forth. However, none of the framings above gained sufficient cultural and legal resonance. What finally did in several countries was the framing of 'occupational health and safety'. This is an area with a strong legal tradition in a number of countries, a tradition against which the side with interests in free smoking in restaurants, bars, and other public spaces where people work, had no chance of winning (Hyland, Barnoya, & Corral, 2012).

The social rationality of prioritising esteem

That social esteem, along with its more elegant soul mates glory and honour, is an overriding, human universal seems to be supported by several parts of the human sciences. Social science, despite its usual reluctance to discuss universality, has through the years done both cross-cultural and historical comparisons where struggle towards glory, honour, and esteem turn out to be far from particular phenomena in specific cultures.

In evolutionary science, evolutionary anthropologists have collected and analysed overwhelming data on how the struggle among people and groups for raising or, at least, maintaining their social esteem is a main driving force universally. Comparative, evolutionary anthropology aims to find traits that are common to all humans (absolute universals), or, at least, to humans in all cultures (conditional and statistical universals). These traits have evolved genetically during mainly the long period of hunter-gatherer society (Brown, 2004, 51). To assume that humans have had time to evolve and adapt to modern urban society, for instance by evolving genetically into having a modern capitalist mindset deeply integrated on their human slate, is, according to evolutionary theory, preposterous.

When studying human universals through cross-cultural, evolutionary anthropology, some 200 traits have been found so far. In a previous book (Klintman, 2012b) I analysed these features, not only to see what traits are included, but also to examine what traits are not on the list, characteristics that in daily speech are still treated as human universals. Evolutionary science downplays that human interests would be static in specific, practical situations. There seems to be little reason economic preferences would be paramount in light of the relative material equality and nomadic ways of life of hunter-gatherers.

That economic rationally (particularly in a material sense) is culturally adopted into mainstream norms in certain cultures, does not mean that this rationality runs in any way as deeply as if it were a genetically prepared, hardwired mental module. This is revealed in the many studies of behavioural economics indicating the biases and heuristics described above that are prepared on the human slate to satisfy human interests that sometimes, but far from always, converge with manifest, material interests. That humans in all cultures are so bad at making economically rational decisions is one among several signs that evolution and its natural selection places economic rationality very low. However, humans do not do poorly in only economic decision making. In the previous book, I bring up the issue of whether humans can ever become good at making decisions that minimise environmental harm (Klintman, 2012b). The short and simple answer is that several of the biases and heuristics that speak against the human potential for rational, economic decision making also speak against the human potential for rational, ecological decision making. For all their differences, economic and ecological decision making share several features, such is their basis in Apollonian mindset and effort. Considering human universals in the research for that book, I soon learned that it is as difficult to find human universals that point towards ecological optimisation as towards economic ditto. The closest we get to ecological concern among human universals is personal hygiene and concern for what is poisonous and what is not. In that book, I interpret this absence as based on the fact that hunter-gatherers were so few (posing a low risk to the environment at large) that minimising environmental harm would not have substantial, evolutionary benefits (for our early ancestors' survival and reproductive success). Moreover, hunter-gatherers were nomads, constantly moving as soon as the local environment could not serve them as an area for hunting and gathering. The evolutionary biologists Ehrlich and Ehrlich, who would confirm my assumptions above, go one step further. They claim that evolution has 'encouraged us to ignore' (Ehrlich & Ehrlich, 2008, 127) abstract and distanced threats, such as the types of ecological harm that people and governments are told to care about today. Caring about and prioritising similar issues would in hunter-gatherer society steal energy and focus from more immediate issues, and would make those who were preoccupied with abstract, environmental issues seem unreliable cooperators to manage more immediate issues.

The manifest interests refer to the interest that contemporary societies are openly preoccupied with – how to reach economic growth, reduce environmental harm, make scientific advances, make productive political decisions, and so forth. Still, from an evolutionary perspective of human interests, these manifest interests do not in themselves run deeply enough in human motivation, and do not trigger comprehensive effort as long as they do not converge with deeper, latent interests, that are universal and genetically prepared on our slate. These deeper, latent interests point far more towards a social rationality. We can see this by contemplating the following human universals, which are only a few of the universals that reflect a social rationality:

> 'resistance to abuse of power' … 'turn-taking' … 'group living' … 'prestige inequalities' … 'cooperation' … 'coalitions' … 'collective identities' … 'judging others' … 'resistance to dominance' … 'customary greetings' … 'awareness of self-image' … 'shame' … 'manipulation of self-image' … 'concern for what others think' … 'statuses and roles' … 'statuses ascribed and achieved' … 'manipulation of social relations'.
>
> (In Pinker, 2002, 371–9, based on Brown, 1991, 2004)

Why then are, for instance, esteem, social status, and strengthening or at least maintaining one's social reputation genetically hardwired, overriding, universal interests? Because surviving and procreating in the hunter-gatherer society necessitated social bonding, collaboration, and the motivation to assess who is trustworthy and who is not, in order for people to survive and reproduce. Those who had this motivation, and the social rationality tied to it, had a far better chance than others not just to hand down not just their own genes, but also to share their experiences culturally, providing narratives to future generations of how to lead a durable life. The social psychologist Baumeister gives further support to this position, by showing how our social motivation, and what I in this book call social motivation, has been, and perhaps still is, a process of coevolution between genes and the social environment (Baumeister, 2005). Those who were most socially oriented among the earliest humans were able to survive (for the reasons mentioned above). They in turn influenced the social environment in ways that this environment demanded even higher social skills and abilities of people to survive. The key adaptive trait became the ability to benefit from culture. Those with a strong social rationality may make better use of culture for becoming appreciated members of groups and communities, becoming more knowledgeable, and getting a good and stable position, factors that have reproductive benefits.

As the reader can see, social rationality is not merely Dionysian. In social rationality, the spontaneous and instinctive motivation to bond and interact with others is in constant interaction with a more Apollonian, measured and calculated way to relate to others. This interplay between the Dionysian and Apollonian is necessary in order to both win other people's trust that we are reliable group members, and by continuously reassessing whether other members of our group are reliable or whether they have cheated on the group. The list of human universals above clearly implies this necessary tension of human sociality.

The interest in doing well in the social game, doing well ranging from the glory of the Machiavellian Prince, via success in prestige of organisations and companies, and to the social bonding and belonging of each of us in our daily lives, presupposes the social rationality mentioned above. People concretise their social rationality by, for example, imitating as well as distinguishing themselves from other people and groups, through practices, styles, and values. Social rationality is also reflected in the efforts of developing knowledge skills and routines, and in the signalling and sharing of these skills to others, thus strengthening one's social bonds and position.

Several of our propositions above indicate that social rationality, rather than, for instance, manifest interests in material accumulation, minimising environmental harm, or producing the most accurate knowledge, is key to the universal interest in social esteem. This means that we should expect social esteem to be prioritised when it is in conflict with the manifest interests. Consequently, groups identifying with the principle of environmentally oriented voluntary simplicity are likely to compromise with their reductions of environmental harm in practices that go against the image of voluntary simplicity. This could take place if they hear that it is better for the environment to purchase new household products, a new car, and so forth. According to this argument, new products use less energy and entail less harmful emissions than do, for example, old automobiles. We should expect people to find it more important to stick to the identity components of their group – often at the aesthetic level – than to pursue manifest project interests when these ends are in conflict with this aesthetics. Another side of this coin is where the immediate material gain is an inefficient means of strengthening one's social esteem and positive recognition. In such situations, it is common that people and organisations compromise with their material gain in order to strengthen their esteem. For instance, wealthy companies and people can be expected to support philanthropic or other idealist projects with some of their wealth when it strengthens their social position, prestige, or the like, more than keeping the money would do.

Finally, people should be expected to (unconsciously) prioritise sticking to the knowledge claims and beliefs of their social and cultural group over weighing evidence in a systematic and unbiased manner. This is why conservatives and liberals in certain countries are so stable in their knowledge claims and beliefs about the pros and cons of capital punishment, private gun ownership, what the limits should be (if any) for abortion, and so forth (Haidt, 2012). People on both sides downplay even first evidence that speaks against their own position, since it is (unconsciously) of primary evolutionary importance to stick to one's group and culture but getting all knowledge right is only of secondary importance (Mercier, 2011).

The huge benefits that can be associated with the human interest in social esteem and acceptance means that the mental processes that help us constantly move towards esteem and strengthened acceptance are naturally selected and highly sophisticated. These processes are included in people's social rationality. The term rationality implies that human endeavours necessarily include motivation, resources, means, and goals. That social rationality is genetically rooted denotes mainly three things. First, social rationality has general, universal traits, but is at the same time highly adaptive to specific social conditions. What is socially rational in one culture may be highly irrational in another. There is huge space for making use of our social rationality by culturally shaping the content, for instance through manifest project goals. Second, contrary to the rational choice perspective of human endeavours as fully conscious and calculative, the notion of social rationality stresses that humans are only partially conscious in the sense of being fully calculative in their pursuits. Humans have of course developed from more primitive creatures. We have inherited genetically much of the latent, instinctive level, and this frequently serves us well. Whereas behavioural economics implies a wish that humans were 'more rational' (consciously economically rational to pursue our manifest project goals in optimal ways), my approach to social rationality is a recognition that what may appear as 'irrational' from the perspective of behavioural or traditional economics has its basis in social rationality. It refers to productive, albeit often impulsive, efforts to belong to certain groups and distinguish ourselves from others, to develop alliances, and so forth. Third, it is within the social rationality of people and groups not to accept problems and issues as absolutes. How people, groups, and cultures not only create norms but also use them flexibly, often by challenging them, is a key part of social rationality. This flexibility and dynamics take place through framing: how groups, organisations, parties, countries, and regions frame certain issues as problematic, whom to blame, and how these 'problems' should be solved. At least as important for the social and economic sciences is how such framing processes entail exclusion of other conditions as irrelevant, unproblematic, 'normal', by various actors of society. People and groups often pursue their manifest interests with much energy, focus, and pathos. At the same time, the notion of social rationality helps to acknowledge the need for the human sciences to search beneath this manifest level, to see how people use norms and framings. There, the latent interest in social esteem, honour, and glory – or just in mere social acceptance – can be expected to be the ultimate goal.

Conclusions

This chapter has provided some basic ideas, mainly based on evolutionary science, for what types of factors are genetically prepared on the human slate. Extensive research has been done in this area in a number of disciplines, and previous knowledge claims constantly need to be falsified or revised. Therefore, this chapter has mainly shed light on very general and broad patterns and processes. Its emphasis lies on human scientific findings that indicate how the old dualism of nature and nurture is most often invalid, and what the intertwining of the two looks like concerning human interests.

The chapter has explained the close interplay and coevolution between nature and nurture of humans that has turned us into a species somewhere in the middle of the continuum between a tournament species and a pair-bonding species. If we add the immense human potential towards social learning and cultural adaptations, it becomes clear how cultures may pull humans significantly (but never entirely) in one or the other direction along this continuum. Several social and evolutionary scientists argue that many cultures over the centuries have become increasingly 'civilised', manifested in monogamy (yet in the form of serial polygamy), reduced violence, improved rights for women, increased tolerance of ethnic minorities, and so forth. Regarding the continuum above, this has been a move in the direction towards humans as a more pair-bonding species. The crucial role of women's movements and feminism are typically highlighted here as a highly positive factor.

At the same time, the fact that humans are not blank slates means that certain tendencies and inclinations are genetically rooted. The human sciences need to have a constant focus on these as well. Social science repeatedly identifies the enormous differences in violent aggression between men and women universally in extensive, statistical examinations. Although male violence has been reduced dramatically in certain countries, the difference in violent aggression between women and men remains huge globally. Evolutionary scientists search for the root of this difference in the different conditions under which male and female reproduction takes place, entailing certain differences in the latent interests of women and men. Nevertheless, individual differences in interests, personalities, and abilities are far bigger than are these differences between women and men.

According to many evolutionary scientists, the human slate is also prepared with foundations for language, morality, and for some heuristics. The latter has the function of reducing the energy use of the brain and to help people make quicker decisions. At the same time, particularly behavioural economists focus on how heuristics are sometimes not well suited for satisfying certain Apollonian interests of contemporary society, such as interests in long-term planning. Whereas this is certainly true, it is nevertheless important to keep in mind that human interests are at least as strongly connected to latent, Dionysian interests (in social bonding, esteem, and so forth). To some extent the genetically prepared heuristics may in some cases point to an – often sound – priority of these latent interests, in cases where the Apollonian and Dionysian interests are in conflict.

All human sciences take a strong research interest in how such heuristics are used in society, and how society and culture are highly dependent on framings and metaphors for making sense of the world and for uniting people in a community. People and groups also make creative use of framing and heuristics for influencing others, and for gaining esteem.

Part III

Interests, continuity, and change

Prologue

A central theme of the human sciences and all life sciences (including biology) concerns tensions between continuity and change. In a liberal democracy, having its ideological basis in the Enlightenment, change is often embraced almost as something of intrinsic value. Politicians, companies, and leaders of organisations are constantly expected to present new ideas for political, social, and economic change. Even continuity requires change, this view contends. Someone who does not want change, and does not have a vision of something different from the current state, is seen as lacking will and fire. However, the interest in continuity is at least as strong. Although less attractive a sentiment in the culture of liberal democracy, interest in continuity and even in status quo is easy to identify in all segments of society. Several human scientific terms are used for understanding and explaining the reluctance to change. Inertia, path dependence, and status quo bias are only a few of these. Comprehensive research findings indicate that resistance to change is probably as strong as the drive towards change (Hopf, 2010; Polites & Karahanna, 2012).

Interests in continuity and change cannot be directly reduced to conservatism versus radicalism, as in right-wing versus left-wing politics. Both these sides of politics incorporate interests, not just in change but at least as much in continuity, depending on, for instance, what side has the most political power in the local area, region, or country in question (Tuschman, 2013). Nor are conservatism and radicalism constant, as in being able to host the respective of its 'classical' social and economic thinkers permanently, regardless of the social context. For instance, most current political parties and economic thinkers who consider themselves conservative today embrace the main ideas of the founder of traditional economics, Smith (1776/1843). However, in his own time, the eighteenth century, Smith was considered a radical. He challenged the land-owning aristocratic society of his time. The conservative aristocracy wanted anything but an invisible hand and equality before the law, two notions that Smith strongly endorsed.

Human interests in continuity and change constitute a theme that contains two issues, at least. Table PIII.1 below indicates this. One issue concerns whether

Table PIII.1 Interests, continuity, and change

	Interests in continuity	Interests in change
Actors and groups	1 Stable interests: interests in maintaining usual activities, habits, routines; stable interests	2 Flexible interests: interest in changing one's activities in order to better adapt to the current structure, or participate in changing the structure
Structure	3 Interests in traditions, norms, conventions, and economic, political, social structures being kept constant	4 Interests in structural change ('game change')

people, groups, and organisations favour the current state of affairs (Square 3) or if they would prefer a more or less radical change (Square 4). Another issue refers to whether interests among people, groups, and organisations are stable (Square 1) or whether they are highly flexible (Square 2). This chapter focuses mostly on the former issue – interests in structural continuity and change – although the latter – stable and flexible interests – is brought up where the two issues are inseparable.

The social and economic sciences should become better aware of the evolution-rooted forces of inertia, of resistance to change. This includes getting a deeper understanding of the benefits of continuity. From an evolutionary perspective, getting rid of all continuity and inertia would be disastrous. Extensive change, including social change, always implies a state of unrest and uncertainty, demanding much additional energy use of the actors and organisations. Many negative, unintended consequences may lie around the corner. Change always implies a motivational challenge for the leading segment of society, whether to the left or right. Intriguingly, this evolutionary principle – with several translations in social science where the term powers is always core – is not vastly different from what economists with a public choice perspective express. This perspective implies a constant, critical eye of traditional economics on political power. Whereas public choice economists have a basic faith in the corporate world, given that the right institutions are in place to allow the invisible hand to operate freely, the political realm is constantly under the risk that political actors and groups will prioritise their direct self-interests over the interests of the general public and companies. Those who are in power are accordingly inclined to compromise with the interests of the public in order to better satisfy their Apollonian interests in maintaining and gaining influence, accumulate resources for themselves, and perhaps also to meet Dionysian interests in maintaining their esteem for its own sake. From the public choice perspective, this is the main reason why politics and in extension the public debate do not more often follow the advice of economists about how to maximise efficiency and make society better at economising with its resources:

Economists know what steps would improve the efficiency of HSE [health, safety, and environmental] regulation, and they have not been bashful advocates of them. These steps include substituting markets in property rights, such as emission rights, for command and control ... The real problem lies deeper than any lack of reform proposals or failure to press them. It is our inability to understand their lack of political appeal.

(Peltzman, 1993, 830)

Even if social, economic, and evolutionary scientists would disagree about what alternative policies are most likely to increase the satisfaction of the interests of various groups of the general public, they would probably agree on a formulation similar to our following proposition:

Proposition 7: actors and groups at the top of a hierarchy have as their latent interest to stay at the top (in power). If this interest is in conflict with their tasks of satisfying the manifest interests of the people or groups they represent, their social rationality often implies that they prioritise the satisfaction of their latent interest.

One area where the three sciences would definitely disagree is public choice economists' intense focus on 'political' power, as if 'corporate' power would be far less problematic.

Segments 'below' the leading one always include some actors and organisations who have the social motivation to challenge the leading segment to reach towards power, glory, honour, esteem, or, at least, dignity. At the same time, this seemingly logical pattern is not carved in stone. Particularly a constant readiness for unprivileged groups to actively challenge the establishment or leadership is frequently conspicuously absent. Social science has a particularly long tradition of analysing such absence, whether called false consciousness, false belief, or political apathy. An intriguing pattern in history has been that not just the elites, but also parts of unprivileged groups, are sometimes resistant to social change. This is one among several issues where mutual learning is needed between the three human sciences to reach beyond description towards explanation.

7 Economics

Interests, continuity, and change

Stable interests

Homo economicus – like real individuals, according to economics – has stable interests and preferences, and these have a utility function. His or her stable interest and motivation is to maximise his or her own expected utility based on limited resources (Folmer, 2009, 258). Homo economicus aspires to be perfectly informed, and uses this information for satisfying his or her stable interests. Economists and many non-economists describe such an (illusory) individual as rational, as if it would be rational to behave in this individualist, consciously, and purposefully self-interested manner, concerning manifest interests.

There is something admirable in that traditional economics attempts to grasp humans and society in this elegant way in order to at least try to predict economic and social behaviour, as described in textbooks in economics (MasColell, Whinston, & Green, 2006). Moreover, we should not forget that the notion of Homo economicus and his economic rationality was developed to describe human behaviour at the aggregate level of many humans in society, not to describe and predict the behaviour of single individuals. Still, although the Homo economicus perspective is certainly elegant and rigorous, enormous amounts of criticism have been thrown at this view of human interests. Its crude abstraction of human and social life, the critique contends, entails limited potential for explaining and predicting human action and social development. Thus, it is, according to the critique, of as limited value for understanding humans and society as it is for policy (Rol, 2008).

At the same time, as in many caricatures, there seem to be certain grains of truth when using Homo economicus to describe an influential part of how economists understand human interests. One part is 'conservative' (in a wider sense than in narrow party politics), and another part points towards the great dynamics of human decision making. The conservative message is that we should not expect humans to change their nature. Humans will always be what they have always been. Moreover, according to traditional economics, people are highly dependent on external stimuli, often regarding incentives and disincentives.

History has been replete with economic and social thinkers who argue for making sure that the poor be kept poor. If not, the poor would not work (since people these scholars assume, tend to be passive unless incentives and disincentives stimulate them to be active). To make the poor better off would be bad not just for the affluent parts of society but also for the poor people themselves. These thinkers conclude that it is fair to favour continuity where the poor remain poor. It is fully understandable that many economic thinkers a couple of centuries ago are worried about laziness and passivity, in times when the rich consist of nobilities who have as their rule of life not to work, and to expose that they do not need to work. It is logical that these thinkers assume that if workers be better off, they will refuse to work to any serious extent (Manderville, 1714/1989). Extra incentives that are provided for particularly hard work run the risk of creating economic and social mobility (upward), which back in those days are seen as inadvisable.

Today, the mainstream view in economics is, of course, that people who work particularly hard should be financially rewarded. At the same time, the view among economists of humans as economically rational contends that the level of material incentives and disincentives to employees as well as to employers have huge consequences for their interests in working hard to provide for themselves. By extension, this selfishness and propensity for laziness – unless (usually material) incentives are sufficient – is highly relevant to the welfare of society as a whole. That a certain degree of unemployment is healthy for the economy can sometimes be heard, the argument contending that a degree of job insecurity may energise and strengthen people's motivation to work hard. That hungry wolves hunt best might be seen as common wisdom in many work environments, at all socio-economic levels.

Even if economics, like most other disciplines, is represented by people of several political colours, its general message is that no society can be expected to handle successfully societal problems without taking into account, and making use of, what economists perceive as (genetically hardwired) stable human receptivity to material or other Apollonian incentives and disincentives. This notion is core to the view in economics about the economic rationality of individuals and organisations. It is futile to try to bring about an entirely different society where humans are changed into becoming uninterested in material incentives and disincentives, and instead intrinsically motivated to do only beneficial things to the world. However, society can do something else. Since a stable trait of humans is to be highly receptive to incentives and disincentives, and since people have a fundamental interest in actively improving their own lives, financial carrots and sticks are the keys to improvements of society. Through economic instruments, society can help people voluntarily enrich their lives and channellise human selfishness into the strengthening of the common good. Economics embeds both a strong view of stable human interests, and of a human susceptibility to stimuli that can help individuals and society become authoritative agents constantly making active, voluntary choices.

Changing interests

One of the most common definitions of economics comes from Robbins: 'Economics is the science which studies human behaviour as a relationship between ends and scarce means which have alternative uses' (Robbins, 1932, 15). Understanding the world as one of trade-offs between different choices of means, as economists do, implies a view that choices should constantly be recalculated and reassessed. However, such recalculations are done, and should be done, on the margin, not in a binary, all-or-nothing manner. This becomes apparent in economists' recipes for how to solve various societal problems. According to traditional economics, the issue of solving climate change does not concern ending entirely the use of fossil fuels or abandoning completely other uses of greenhouse gases. A so-called zero-emission target is something of which traditional economists are highly sceptical. As long as the emission does not refer to a chemical that is lethal even in tiny quantities (which it does not in the case of CO_2), economists find zero-emission targets sub-optimal. The reason is that economists assume that there is an optimal level of CO_2 emissions, a level that could be far higher than zero. Accordingly, natural scientists should assess what is the critical level of emissions, which must not be exceeded if the planet is to avoid highly problematic temperature changes.

Example: carbon offsetting – continuity of market liberalism with a green twist

Carbon offsetting is an example of an instrument that intertwines interests in strengthening the continuity of market liberalist-based problem management, at the same time as it may entail voluntary changes in interests (into practices that do not emit climate gases). Carbon offsetting for flight transport, at least in its earlier versions, has by some been said to be an example of this. Guilt concerning fossil-fuel-based transport (Gans & Groves, 2012), and the handling of this guilt by offsetting the emissions by paying a certain fee to compensate for one's emissions, can be associated with several of the human interests described in this book. First, carbon offsetting to reduce feelings of guilt represents a change of interests, from a fully economically rational purchase of transport services into a wider interest in compensating for one's climate-gas emissions. Second, offsetting represents the dynamics between manifest interests in efficient and price-worthy transportation services, and a socially rational striving towards marking social position. This latent interest entails efforts towards being respected by others, both based on one's financial (social) position, and furthermore in being esteemed for one's benevolence. Yet, this latent, Dionysian interest presupposes the means of signalling the offsetting efforts to others. Signalling is an area where the offsetting instrument is weak so far, at least for private travellers (Blasch & Ohndorf, 2015). Third, offsetting to reduce guilt represents the dynamics between individual (short-term) interests in efficient and comfortable transportation at minimal costs, and collective interests in reducing climate harm and in extension health harm at a global level. Finally, and most relevant to this section, offsetting to reduce guilt is relevant to interests in continuity and change. Carbon offsetting and other 'green consumer instruments' may seem progressive and even radical. Still, it is not unfair to conceive of many of them as tools aimed at maintaining structural continuity of market liberalism with a green twist, instead of instruments of latent, structural change (of power relations, etc.; see Table 1.1, Square 4). For instance, carbon offsetting may, to be sure, help mobilise some money for reducing climate-gas emission. Yet, as long as offsetting is voluntary, and at the same time a weak device for social signalling, it cannot be expected to be used very extensively. Designed in this way, carbon offsetting does not meet the social rationality of private travellers, at least.

Voluntary carbon offsetting is, moreover, an example of the narrow focus of economic instruments towards reducing specific harm to global commons. Critics complain that carbon offsetting only addresses reductions of total climate gas emissions, rather than helps to reshape the modes of transportation into fossil-fuel-free transportation, and so forth. Still, instruments that economists suggest are usually aimed at not doing more than meeting a specific, manifest, Apollonian interest. According to economics, economic instruments cannot be expected to solve several broad problems at the same time. Economic rationality implies focus and results in specific predefined areas. At the same time, in the case of carbon offsetting, people's offsetting is invested in a broad range of schemes directed towards renewable energy.

From the perspective of economics, very drastic emissions reductions or entire removals of all emissions of a certain kind will be subject to reduced marginal utility. It is very expensive, and of very marginal utility, to reduce the green-house gas emissions more extensively than to the critical level. Instead, the changes that economists prescribe take place on the margin. The same applies to changes in people's daily practices. It is not realistic, or even desirable, that everyone quits using a car. Instead, through modifying price mechanisms so that the 'negative externalities' associated with using a car (local and global environmental impact, health risks, etc.) are integrated in people's expenses for their car use, economists assume that people will change their transportation behaviour on the margin. People will perhaps drive less than every day. Some will share a ride with colleagues, and so forth. Increased taxation on gasoline or congestion fees are a couple of methods for correcting the price of car use in ways that make people aware of the opportunity costs of using a car daily. Opportunity costs are the costs (in time, money, and effort) people pay by, in this case, insisting to use a car daily despite congestion fees and gasoline taxes, thereby missing other opportunities, such as sitting and reading a book on the commuter train and still saving some extra money.

The reasonable way of relating to the world is to be continuously prepared to alter one's past means, and to question the means that oneself and others have previously taken for granted. This is where economists' understanding of human interests in change comes in. One of the few things that economists do not want to be changed is the societal effort towards maximising the possibility for independent individuals to become increasingly active in making voluntary choices, doing voluntary exchanges of goods and services with others in the market.

A conservative feature in economics is its contention that human interests (preferences) are stable and that people's rational efforts lie in maximising these interests. At the same time, economics conceive of human interests in a non-conservative view, by claiming that people want to, and should, constantly question previous choices.

Throughout history, such questioning has concerned traditions of material moderation, of frugality, and so forth. The criticism in economics of the notion of sticking unreflectively to values and traditions has roots in the Enlightenment. In that stream of thought, beginning in the early eighteenth century, there are philosophers holding views with which many economists of today would agree. Voltaire, for instance, maintains that 'abundance is the mother of the arts'. He connects changes towards material abundance to positive social change. The quest for prosperity, he holds, may even reduce violence and tension between peoples of different traditions and religious faiths. Voltaire comments on the London Stock Exchange as an institution that fosters toleration. After a day of intensive business interaction, people of different faiths – mainly Christian and Jewish – go back to their separate lives: 'On leaving these peaceable and free assemblies, some go to the synagogue, others in search of a drink ...' In the end, 'all are satisfied' (Voltaire, 1733/2003, 26).

From Voltaire's perspective, material prosperity is necessary for the development of a more advanced civilisation (Muller, 2007). Repercussions are heard today when, for instance, economic growth-oriented environmental scholars and politicians assert that economic growth and its increased material prosperity must come first. In the long run, material prosperity will inevitably entail an interest among individuals, companies, and society in refining production and products so environmental harm be substantially reduced. A more prosperous society is a higher civilisation with more refined interests in reducing negative externalities derived from material abundance, externalities such as environmental harm. At the same time, there does not seem to be an end to manifest, material interests, and an end where people are content. Only the objects of our material interests keep changing, often by expanding in quantity.

Traditional economics emphasises that human interests are, and should be, open to change (except the stable interest in choice itself). Even on this issue, Voltaire's thinking resonates with economics as well as with capitalist thinking. In his essay 'About scissors', Voltaire notes that cutting one's hair and nails using the new invention of scissors was at first seen by most people as a luxury, an excess. However, after some time, it became a natural part of daily life for wider segments of society.

> When scissors ... were invented, what wasn't said against the first people who clipped their nails, and who cut some of the hair that fell down over their noses? They were doubtless called dandies and squanderers, who brought an expensive instrument of vanity to mar the work of the Creator.
>
> (Voltaire, 1764/2012, 224)

People's interests change so that what they earlier perceived as their wants are transformed into needs. The most important trait of capitalism is that it is dynamic, always changing. The easiest way to see this is, as above, to note how our views of needs and wants change, and how material abnormalities may soon become normalities. In personal and home electronics, this is particularly evident. When computers and mobile phones were first introduced, many consumers found it impossible to believe that they in the future would sense a need for these products. Capitalism stimulates new wants and helps people satisfy these wants, only to have these wants be expanded or changed again. In each such change, a new series of market exchanges may take place, new positive-sum games, where both buyers and sellers increase the satisfaction of their interests, economists contend.

Creative elites benefit the most from change

Even if economists may claim that all actors involved in market exchange are, per definition, better off after the exchange, some actors gain more than others in an ever-changing society. In the early twentieth century, the economic and political thinker, Schumpeter, takes a particular interest in a highly influential, but at the time not very well understood, category of people: entrepreneurs. This intriguing type of actor on the market plays a major role, argues Schumpeter, in teaching consumers to change their interests into wanting new and better products and services. Moreover, and perhaps more importantly, entrepreneurs help producers constantly modify their practices in order to lead or follow the dynamics of capitalism. For example, producers may want to integrate their production horizontally, by not only making rubber wheels but also other items out of rubber, such as soles of sports boots. Entrepreneurs can help producers integrate their production vertically, so that it becomes active in several steps of the supply chain, for instance, from producing and selling vegetables to delivering these products as well. Entrepreneurs help triggering change and are also highly dependent on change. Schumpeter has influenced numerous recent scholars in economics and innovation, but also in social science. The sociologist Dahms (1995) notes that Schumpeter's entrepreneur is a creative and (in the terminology of my book) a socially rational actor, rather than an economically rational one. In the same vein, Cole points out that Schumpeter's analysis always has a sociological content (Cole, 1952), for example by inspiring subsequent social scientific concepts and analyses, such as of 'leaders', 'laggards', and 'the creative class'.

Key is the susceptibility of entrepreneurs to a constant change in which they survive and prosper. In a sense there is an evolutionary perspective here, concerning the 'survival' (albeit a term reflecting a misunderstanding of biological evolution; procreation, not survival is key to biological evolution) of those who can best adapt to, or even to steer, changes in the (social, political, cultural, economic, and technological) environment. Schumpeter accordingly points out that the constant change embedded in capitalism has winners and losers. The clearest winners are the creative elites, who have a deeply rooted interest in change. The creative elites drive what Schumpeter calls 'creative destruction' of old and inefficient production processes, for instance, giving way to new and more efficient ones. To avoid the possible impulse of seeing such dynamics as heartless and inhumane, creative destruction could be exemplified by the destruction of fossil-based transportation and heating systems, instead giving way to transportation and heating systems using renewable energy sources. Still, despite the fact that the entrepreneur-driven development through creative destruction often helps increase most or all people's satisfaction of manifest, constantly changing interests, the creative elites, particularly entrepreneurs, are the clearest winners in such a system.

To be sure, entrepreneurs have their manifest, Apollonian interests satisfied more than others, such as in rapid increase in financial wealth. However, at least as importantly, their latent, Dionysian, interest of getting an improved social position is satisfied, by fulfilling 'the dream to found a private kingdom', by creating, and by leaving a mark, developing his own 'kingdom' (Schumpeter & Elliott, 1911). This motivation is far more in line with people's social interest in esteem, honour, and even glory, than in the interests that Homo economicus represents. Monetary wealth is only of secondary importance to entrepreneurs, and probably to most people, according to Schumpeter.

Since he focuses on the talented few, Schumpeter has been criticised by leftists for elevating the elites. Still, one of his points is that the creative elites need not come from the upper segment of society. To the contrary, it is more likely, according to Schumpeter, that creativity comes from somewhere below the upper segment. Consistent with evolutionary theory in biology, Schumpeter sees little reason people in the upper segment of society would make efforts to be creative since they were already at the top. Moreover, entrepreneurs do usually not own the capital that they use. Even if capitalism might make most people better off, Schumpeter points to the unavoidable fact that capitalism at the same time has winners and losers. Social science has been particularly active to try to explain, and in some cases to reduce, the division between winners and losers, which I show elsewhere in this book.

Social indifference or respect for individual integrity?

Economics embraces a stable human interest in the freedom of choice in making independent decisions to engage in extensive and ever-increasing market exchange. People are accordingly deeply susceptible to the process of weighing costs and benefits, incentives and disincentives. The latter part, of being highly inclined to actively weight costs and benefits, economists often use as a definition of an economically rational human being. This view of human rationality has certain advantages. It triggers a never-ending hope among economists to find the (often economic) rationality behind a certain behaviour of people, instead of too early dismissing people's seemingly counter-productive or destructive behaviours as irrational or as plain dumb. This rational choice perspective (an Apollonian perspective of how people handle their interests) arguably holds a very high respect for the individual's integrity, and for the person's potential to make her or his active choices in line with her or his interests. There is something socially (and scientifically) appealing about a perspective that does not judge 'the others' with one's own yardstick, even in activities that may appear strange to an outsider. The rational choice perspective (rooted in the view of economic rationality as universal) does not judge upfront the behaviour of poor people or of people in ethnic minorities as 'irrational', plain stupid, or as acts made by complete captives of their traditions, a view which has been common among policy makers and government officials, and still is today (Wilk & Cliggett, 2007).

This does not mean that rational addiction scholars, or any economists, maintain that all rational choices are good choices. Still, even to engage in risky sexual practices and to commit crimes are active choices, and in a formal sense voluntary ones, and should not be judged as irrational. According to economics, rationality merely refers to whether the means are the best ones for reaching a goal, the latter that economists maintain that they never judge. In this sense, economists hold that their science is amoral. A problem with this view of rationality, however, is that it makes it tough to legitimise most of the policy interventions that many societies consider for reducing or preventing various harms. It is hard to promote anything else than libertarianism if one's view is that anything people do, including self-destructive things, has a rational basis. Should the government or civil society then ever interfere, as long as people do not harm each other directly? Even people on the social margins, at least as long as they are not strongly mentally ill, accordingly act rationally. They may potentially respond to costs (in the widest sense of the term) and benefits of the deviant behaviour that they behave. They have actively and consciously made their own choice, voluntarily, out of individual freedom and power. In addition to the moral dilemma this notion of rationality entails, there is a conceptual and analytical problem here. It becomes hard to imagine how any human behaviour could be irrational or peccable, as long as the person does not harm others directly. This position runs the risk of becoming circular. Some critics find economic rationality, in the definition used by traditional economists, as tautological, vague, and thus meaningless. Consequently, it can neither be proven nor falsified, and is thus pseudo-scientific, the argument goes (Zafirovski, 2003). To be meaningful there needs to be a possibility for negation, a counter-factual practice that is irrational.

However, several concepts and approaches within traditional economics might challenge the aspiration of neutrality. For instance, the term 'opportunity cost' denotes the costs of not seizing a chance (Polley, 2015). If taking drugs makes people miss the opportunity of getting an education of a job, an economist could start to compromise her or his initially value-free, non-interfering position. Moreover, in parallel with a simplistic view of conscious, rational choice, there have run streams of thought about how people do not respond to incentives and disincentives in fully rational manners. The main topic here is closely related to that of interests in change: How should we understand and evaluate short-term versus long-term interests?

The threats to long-term interests

While economics embraces individual judgement, and even if this discipline understands as rational and sound the continuous weighing of costs and benefits in the individual's personal way, we should not forget that economics is largely based on the Apollonian model. This is reflected in their favouring of long-term planning, and long-term interests. This concern for long-term interests (perhaps it should be called the 'bias' of far-sightedness) is shared among traditional economics and behavioural economics. This concern has long roots. Schumpeter, the economist discussed in the section about entrepreneurs and the creative elite, has thoughts about the same line. In the late 1930s, he tries to explain why people were having fewer children than had been the case previously. Giving people incentives to work and consume more capitalism gives limited room in life for having more than a couple of children. Interestingly, Schumpeter raises the argument that much later became common in behavioural economics. People miscalculate the costs and benefit in the sense that they under-estimate the long-term benefits of, for example, having children, and over-estimate the short-term costs of having several children. Importantly, the long-term interests of having children are deeply emotional and social, and have a strong impact on human wellbeing, in the long run, Schumpeter argues. People over-estimate the short-term economic costs and the sacrifices needed to reduce their focus on consumption and work temporarily. This 'miscalculation' tends to steer people's decision into avoiding having more than a few children until biology restricts the adults' option of having more children.

Underlying Schumpeter's analysis is that there is a human 'bias' towards short-sightedness, which among other things entails taking one's short-term interests as stable, while overlooking that one's interests are in fact highly variable. Economists study this bias at several levels and areas of society. The conservative economist Buchanan, for instance, makes a similar point in his criticism of the economic recommendations of the progressive economist Keynes. The latter-mentioned economist's version of political economics includes generous use of subsidies and public services. According to Buchanan, this state generosity satisfies the shortsightedness of politicians as well as of the public. Politicians receive more votes as a result of having raised financial subsidies. Reversely, they receive fewer votes when they remove or reduce such subsidies and other public expenses. The system of incentives and disincentives thereby has perverse effects, stimulating politicians to spend more of the public resources than a neutral, economically rational agent would do. They spend more resources than were brought into the state (Buchanan, 1977/2000). To be sure, Keynes bases his approach on a hope that the good times and bad times would be evened out through democratic processes, but Buchanan maintains that this has often turned out to be difficult.

Behavioural economics is probably the sub-field of economics most active in making judgements about people's 'irrational' and 'biased' way of understanding and handling the relationship between their short-term and long-term interests. A main problem of humans is, according to behavioural economists, that they hold 'myopic' preferences (Haisley, Mostafa, & Loewenstein, 2008). People are irrational in their bias towards their short-term interests at the expense of their long-term ones. They have difficulties being as Apollonian and long-term planning as economists, and sometimes themselves, would like. Behavioural economics usually views and treats this human characteristic as a mental bug. The Apollonian ideal, which behavioural economics shares (even if it recognises Dionysian traits), generally favours as more 'rational' a long-term perspective of planning and restriction. Consequently, all economists hold that it would seem highly irrational to prefer 100 Euros today to 110 Euros in a month. Unless a person needs the money urgently already today, this preference would be highly irrational, according to both traditional and behavioural economics. To receive 110 Euros after waiting only one month corresponds to a guaranteed, yearly interest rate of 314 per cent. By sharing the Apollonian character of other economists, behavioural economists cannot, and do not want to, hide their frustration of how myopic preferences and other human biases lead people in economically sub-optimal ways.

Conclusions

Economics emphasises the human interests in continuity and expansion of free and active exchanges of goods and services on the market. Since such exchanges increase the satisfaction of certain manifest interests of all parties involved, this individual interest converges with interests of society as a whole, economists maintain. Importantly, the stable interest in free choice and open exchange does not just concern the opportunity of free choice, but also the acting on these opportunities to maximise utility. Given the nature of capitalism, of always being in motion and of always changing in its content, human interests in the specifics of goods, services, and exchange are constantly changing. To be an active chooser, calculating, reassessing, comparing, and translating between different possibilities concerning their pros and cons are essential to being human, traditional economics contends.

As mentioned in several parts of this book, being a rational human being, according to economics, is to be responsive to incentives and disincentives. Incentives and disincentives need not be financial ones. If one understands rationality this broadly, being responsive to incentives and incentives of whatever kind makes most if not all types of behaviour and lifestyle rational, unless a severe mental illness is involved. Also criminal, health-threatening behaviour, such as an unhealthy diet, drug addiction, or unsafe sex ought to be labelled rational from this perspective. On the one hand, this understanding of rationality may lead to a refreshing and respectful analytical perspective where scholars search for the logic of social deviance. On the other hand, such a view might be hard to combine with a policy perspective implying the need to help and to use collective resources to help. Why should society use the resources to change the lives of rational individuals? Why should society – or anyone – question the life choices and integrity of rational individuals?

There are other strands of thought in economics as well. Behavioural economics is the most active one in claiming that humans are not rational in the sense of Economic Man or the rational addict. According to behavioural economics, it might be that people always respond to incentives and disincentives, but do not respond in a formally rational way. Human biases towards myopic preferences and towards favouring sub-optimal continuity are two of several examples of human irrationality that behavioural economics highlight. By responding to incentives and disincentives in a shortsighted way, people often do not take opportunity costs into sufficient costs, the costs of not taking opportunities (of education, bringing children to the world), which are in their long-term interests.

Despite these differences, economists, including traditional and behavioural ones, have their intellectual roots in Apollonian, Enlightenment thinking. Thus, they are particularly concerned about the challenges of taking long-term interests into account. Studies of human and organisational behaviour with consequences on environment and health put much focus on how humans, companies, and governments could become better at taking long-term interests into full account in their decision making. This leads to a dilemma: Behavioural economists, in particular, have concerns about myopic preferences and other human biases. These economists do not just want to analyse human biases. They also wish to do something about them, not least by suggesting effective ways for society to intervene. At the same time, these economists come from a strong tradition honouring active and free choice as the interest that makes us human. A solution that some behavioural economists have suggested is 'paternalist libertarianism': of providing the same amount of free choices, yet by using 'choice architecture' by rearranging, restructuring the goods and services, modifying default options, changing reference points, and so forth. In the terms used in this book, adapted from Haidt (2008), these economists thus try to reconcile and find perfect consistency in the application of the moral foundations of care, liberty, and economic efficiency.

From a perspective of economics, this might be seen as solving the dilemma. However, other moral foundations are not taken into full account even in behavioural economists' notion of 'paternalist libertarianism'. Two of the moral foundations that some human scientists would claim to be overlooked or downplayed are fairness and sanctity. Moreover, it is not obvious that the moral foundation of care can be fully recognised (on a collective level) through the recipe of paternalist libertarianism. As we shall see, these gaps are regularly addressed by social science.

8   Social science
Interests, continuity, and change

Interest in continuity

Previous sections show how economics emphasises an essential human interest in a continuity and expansion of free market exchange. How about social science? As discussed in the book part on universal and culturally specific interests, social science does not conceive of free and expanding market exchange of independent individuals as a universal, genetically hardwired, interest. From a mainstream social science perspective, market liberalism – frequently used as synonymous with capitalism – is a cultural specificity, albeit an extremely widely spread one. Some social scientists are in favour of it, whereas others – most notably Marxists and neo-Marxists – problematise it. To be sure, it would be difficult for orthodox Marxists to be *against* capitalism, since Marxism conceives of capitalism as a necessary step towards their envisioned, classless society. Still, we can roughly summarise that mainstream social science (consisting of non-Marxists and Marxists) sees it either as a culturally specific phenomenon or as a specific, transitory stage of societal development.

This discipline instead stresses the human interest in a continuity of other Apollonian interests, as well as Dionysian ones, such as in relative welfare, along with social bonds, traditions rituals, community interaction, and so forth. As several classical sociologists have shown, for instance Durkheim and Tonnies, social bonding is not easily created. Nor is it easily fixed once it has been disturbed. Society is founded on traditions, rituals, habits, institutions, and other social phenomena that are often taken far too lightly by some economists, social scientists maintain. These social phenomena take time to establish and take hard work to maintain and strengthen, especially in liberal democratic societies with the strong pressures from the constantly swirling capitalism.

This view represents a conservative, highly Dionysian trait of social science. It is concerned with what is lost in an ever-changing society, particularly when capitalism exerts pressure on people, groups, and their institutions. A concern for the moral foundations of sanctity, loyalty, and even authority can easily be traced in social scientific analyses of the risks and downsides of capitalist society. Similar to conservative political parties, parts of social science evaluate society with a voice of guardians of a civilisation that is endangered. Among social scientists, this is regularly extended to a concern for conserving and protecting the natural, physical environment. The apparent inconsistency among many political conservatives – of wanting to conserve traditional values while making far fewer efforts conserving or preserving the natural, physical environment – is one which environmental sociologists often point out as severely problematic (McCright, Xiao, & Dunlap, 2014).

In societies where the satisfaction of human interests is threatened, as to the continuity and strengthening of group bonds, shared culture, traditions, and institutions, social scientists highlight what they see as the importance of these human interests in continuity. The vast majority of social scientists hold this concern for social bonds in a manner that also embraces cultural pluralism. Their ideal is usually to help preserve and develop the bonds and traditions within a society, without compromising the mutual respect and integration between cultures. However, this pluralist view of human interest has not always been the prevailing one among all parts of social science. The political philosopher Schmitt, for example, moves his conservative, Dionysian perspective to the extreme political right. His critique of the changes brought about by capitalism is most relevant to our discussion here. Capitalism may, just as economists maintain, give people many choices. However, capitalism is amoral as to what choices people favour, and as to what manifest interests people choose. According to Schmitt, capitalism is a cold, dispassionate, and arbitrary system that exaggerates the degree and width in which humans hold an interest in change. Capitalism goes against what Schmitt conceives as human interests in continuity, of sharing a collective sense of purpose and meaning. What Schmitt fears the most is a world becoming increasingly like a global trading company, with no local roots, no continuity, no deeper social and cultural bonds (Schmitt, 1932/2007). This is a world adopting a disproportionately Apollonian mindset, without recognising people's Dionysian interests in continuity and social bonding. Schmitt's conservative and communitarian arguments draw to the far right, towards nationalism, even ethnic nationalism, by favouring ethnicity as the basis for a nation to become or stay united.

Capitalism for winners; Fascism and Marxism for losers?

Market liberalism and capitalism have been subject to strong criticism both from the social scientific left and right. This two-sided pressure on capitalism has been analysed not just by the left and far right, but also by strong proponents of capitalism. For example, the neoliberal economist Hayek portrays the far right, fascism, as an ideology perfectly suited for losers in the capitalist system. Counter to the common picture of fascism as elitist, a picture partly based on the emphasis on strength and contempt of human weakness, fascism in the twentieth century, Hayek (1944/1994) claims, mainly attracted lower middle-class people who had ended up in a void. They had lost their middle-class position through capitalist development. They were not part of industrial workmanship, since they had had their social status slightly above industrial workers. (The latter group, by contrast, had something to gain from capitalism.) Nor were lower middle-class people considered belonging to the true middle class, the latter holding professions that could be adapted to the capitalist system. People of the lower middle class were stuck in between. They had been unable to adapt to extensive changes in society. The reactionary character of fascism gave them hope that each class would be moved back where they belong and stay there: back to an (imagined) social and cultural continuity. Strong interests in the idea of a stable past among this marginalised category of the lower middle class led to much of the violence initiated by people of fascist ideology in the twentieth century, according to Hayek.

Schumpeter brings similar arguments forward in his analysis of winners of capitalism. However, his focus is not on fascism, but on capitalism's enemy at the left: Marxism (and even socialism as a whole). Schumpeter sees sentiments of envy, resentment, and inferiority as the foundation of Marxism. These sentiments, Schumpeter maintains, can be found among those who did not have the ability to adapt to the dynamics of capitalism and to have their manifest or latent interests satisfied there. It is easy, according to Schumpeter, to have people unite based on a shared feeling of having been treated unfairly. In his book entitled *On Socialism*, he summarises socialism as 'An auto-therapeutic attitude of the unsuccessful many' (Schumpeter, 1942/2010, 6). What Schumpeter misses is, among several things, that socialism-oriented protests against capitalism are often triggered in regions, sectors, and times where the theoretical principles of capitalism have failed in practice. To function properly, the invisible hand demands, among other things:

- that each harm that occurs (not least to workers) be compensated for;
- that prices and wages be set appropriately (so that workers are not 'exploited');
- that people's rights be clearly defined, that information on which all parties make their decisions be accurate and complete.

To be sure, the traditional economic notion of 'exploitations of workers' differs from the Marxist definition. Marx argues that any use of workers (who do not control the means of production) is per definition exploitation. Traditional economics, on the other hand, usually contends, based on the notion of Schumpeter himself, that a worker is exploited only when she or he receives lower compensation than the additional profits the employer earns from that single worker (Schumpeter, 1949/2012). This 'only' happens in cases where there is not pure competition on the labour market. Despite this difference in how exploitation is defined, it is safe to say that what Schumpeter contemptuously calls 'an auto-therapeutic attitude' behind workers' protests many times originate in the deliberate or unintended failures of industrialists and employers to meet the long list of criteria for a fully functioning capitalism. Schumpeter was not around to witness developments that speak against his thesis about resentment on a selfish basis as the only root to socialist protest. For instance, the so-called New Social

Movements in the 1960s and onward consisted of people of the stable middle classes. In several cases, they protested against a capitalist system which would probably have rewarded them financially more than the leftist ideology to which they subscribed. Moreover, even economists sceptical of most notions of 'exploitation' as long as people are not by physical force coerced to work at an individual workplace, ought to recognise the many cases where the invisible hand of a labour market based on clean competition has not been able to operate.

In sum, the two, polarised sides, the far right (even fascism) and Marxism appear to share certain traits. Both sides frame at least some versions of capitalism as a decadent, cold, and uncontrollable force threatening people's Dionysian interests in continuity and social bonds.

At least as often as social science criticises the lack of continuity in the capitalist system this discipline attacks capitalism from the reverse side. In analyses of market liberal societies, most social scientists frame capitalism as the old, and conservative, as status quo, the condition taken for granted, and the system supported by the powerful and by the establishment (corporations and the mainstream political realm). Social scientists here interpret capitalism as appealing to the moral foundation of (stiff) sanctity among most economists: Maximising market exchange is, according to capitalism, an essential human interest, that should be treated as sacred. Thus, not even economics can be the dispassionate and amoral science that it portrays to be. Even economics, and perhaps economics more so than in the social and evolutionary sciences, rests on strong normativity, and even moralism, this view contends. Economics implicitly stipulates that the moral foundation of sanctity concerns specifically the sanctity of free, voluntary, and ever-expanding market exchange.

Women as more adaptive to service and knowledge society?

A more recent structural change is one from the industrial society to what the sociologist Bell, introduced in Chapter 2, calls post-industrial society. Other terms are service society or knowledge society. There are certain differences between these terms, but these differences are not relevant for our purposes. The changes to post-industrial society refer to more activities in the service, information, and knowledge, and less to energy and raw muscle power than in industrial society. Industrial activities remain, of course, a large part of contemporary society. Yet, a transition to a post-industrial society implies that more than 50 per cent of people who are active in the workforce work in the information and knowledge economy. This description is sometimes used as one of several definitions of a post-industrial society. Who are the winners and losers here? Bell highlights human relations and social skills as particularly important competencies in post-industrial society. He claims that women have, or are at least attracted to these competencies to a greater extent than are men. Simply from the fact that the 'service industries' were expanding (in the 1970s), Bell (1976/2008, 146) draws the conclusion that the proportion of women in the workforce was bound to rise. He perceives this structural change as an increase in the satisfaction of women's interest. It is unclear whether he perceives work in the service sector, such as in human services, activities being close to women's 'nature', or whether it is mainly that culture moves women closer to these areas. Yet, he understands the structural changes as doubtlessly providing entirely new opportunities for women. By 'opportunities', he mainly refers to the reduction in women's economic dependence on men, that participation in the labour force entails. Alongside the advantage that Bell perceives of women's competence in work tasks demanding social perceptivity, he stresses the increased pressure that the structural changes towards information and knowledge production place on people's Apollonian character. Those making use of their social rationality through long-term planning, educational discipline, and self-control have far higher chances of succeeding in the new social game of the service and knowledge economy (see Chapter 2).

Interests in change

As mentioned above, economics downplays that social and economic equality would be a necessary part of the moral foundation of fairness. As long as everyone is better off than he or she used to be, people should not compare themselves to others in an envious or resentful way. Instead, people should redirect their comparison and envy into harder work to become better off themselves. Social science, in contrast, underscores the human inclination of constantly comparing oneself to others, and for groups to compare themselves to others. From this perspective, social scientists perceive capitalism as conservative. In this light, they hold that there is a need for radical and progressive forces in society. All this constitutes the background to the common social scientific embracing of human interests in social change. The people in focus, whose interests in change should be taken into better account and become more visible, are unprivileged groups, the working class, and to some extent the 'middle class' (in the wide, American sense of the term). Social scientists, particularly sociologists, often conceive of themselves as intellectual spokespersons of such progressive and radical interest, with a focus particularly on the moral foundations of care and fairness. Social sciences, along with economics, hold that care is a moral foundation that needs particular attention. Moreover, the views in these two sciences of what they should define as care – such as reducing suffering and environmental harm – are probably quite similar.

As to another moral foundation, of fairness, however, their views may diverge substantially, probably in parallel with divergences in political ideology. Being a moral foundation, fairness is something that people consider universally, regardless of political sympathy or whether one has a mindset of an economist or social scientist. However, views on the meaning, content, and extent of fairness obviously differ.

Social science is the human scientific approach most well known for analysing, discussing, and suggesting alternatives to situations that they perceive as unfair, namely a lack of social and economic equality. Social scientists conceive of social comparison and the struggle towards fairness as a stable interest. Nevertheless, they recognise how vastly differently fairness is understood, framed, interpreted, and so forth, depending on what culture they refer to, as well as what position and situation in that culture they refer. Human interests seem to be highly flexible concerning how people in various cultures, norms, social positions, and situations understand the content of fairness. Here, social science may even imply a blank slate: People's views on fairness are highly or wholly dependent on their social position, context, and situation.

The question then is which human situations are most important to highlight, and whose interest in status quo should be taken as most important to understand and change. Many social scientists find this easy to answer: unprivileged people and groups, the working class, and possibly the middle-class people (the latter in the sense of 'ordinary'). People of cultural minorities, as well as women, are common categories. Economists are quick to point out that groups in all socio-economic segments world-wide have enjoyed increases in their material standard of living during the last century (albeit the absolute number of poor people in the poorest countries has also increased). Endorsers of liberal market societies often label this the 'win-win' of capitalism. However, this does not satisfy most social scientists, even when they agree with this factual claim. Social scientists are quick to point out the fact that the economic inequality has been widened. Thus, fairness has been reduced – in the eyes of social scientists.

Should economic inequality become an issue beyond the moral foundation of fairness, entering a moral foundation that all human sciences emphasise: care/harm? Several research findings point in this direction (Layard, 2007). Remember the abundance of studies mentioned earlier indicating that the relatively of people's income matters deeply to their wellbeing. Thus, a market exchange that benefits the richer one more than the poorer one may raise the reference point (see Chapter 6) for the poorer person more than the satisfaction of her manifest interests have increased by the market exchange. She may have increased the satisfaction of Apollonian interests to some extent, but has decreased her satisfaction of Dionysian ones. In other cases, where another person or group who has already a high material standard further increases its level, this should perhaps be seen as a negative externality inflicted on poorer people. After all, there is plenty of empirical evidence that increased material standard of groups who are already doing well creates stress for people at the lower material level and reduces their wellbeing (Wilkinson, 2001). 'Negative liberty' might not prevail in all the activities that economists, and perhaps the rest of us, once thought it did.

The particular recognition of the interests of unprivileged groups and groups up to parts of the middle class makes intuitive sense to many, if not most human scientists with a humanitarian pathos. However, this does not mean that these issues are always easy to translate into clear-cut social scientific, normative interpretations of concrete empirical cases. Nor are these questions easy to categorise in social scientific theory.

As Table 8.1 indicates, there are, as all human scientists recognise, unprivileged groups in both traditional and market liberal societies. For the sake of

Table 8.1 Analytical and ethical challenges of the human sciences

	Traditional society	Market liberal society
Less analytically or ethically challenging	1 The unprivileged express frustration, develop social movements, unveil false consciousness	2 The unprivileged have unveiled false consciousness, such as concerning illusorily equal opportunities, and consequently carry out protests and social movement activities
More analytically and ethically challenging	3 The unprivileged accept oppressive continuity, as long as the principles and rules are clear and consistent; 'the contended slave dilemma'	4 The unprivileged accept increasing inequality, as long as they are better off than before

simplicity, the table draws a clear line between the two, although they are much more intertwined and blurred in many parts of the world. Social science frames the moral foundation of fairness not only as '*negative* liberty' (absence of external restraints, for instance, restraints to free market exchange). They understand fairness also as '*positive* liberty', which denotes the resources and power to fulfil one's potential, through equal access to health care, education, culture (Berlin, 1958). Therefore, social scientists usually conceive of interests in not just economic but also social and cultural change as a latent universal that ought to be obvious interests among unprivileged groups.

Squares 1 and 2 of Table 8.1 refer to situations and cases where social scientists have identified how unprivileged groups – the poor, women, oppressed ethnic minorities, and so forth – express frustration about their situations. Square 1 indicates this situation in traditional societies. Social scientists enthusiastically examine and interact with grass-root movements, social, and cultural movements. Social scientists may play a variety of roles here, as distant observers or as action researchers, trying to facilitate and stimulate the social movements to mobilise their resources in the most efficient ways. Scholars here frame the moral foundation of fairness as one of gender equality as well as of more negative as well as positive liberty for the unprivileged and privileged. Square 2 refers to cases where unprivileged people in modern, market liberal societies have unveiled illusory master frames of market liberal societies, either themselves or with the help of media, NGOs, and possibly social science. These disadvantaged people may have unveiled the 'false consciousness' under which people in their position are assumed to work increasingly hard. The basis for the false consciousness is the mistaken belief that they have a fair chance of reaching the economic, social, and cultural conditions of the handful of music and sports stars, who have been able to move from the bottom to the top. This unveiling often demands knowledge based on statistics and probability calculations, something that social science produces and aspires to share among the disadvantaged. Another type of unveiling refers to analysing how, and why, 'free' market and 'pure' competition are many times far from the real condition in capitalism. Corruption and hidden influences of affluent interest groups make the free and fair market an illusion, the argument contends (Harvey, 2011). Collective protests and mobilisation in capitalist societies of unprivileged groups, often supported by groups that are better off, are also a favourite theme among social scientists, as analysts, proponents, marketers, and sometimes participants.

Does engagement in collective efforts to reduce inequality make people more satisfied with their workplace and working condition? In the United States, several studies indicate that unionised workers have approximately 15 per cent higher wages, and – at least among those who have been employed for a long time – greater job security than their non-unionised colleagues (Bennett & Kaufman, 2007). Despite this, the unionised workers are significantly less satisfied with their workplace and working conditions than non-unionised workers in similar occupations and workplaces, regarding physical safety, recognition, job security, and so forth (Gallup, 2015). Why? An apparent reason is that some workers become members in labour unions because they have negative experiences from their current or previous workplaces. Still, we cannot overlook the fact that unionised workers often have better working conditions, wages, security, and so forth, than their non-unionised counterparts. A reverse causality may also operate here: As people learn about a labour union, prepare to become members, and gain experience from union membership and engagement in such issues, their reference points for what are the realistic levels of fairness and equality can be raised. They start to reframe their conditions, to change norms or to adapt to social norms of the union, which might favour a somewhat critical and change-oriented attitude towards the working conditions. It may also be that union members look beyond their own, somewhat better working conditions than their colleagues, instead focusing on the conditions of the collective. In normative, Marxist parlour, a false consciousness might be in the process of being corrected. This apparent gap between lower satisfactions even as improved conditions have taken place in a spirit of activism and protest can also be seen in other areas. From a social scientific perspective, what constitutes a good or improving society should not be assessed merely by opinion polls about happiness and satisfaction. Social scientists (as all human scientists) should dig far deeper and analyse all polls in their context. A low level of expressed satisfaction and contentment may often be a sign that social norms are about to change, awareness is raised, and so forth. For instance, Pinker indicates how people, despite substantial reductions in violence, have become far more inclined to perceive their physical environments as unsafe, ready to go out and protest against violence, and so forth (Pinker, 2011). From a social scientific perspective, this may be a sign that the social norms against violence are strengthened. People, not least women, may have become aware of the unacceptability of violence. People might, to be sure, have become less happy, in the simple sense. But they have become more aware of that a change towards far higher levels of interest satisfaction of themselves and the collective is both reasonable and realistic.

Protests as in requirements of better material conditions are only one part. Social scientists place their focus at least as much on protests against what they interpret as market liberal societies' constant movement towards making greater parts of people's lives commodified, tradable, and so forth (Burawoy, 2014). The term 'commodification' denotes this, and was introduced in Chapter 3. The moral foundations that social scientists emphasise, not only of fairness but also of sanctity (of social bonding and community undistorted by trade relationships), entail the social scientific call for change. More specifically, it is often a call for change away from the seemingly static capitalist principle of making as much as possible tradable.

Social science here tries to support the preservation of not least Dionysian factors that otherwise runs the risk of being lost: culture, tradition, social bonds, sense of community, and belonging. Implied by social scientists (as by large parts of the general public), the earlier mentioned unprivileged groups do what they should do: follow their 'obvious' interests, given their situation, and try to reach the satisfying of these interests by struggling towards social and economic change.

Yet, the social settings that social scientists analyse are not always this straightforward, oriented towards unambiguous enthusiasm of social scientists. Much more challenging – and more intriguing – is how social scientists should understand, analyse, and act in situations described in Squares 3 and 4.

In market liberalism, but also in other types of societies, one may note how not just the higher social segments, but also groups far down on the socioeconomic ladder, express as favourable what social scientists often conceive of as an unfair structure of society. (This is briefly mentioned in the introduction to Part II.) Such conditions are paradoxical from the social scientific perspective that stresses the moral foundation of fairness as universal interests in a social and economic change of the people at the lower socio-economic levels. The situation is one that has puzzled social analysts, at least since Nietzsche (1908/2009), with his ideal of 'amor fati' (to love one's fate), and later by Camus (1942/1955), in his interpretation of the Sisyphus myth. Sisyphus is a mythological figure in ancient Greek thought made to roll a boulder up a mountain, a boulder that rolls down over and over, forever. The question is how a human scientist should interpret this situation when given the additional information that Sisyphus is happy, contented. Camus, influenced by Nietzsche, perceives the contented Sisyphus as an ideal human condition of 'self-overcoming'. To be sure, it would be tasteless, insensitive, and probably wrong to translate 'amor fati' into the mindset of people in precarious situations. At the same time the sense of absurdity that we all get from learning about the contented Sisyphus, might be comparable with the frustration social scientists may sense in concrete situations of inequality, oppression, exploitation, and so forth, in cases where unprivileged people express acceptance (either as contentment or resignation). This frustration among social scientists is plausibly shared by any group of human scientists analysing people in precarious situations. Rational addiction scholars in economics (discussed in an earlier section of this book part) are only one additional example of human scientists who try to make sense of suffering and misery. Still, the theory of rational addiction forces these scholars to always identify a humbling 'rationality' behind addictive people sticking to an apparently miserable continuity. As to the unprivileged groups in Squares 3 and 4 studied by social science, the acceptance of continuity may not stem from what some economists understand as situations where 'rationally addictive' individuals have actively and purposefully responded to incentives and disincentives. Instead, social scientists understand Squares 3 and 4 more in line with the 'social rationality' that interests in continuity may regularly imply at the latent level.

In market liberal societies, social rationality may sometimes be manifested in unprivileged people identifying with other people of a similar, unprivileged background as oneself, but who within the current social order have reached great success (for instance, music stars and sports stars). However, social scientists have to admit that there sometimes are no anecdotal role models, whose immense (yet immensely unlikely) success triggers unprivileged groups to support policies and politics working against an egalitarian society. Social scientists thus continue to analyse, not without frustration, the frequent occurrence of unprivileged or, at least, the lower segment of the working class favouring politics that combines value conservatism and economic libertarianism (reduced subsidies, reduced economic redistribution, and a focus on satisfying negative but not positive liberty). This political and ideological stance, that 'ought to' be held mainly by the affluent, is to a significant extent held by the unprivileged as well (Huber & Ting, 2013). By placing most of its efforts on answering how-questions, mapping out how people of various social segments describe and act based on their perceived interests, social science has few analytical tools for answering the deeper why-questions behind paradoxical interests. Intriguingly, it is not uncommon that social scientific publications present the identification of paradoxes as the final research result. Sometimes social scientific analyses dive into such 'paradoxes' by examining them as habits that are separate from anything rational and conscious. Particularly frustrating to sociologists might be the dimension of habits that de Vries and colleagues call 'non-acting habits' (de Vries, Aarts, & Midden, 2011). Just as habits can be ways of acting, habits not to act are just as puzzling. From a sociological viewpoint, habits of non-acting are often more intriguing than acting habits.

For instance, does the omittance of public protest against local air pollution, urban crime, or against the production of goods without sufficient environmental and humanitarian consideration mean that people do not care, that the one who is silent consents? What might it otherwise mean?

When Hopf investigates international relations and habits – non-active as well as active ones, he states that '[T]he logic of habit necessarily precludes rationality, agency, and uncertainty' (Hopf, 2010, 539). Such claims only make the paradox more puzzling of why some unprivileged groups seem to act against what they 'ought to do', namely act, or, at least, speak, for social change. Could the concept of social rationality be of use here? In a more traditional society, social rationality may refer to an interest in social bonding, belonging, of sticking to a situation of which one is familiar: one's community, however oppressive. To give an example of interest in continuity in traditional societies, social scientists have studied women's living conditions and roles in Somali cultures. A common focus has been female circumcision, something that Western social scientists along with most people in the Western world, find appalling and oppressive (Sweetman, 1998). Still, when spending lengthy times in these cultures, social scientists have been struck by this: The strictest explicit proponents of female circumcision are often not men but in many cases women. Young girls who are to be circumcised typically claim that they prescribe to this practice. This is not mystifying, in light of the pressure under which we can assume that they are. It is more bewildering that their older sisters, mothers, and grandmothers, sometimes more than their male relatives, are those who most strongly prescribe to female circumcision (Moseley, 2004). However, from the perspective of Dionysian interests, of which social scientists have extensive insight, it is possible to understand and explain such paradoxes. Traditions and routines, albeit patriarchal and apparently oppressive ones such as this, may still fill a latent function by contributing to community bonds in a culture. If this particular ritual is removed, this, of course, will be a removal of a painful and oppressive practice. At the same time, removing a cultural practice possibly creates a void that involves uncertainty of what ritualistic practice should fill this void and hold the culture together. Discontentment among social scientists cannot go away despite such sober social analyses. The frustration often raises questions of a philosophical kind. An ontological matter is whether we can assume that people have 'true, latent interests in change', beneath the verbal claims that one may assume girls to make under cultural pressure and influence. Supplementary, epistemological, and methodological questions include the following one: If there are such genuine interests in change, is it possible for the social scientists to identify them? Still, there is the mainstream social scientific claim that individuals are unthinkable in separation from the social situation, the institutions and norms in which they live. Given this, it becomes challenging to try to separate groups that from the outside may seem oppressed by their social milieu, and try to trace their 'genuine interests in change', interests that go against what people say and do. To be consistent, social science sometimes establishes a long-term dialogue with the entire communities, trying to create interest in social change among the oppressed. This requires a respectful dialogue in which oppressed groups themselves reframe the situation into one where valuable parts of their cultures are preserved, while removing the parts that cause suffering and oppression. As social scientists are highly aware, it is far from easy, and not always advisable, for Westerners to try to impact a traditional society to start picking and choosing some of their practices and reject others.

Proposition 8: human scientists should never take as a given that people's passive consent or active protests reflect these people's interest satisfaction or lack thereof. Protests may indicate that social change is already taking place towards increased interest satisfaction, and passive consent may indicate that people's dignity and esteem are so far from being satisfied, that they do not find it reasonable and realistic to protest.

Conclusions

Social science stresses the human interest in a continuity of certain social bonds, traditions, rituals, and community interaction. Well aware of the risk of constraints embedded in social bonds and tradition, social scientists try to identify ways in which social bonds and personal freedom can be reconciled and balanced, in traditional societies as well as in liberal democracy. Instead of, as in economics, conceiving of each market transaction between free individuals as – per definition – a rise of mutual benefits, social science highlights the possible downsides of a transformation of human relations into market relations. To a much greater extent than economists, social scientists express worries about what they perceive as the degrading of social relations through market liberalism's transformation of social norms, morality, and culture, into the principles of market exchange. In this respect, social science is conservative, whereas economics seems to be radical in the values its scholars embrace, albeit often implicitly.

As to interests in change, social scientists note, similar to economists, how capitalism triggers extremely rapid changes in human interests concerning what specific goods and services are preferred. Human wants are quickly transformed into 'needs'. However, contrary to economists, social scientists stress the downsides of these constantly changing interests. Although Marcuse (1964/2002) with his pointed critique of capitalism is certainly not embraced by but a fraction of social science, some of his concepts, such as 'euphoric unhappiness', would probably appeal to many social scientists, when analysing market liberal societies concerning human interests. Accordingly, it is largely an illusion that people have this interest in change, in any deeper sense of the term 'interest'.

Instead, people, predominantly the unprivileged and their sympathisers, have a deep-rooted interest in change towards another goal than towards a maximisation of utility in a specific, Apollonian sense. The change in which these groups have a major interest is a social, economic, and political change towards what social science stipulates as the moral foundation of fairness: reduced inequality. Traditionally, social science has focused on, and has problematised, unequal access to goods, services, and political influence. Through the strongly increased research focus on environmental and health-related problems, inequality has become more widely understood among social scientists. Nowadays, it also refers to the unequal distribution of 'bads' – often the negative side-products of unsustainable, industrial production: environmental and health-related risks and problems (Beck, 1999).

With its point of departure in an understanding of fairness as reduced inequality, social science examines what they perceive as unfair and oppressive traits in both traditional and market liberal societies. All types of societies accordingly have winners and losers. Both types of societies hold not just social resistance and insurgency by unprivileged groups and their sympathisers, but also more challenging phenomena, such as false beliefs and 'the contented Sisyphus', both challenging the normative, social scientific view of the need for social change.

Social scientists typically address the need for social change through education and increased involvement of social science, NGOs, and possibly state agencies with unprivileged groups to unveil false beliefs (Archer, Bhaskar, Collier, Lawson, & Norrie, 2013). Furthermore, a redistribution of wealth, taxations, or hard regulation targeting environmentally harmful corporate activities, are common in social scientific article sections titled 'policy implications'. More generally, how social scientists conceive of interests in continuity and change among people in various societies and positions is typically assessed by these scientists after an analysis of the prevalence of negative as well as positive liberties, along with people's efforts to reduce economic, social, and political inequality.

9 Evolutionary theory

Interests, continuity, and change

How does evolutionary science conceive of human interests in continuity and change? Moreover, what challenges and promises does evolutionary science see for the satisfaction of human interests, and by extension future and non-human interests, based on their view of continuity and change? Misunderstandings have long been around as regards perspectives in evolutionary science on continuity and change in society. The worst misunderstandings are, on the one hand, that evolutionary science would contend that everything that takes place with as little social or political intervening as possible is good. Evolutionary science is still sometimes misunderstood, despite decades of clarification, to hold a laissez-faire ideal of social, political, and economic continuity and change. According to this misunderstanding, evolutionary science would endorse a continuity of old and cemented power structure and hierarchies, or of changes under conditions of unfettered deregulation of everything that may intervene with a 'natural order of things'. However, this ideal, with the naturalistic fallacy on which it is based (that everything that seems to exist 'naturally' can be directly translated into an 'ought'), is worlds away from where any serious scholarship in evolutionary science takes place. Darwin himself found such a view completely alien to him (Lewens, 2006).

Interests in continuity

A part of the evolutionary scientific perspective on continuity concerns human habits. A simple definition from an evolutionary perspective is that habits are 'not fully conscious forms of behaviour' (Marechal, 2009, 69). Habits should not be equated with frequent or repetitive behaviour. Concerning the latter behaviours, it remains an open question to what extent they have been preceded by extensive, reflexive thought and calculation (as in non-habits) or through a degree of automacy.

Habits are not taken lightly by evolutionary scientists, not even by history's greatest one. Darwin expresses amazement at the strength of habits, both in the animal kingdom and in human society. He claims that 'It is notorious how powerful is the force of habit' (Darwin, 1872, 29). Darwin is not alone to be intrigued by habits during the age he lived. In the book with the strikingly modern title *Self-Help* from 1859, Smiles maintains the following: 'It is …

generally felt to be a far easier thing to reform the constitution in Church and State than to reform the least of our own bad habits' (Smiles, 1859, 283).

An important evolutionary perspective on human interests in continuity, manifested by habits, has to do with energy. The resource efficiency of habits is where evolutionary science finds parts of its understanding and explanations of habits, and of human inclinations towards continuity more in general. At the neurological level, scientists indicate how it is only through changes that neurons react. In a mode of continuity, the neuron is quiet (Barnett & Larkman, 2007). Neurons are highly selective, only responding to very specific combinations of impulses (Squire & Kosslyn, 1998). The human brain is an immensely energy demanding organ, using at least 20 per cent of our energy (Fonseca-Azevedo & Herculano-Houzel, 2012). In order not to have the brain demand even a larger share of our energy, and thus jeopardise survival and reproduction due to energy shortage, evolution has provided the brain with several ways of economising on its energy use. A tendency towards not using more energy than needed to survive and reproduce can be found in most organisms, including humans. Habits and a partial tendency towards continuity can probably be derived from the above-mentioned conditions, which is a tendency humans share with other organisms.

In this respect, it seems to be deeply human to have a conservative trait within one's motivational repertoire. Children, not least, are strikingly conservative and habit-oriented. They want to eat the same kind of food over and over, and they wish to hear the same stories repeatedly. Despite economists' focus on the importance of providing improved conditions for new options, alternatives, and choices, most people stay close to where they have always lived. This is true even in the United States, despite its rumour as one of the more rootless countries (Compton & Pollak, 2009). As adults, people want to eat similar things that they are used to, albeit with a few tests of new foods out of curiosity. People enjoy travelling on their vacations, but most of them are happy to come back home again. It is common for immigrants, even who have moved from tough conditions, to dream about being able to return to their home country (Long & Oxfeld, 2004). This makes full sense, from an evolutionary approach.

At the societal level, getting rid of all continuity would be disastrous. Change, including social and economic change, implies much uncertainty. It demands much energy from individuals and groups, both mental and physical. Humans and organisations are usually more accomplished at the things they are used to doing, since they are trained in it. They often experience that their regular habits, routines, and practices have worked so far. To be sure, potentials may emerge for changes that may provide better opportunities. Yet, changes come with high risks. Change demands much energy, and one's current social status may become subject to uncertainty in the event of change.

One way in which the brain saves energy is by having people constantly seek patterns that are related to other patterns with which they are already familiar. In the brain, it is the prefrontal cortex that makes it possible to seek and create patterns. Humans are strongly inclined to seek patterns. Patterns imply something regular, predictable, and continuous. The activity in the prefrontal cortex is reduced each time people perceive occurrences that look increasingly like a pattern. This process where the brain seeks familiarity and regularity is highly energy saving, compared to its alternative: to constantly try to make sharp sense of each distinct impression without the use of the person's already acquired experiences.

This human interest in continuity, patterns, regularity, and familiarity is not only energy saving. It is also very helpful for making sense of, and finding meaning in the world. By extension, this helps people to bond with others based on shared understandings of how practical matters should be efficiently handled. Thus, people constantly try to seek regularities and non-randomness in their physical and social environment, when they are to make decisions. This is what human biases, heuristics, and framings are about. Through their ability to identify regular and continuous patterns in the behaviours of their fellow human beings, people can develop social trust and build alliances. The human characteristic of being dependable and trustworthy refers to people assessing other people as regular, continuous, and predictable to an extent that these features can be trusted. This characteristic is key to cooperation (Fehr & Fischbacher, 2005).

From an evolutionary perspective, all this is crucial to understanding what may seem so puzzling in human life: the seemingly awkward interest in sticking with the prevailing state of affairs. Even the quote above by Darwin, who is well aware of several of the benefits of continuity mentioned, implies that he is mystified, and even frustrated, by the strength of human habits. The human interest in continuity has even provoked a diagnosis of the entire humanity, namely 'status quo bias' (Samuelson & Zeckhauser, 1988). This reflects the fact that the frustration with a habit-driven humanity is shared among significant parts of all human sciences. Although evolutionary science is probably the science that puts most weight on the benefits of continuity, this science shares this frustration with both the social and economic sciences.

Also, evolutionary science, together with behavioural economics, often highlights how people and organisations seek regularities and continuity also in random events, and between uncorrelated occurrences. Particularly evolutionary scientists with an Apollonian emphasis, along with other human scientists with this emphasis, problematise how the human interest in seeking patterns also for random events ends up with beliefs that are not rooted in reality: from false religious beliefs to false beliefs about a higher purpose or meaning of oppressive, traditional practices or the inevitability of the current societal structure. Furthermore, evolutionary science recognises how an interest in continuity is often the strongest among the leading segment of society. The same pattern can be found among many non-human animals, and it would be peculiar if it would not be found among humans. Those individuals and groups who are already at the top of the hierarchy (a position that gives higher chances of successful reproduction among all species), tend to prefer continuity. Very few individuals or groups who are at the top of a hierarchy are immune to this status quo bias. Eminent scholars are no exception. To be sure, there is a well-established scientific norm of 'organised scepticism' implying that new scientific findings that differ dramatically from old ones should be thoroughly examined (Merton, 1942/1973).

However, when human scientists have examined openness to novelty among scientists, they have been able to control for this, often constructive norm. What the psychologist Simonton has shown from extensive, quantitative studies is that 'disciplinary age', rather than 'chronological age', co-varies very strongly with the openness to change among scientists. Why is disciplinary age so significant here? The longer someone has been in a research field (scientific eminence typically involves high, disciplinary age), the more closed they are to novelty. In a comprehensive study of the reception of Darwin's theory of natural selection, the following has been shown through detailed research. The more eminent the scientists were (e.g. the higher their disciplinary age) during the time of Darwin's publication of his revolutionary book that explained the principles of natural selection, the more likely they were to try to reject these novel Darwinian ideas (Simonton, 1999). Why would disciplinary age have this strongly inverted relationship to people's interests in novelty, and thus to changes in paradigms? Because we can here see a conflict between the manifest, Apollonian interest in improving knowledge (through accepting novel findings once they have been thoroughly scrutinised), and the latent, Dionysian interest of eminent scholars of staying at the top of the hierarchy. In this sense, it is socially rational to become increasingly interested in continuity with increasing disciplinary age.

Evolutionary and social scientists recognise the following corresponding tendency: Individuals and groups slightly below the highest levels of the hierarchy typically have an interest in change.

Example: interests in continuity and change – the battered child syndrome

Child abuse as an objective phenomenon has, of course, existed as long as has humankind. However, before the early 1960s in the United States, it was not framed as a social problem, in the sense of a problem relevant to the government. Intriguingly, paediatricians who would be expected to have long recognised the phenomenon, did not take much notice before that period. The main reason that paediatricians did not raise the problem of child abuse into a wider scientific and political discussion was their role in relation to parents. The parents were their clients, a fact that seems to have reduced the motivation of paediatricians, even to the degree of denial of the phenomenon, to be open to the possibility that some parents sometimes abuse their children 'savagely' (Boardman, 1962). A decade earlier, the articles by Silverman (1953) and by Wooley and Evans (1955) moved the issue from 'uncorrelated observations' to the 'controversy' stage. At that new phase, there was still some doubt about the reality of child abuse. One social worker, Elizabeth Elmer, who made her own discovery of incidents of child abuse, related: 'I can remember some of the tumultuous meetings in which, for example, a paediatrician would say, "If I believed the parent could abuse the child, I would leave paediatrics immediately"' (Elmer, in Shadish & Fuller's personal communication, 18 November 1981 (Shadish & Fuller, 1994). 'One physician, Roy Astley, wrote a paper suggesting that the problem was merely bone fragility. For the majority of doctors who dealt with children, awareness grew slowly' (Shadish & Fuller, 1994, 335).

From the perspective of this book, of esteem, latent interests, and social rationality it is apt to ask the following question concerning the mysterious inertia before child abuse became a problem fully recognised by paediatricians and national government. What occupations did the people hold that made the crucial efforts to frame child abuse as a social problem, and to make it subject to the law? The sociological and historical literature highlights the following occupations. A first whistle-blower was a veterinarian who raised the initial awareness in certain NGOs in 1874, by claiming that child protection ought to be recognised as important in the same way as animal protection was already (Markel, 2009, in Pinker, 2011). Concerning the process moving towards governmental recognition, there were social workers and radiologists. Paediatricians as a collective were conspicuously passive for a very long time. Analyses point to both Apollonian and Dionysian interpretations of the 'career' of child abuse as a social problem to be taken seriously.

On the one hand, veterinarians, who had previously struggled to elevate animal abuse into a problem of society to deal with at the national level, used their simple reason and logic when pointing out that excessive violence to children should also, in the name of consistency, become subject to the law. Moreover, the crucial role of radiologists here can be seen as the fresh, critical eyes of people aside from those who worked daily and closely with children as patients, namely paediatricians. Paediatricians had parents as the paying clients on which paediatricians were financially dependent. Free from the financial dependency of parents, and with fresh critical eyes, radiologists and veterinarians managed to elevate child abuse into a social problem. This is the Apollonian interpretation, which in ethical analyses is supported by the philosopher Singer and the cognitive scientist Pinker, among others.

On the other hand, there is the Dionysian interpretation. It takes more interest in the latent level of interests in change. What social positions did veterinarians, social workers, and child radiologists have at the time when child abuse started to be framed as a social problem? The answer is: considerably lower than paediatricians, who were the 'real doctors'. What is the most powerful way of raising one's social position in the sciences? Radiologists have a high status today, with all the advanced technology that has been developed in recent decades. However, radiologists had a much lower social position than paediatricians in the mid-twentieth century and earlier. A powerful way for people of a certain profession to increase both individual and professional status is to be the first to identify and lead the labelling of a phenomenon as a social problem, syndrome, or disease. This function is exactly the function that the new, social career of child abuse had, strongly benefitting the social status of the veterinarians and child radiologists active in this process. Whereas most people today conceive of these efforts of people in the occupations mentioned above as necessary social progress, the Dionysian interpretation implies that the manifest, positive social change was mainly the means to, or the side effect of, the latent interests in raised social status. We should emphasise again that the Dionysian interpretation has been made by sociologists, who have not made any explicit use of evolutionary theory or Darwinian thinking. Nevertheless, this interpretation of interests in social change constitutes a coherent one between sociology and evolutionary theory. Importantly, this interpretation does not contradict the Apollonian one. Both Apollonian and Dionysian processes may have operated simultaneously, here, as in many other cases.

Evolutionary science fully recognises the bases for human interests in continuity. Habits, repetition, and continuity save energy, provide comfort, a sense of control, even for disadvantaged groups, and often correspond to the interests of the higher segments of society to stay at the top. From a neuroscientific perspective, the interest in repetition and predictability increases with disciplinary as well as chronological age. At the same time, neuroscientists point towards a conflict here. It turns out that there is a latent interest in change among all of us. The latent interest is not just a social one, but also concerns the health of the brain itself. Extensive research in neuroscience shows how an enriched environment and exposure to novelty rejuvenates the brain dramatically. Previously, neuroscientists believed that it was only meaningful to stimulate the brains of young people. The old (erroneous) idea was that the brain inevitably deteriorates by 10,000 or more neurons dying every day, and that there is nothing we can do about it. Sticking to habits, routines, and repetition was the only interest that neuroscientists recognised among middle-aged and elderly people (Sapolsky, 2012). Through controlled experiments about whether enriched environments may also stimulate and improve the health of the brains of adults and elderly people, Diamond (1988) shows strongly positive results. By providing people with an enriched social, physical, and cultural environment, this results in stronger synaptic connections, more neurones, and more synapses, among aged people. Brains mature throughout human life. Thus, there seems to be a potential conflict between people's manifest interest in continuity – reflected in our increased inclination to choose repetition as we age – and the latent, neurological interest in keeping us exposed to novelty and input that challenge our status quo bias.

Interests in change (and in adaptation)

Interests in changes reducing the human mismatch

An increasingly common claim is that a wide range of societal problems – health-related, social, economic, environmental, for instance – are rooted in a mismatch between contemporary society and the Stone Age existence (in Pleistocene environments), to which humans are genetically adapted (Gat, 2000; Narvaez *et al.*, 2014; Runciman, 2005). Implied in this notion is that humans in modern society, in all its versions, have a universal interest in changes in modern society to take place in order to reduce this mismatch. Although evolutionary scientists have more recently spelt it out more clearly, more implicit concerns with a mismatch between humans and modern society can be found among several of the classical social and economic thinkers (Durkheim, 1895/1982; Freud, 1930; Marx, 1844/2007; Smith, 1790). The fact that classical thinkers discuss this issue across the human sciences reflects the foundational character in human scientific thought of such a mismatch.

In what problem areas have evolutionary scientists identified a mismatch? Areas include:

- food preferences, such as the evolved attraction to sweet and fatty foods (Spencer & Peel, 1983);
- limited drive towards physical activity (a limit that saves body energy), manifested in, for instance, excessive car use;
- the tragedy of the commons (entailing environmental harm due to a conflict between evolved individual interests, and collective interests severely threatened in current society; see Chapter 2).

In addition, all the biases and heuristics mentioned throughout this book can be tied to analyses of a human mismatch with, not least, current, liberal democratic society.

The mismatch narrative addresses the deepest question of *why*, a question that is usually lacking in the mainstream social and economic sciences. Whereas social and economic sciences – when detached from an evolutionary context – often run the risk of providing circular claims (people are aggressive because their culture teaches aggression; organisations exploit common resources excessively because it serves their direct utility to do so), the mismatch narrative instead has the ambition of elucidating how many societal problems exist *because* the human drives and motivations that have shaped these problems (in a global society) used to have significant adaptive value in ancestral times (for survival, reproduction, and welfare of one's offspring). Had our ancestors and we not had these traits – that in many ways may be long-term dysfunctional in advanced society – we would simply not have existed today.

Moreover, its explanatory grand narrative is in many respects a convincing one, I would hold. Alternative attempts at explaining the above-mentioned problems, such as that socialisation and learning may fully explain all aspects of unhealthy lifestyles, and individual exploitation of common resources, are not tenable, I argue. Yet, the mismatch explanation is by no means a perfect, sufficient, and fully developed one. Certain challenges remain for understanding, and managing the societal problems addressed by the mismatch explanation. One such challenge is particularly relevant to this book. The mismatch explanation must be examined with regard to a closely related issue, where there is nowadays increasing scientific consensus, from informed parts of sociology and economics to evolutionary science: That nature and nurture are almost always in close interplay (McKinnon & Silverman, 2005), and that one or the other may rarely determine human activity. When discussed too loosely, the mismatch narrative tends to entail calls for a simplistic solution framing, namely that 'nurture'/culture/society should adapt to a fixed 'nature' (of humans). This narrative overlooks the fact that all human life entails close intertwining of nature and nurture. Understanding the potential and limits to the human mismatch explanation could not merely be a matter of discussing how society can better adapt to a static stone age brain. The human brain, in constant co-influence with society, is far more flexible and plastic than that. This makes it necessary to take into account the immense human potential of the uniquely powerful prefrontal cortex (with its Apollonian capacities, for planning, setting, and completing goals as well as for social control), and for continuous cultural learning. All this is needed in efforts to understand and to reduce the mismatch.

From this discussion on a (universal) interest in societal change that reduces the mismatch between human traits and the structure of society, I move towards elaborating on interests in societal change among particular groups, as interpreted through the lens of evolutionary science.

Individual selection and interests in change

In the simple situation of individual selection, the focus is on the individual's position in the group. In what social and economic positions are people likely to have strong interests in change? Individuals located slightly below the dominating segments are certainly candidates here. This is one of the reasons politicians are many times more inclined to struggle for political and social change when they are not yet in power. It is also one reason why, for instance, environmental grass-roots organisations are highly progressive, only to become moderate when they are institutionalised into well-established environmental organisations. Although far-fetched in political analysis of current affairs, evolutionary scientists insist that interests in social and political change among those who are not yet in power become the means to improve their position, and in the evolutionary extension, to improve their chances of reproductive success (Turner & Maryanski, 2016). A common conclusion in, for instance, analyses of environmental problem management, is that politicians and policy makers often frame as 'policy change' or political progress, measures that at the latent level merely strengthen status quo. Increasing the political focus on 'green consumerism', in the sense of promoting individual consumer activities to reduce the world's environmental problems, is a favourite target in such critique of illusory policy progress (Klintman & Boström, 2015).

Kin selection and interests in change

Earlier in this book indicate how the evolutionary phenomenon of kin selection is often used to motivate genetically unrelated individuals to show complete loyalty and be willing to die for each other in war and conflict. It turns out that kin selection as well as reciprocal altruism, examined below, may also entail a human interest in social, political, and economic, changes towards reductions of violence and increases in 'civilised' social interaction. I begin by mentioning peaceful changes related to kin selection. Obviously, the latent motivations of kin selection are a salient component in a lot of change considered as progressive and positive. To remove political conditions of oppression and exploitation, towards emancipation and democratisation, pseudo-kinship metaphors and rhetoric have often been used to increase the sense of community and unity among the oppressed. The strategy has then been to create the dominant framing that emphasises the us–them dichotomy according to the ideological and political divisions that the oppressed group finds essential.

Yet, there are other progressive ways in which pseudo-kinship can be used. Pseudo-kinship may also be to recognise the similar interests of them as of us. They probably just want a peaceful life work, and be with family and friends just as we do. They are in all ways that matter just like us. In programmes for donations and humanitarian aid, this has turned out to be a successful strategy for increasing the willingness of people in the Global North to support highly disadvantageous people in the Global South: to show that poor people have the same dreams and interests as oneself, of stability, schooling for their children, a job, a 'normal daily life'. Evolutionary scientists have associated such creative ways of making use of senses of pseudo-kinship with an increase of women participation in the public discourse to move beyond male–male association, an association which tends to trigger a negative us–them framing. A further way in which new pseudo-kinship has been created is between people in groups that fall outside of the centre of the bell curve of 'normality'. As the number of diagnoses are increasing, some evolutionary scientists hold hopes that stronger and more supportive pseudo-kinships will be established, of people with genetic disorders expressed as autism, letter combinations, and so forth. The hope is that such pseudo-kinships may help to erase the dichotomy of 'abnormal and sick' versus 'normal and healthy'. Instead, a sense of community among people based on them being just a bit different and with their own, partly unique qualities is accordingly a way towards increased tolerance of a pluralist society. Such tolerance would be a compassion based on the acknowledgement that much of our differences is due to random variation in genetics and biology, and is not anyone's fault. (This hope among evolutionary scientists is strikingly different from the hopes expressed among social scientists. The latter typically call for toning down and erasing diagnoses and discussions of genetic disorders in order to broaden the range of what is considered 'normal'. Some social scientists go further by claiming that diagnoses of the above kind are social constructions without substance.)

Reciprocal altruism and interests in change

So far, I have mainly discussed the obstacles to reciprocal altruism for bringing about social change. This constant caution and search for potential cheating is key to game theory, probably influenced by the wars and unrest of the mid-twentieth century. Such caution remains highly relevant today, in light of our conflicts and wars of today and in the likely future. At the same time, the game-theoretical, Apollonian, character of some research on reciprocal altruism over-simplifies human interests, as these interests look in many settings. This part of evolutionary research inflates the tournament trait of humans, whereas this book has tried to make it clear that humans are located evolutionarily between tournament species and pair-bonding species. That humans do not merely have interests in winning substantive, manifest games is overwhelmingly supported by other evolution-based research.

Enormous changes have taken place throughout history when people have identified the mutual benefits of collaborating between hunter-gatherer groups for hunting large animals, for building protection against flooding, for creating towns and cities to collaborate in the protection against intruders, for agreeing on a shared monetary economy, and for trade exchange. From these highly Apollonian and manifest interests in improved living conditions, exchanges of culture and art have emerged.

A claim that I have made throughout this book is that latent interests, in group bonding, social position, and so forth are where the main human motivation can be found. That humans are gathered in billions of associations and group collaborations indicate partly the efficiency of collaborating for improving the lives of those involved. Importantly, the key part of improving one's lives refers to the latent interest in belonging, in being included in social groups, sometimes regardless of the manifest goals of these groups. Since social bonding is at least as important as meeting manifest, individual ends, humans have evolved fairly strong resistance to the temptation of cheating. The human prefrontal cortex, our Apollonian side, help us resist the eventual temptation to cheat, based on our social motivation to remain accepted by the group in the long run. And when we cheat, we are often good at hiding this even from ourselves. This pattern was most clear in hunter-gatherer societies, in which our genes have been shaped. We share these patterns today, yet with the particular challenges of advanced societies mentioned above. More refreshing than the fact that people are good at hiding their cheating are findings in some intriguing studies in neuroeconomics (rooted in evolutionary science). They examined people's brains and compared brains of the people who, when playing the prisoners' dilemma, won over the other players. Unsurprisingly, the activities of brain regions important for motivation and satisfaction were stronger among the winners than among the losers. Far more surprising are the comparisons between the winners and of other participants: those who had managed to reach cooperative agreements with which both parties were fully satisfied. The intriguing result has already been mentioned in a previous chapter: The latter group showed a significantly higher degree of activity in the ventral striatum, which is part of the brain's reward pathway (Rilling *et al.*, 2002; Ruff & Fehr, 2014). These studies support the assumption in evolutionary theory that collaboration and group bonding is more strongly motivating than merely winning each game. The studies remain to be modified to various settings. Yet they give some welcome hope for future inclination of reaching, for instance, international agreements in issues of environment and health in ways that do not mainly lead to winners and losers, but to a deeper sense of collaborative efforts to reach a common cause.

Conclusions

Evolutionary science conceives of human interests in continuity as a central aspect of a major challenge to the brain: how to economise with energy. The brain has evolved to economise with energy use whenever possible. This is one explanation for the inclination for developing habits, routines, and a degree of 'automacy', whenever possible. Our constant pattern seeking and use of heuristic are, if not a search for continuity, then, at least, a search for patterns of change similar to the previous change. Evolutionary science also highlights the social element of continuity, of inertia, tradition, and shared meaning, even in cases where such continuity constitutes a gap to the actual matters of fact and the latest scientific findings. Religious rites and traditions might be examples of this. Here, the social rationality becomes clear of embracing and sharing certain continuity. Another part of social rationality refers to how there is something particular about the higher status segments in society and their embracing of continuity. In the example of the battered child syndrome, we could see the striking inertia before paediatricians were ready to accept fully the very possibility that parents (the clients of paediatricians) could inflict such harm on their children. This and several other research findings constitute the evolutionary, as well as social scientific, contention about social rationality: that the social establishment can be expected to favour continuity as soon as changes towards improvements would jeopardise their high social position.

As to interests in change, evolutionary science elucidates the mismatch that seems to prevail in human conditions of current society and the ancestral environment to which we are genetically adapted. Accordingly, there is an interest in changes that reduce this mismatch, at least concerning certain factors. One example is stress. To be sure, evolutionary scientists point out that some stress is highly beneficial and stimulating, if it is limited in time, moderate, and takes place in a relatively safe setting. The long-term stress characterised by a sense of complete lack of control, predictability, and where no end to the stress seems to be in sight, is very far from the short-term, intensive stress situations that faced humans in its ancestral environment. This mismatch is particularly apparent for people with low socio-economic status, a position that typically implies a very limited social network to help people manage the stress. The notion of a mismatch does not need to mean that evolutionary scientists need to commit the naturalistic fallacy of embracing all traits of our ancestral environment as 'natural' and therefore as 'good'. Social, political, and ethical analysis and debate is always needed in the 'space' between the description and normativity.

The three evolutionary principles of individual selection, kin selection, and reciprocal altruism all point to interests in change under various social, economic, and political conditions. Individual selection points to the interest in change that people and groups beneath the highest social segments may have. Much of social change has been initiated at the middle- and low socio-economic levels in society, motivated both by the Apollonian interests in better material conditions in absolute terms and at least as much by Dionysian interests in reduced inequality and increases in the social status of the middle or lower segments of society. The other principles, kin selection and reciprocal altruism, can also be directed towards interests in change. The chapter has shown how pseudo-kinship can be constructed to strengthen alliances, and raise awareness among different groups, in turn leading to a shared sense of common interests. Reciprocal altruism may, through trade, cultural exchange, and other types of interaction between groups, organisations, countries, and regions, turn previous zero-sum games into positive-sum games, where the mutual dependence constitutes a change that may reduce the risk of violence. Such change is close to where economics have long developed valuable insights.

Book conclusions

Based on this analysis, I can safely confirm the initial assumption in this book: that concerns with, and about human interests are indeed shared between human scientists in all disciplines. Not least some of the driest, statistical examinations breathe empathy and passion as regards the aim towards understanding and explaining social, economic, and evolutionary conditions for the satisfaction of human interests. Human scientists have, of course, manifest interests in steadily improving knowledge about human interests and conditions, by extension contributing to the improved welfare of also non-human animals and the planet. As the book has shown, however, manifest interests and concerns alone are not a guarantee that all parts of the human scientific disciplines are on the most scientifically well-grounded track towards their own explicit goals.

My ambition with this analysis has initially been twofold. First, I have wanted to highlight and compare how the three human sciences understand and examine human interests, mainly applied to issues of environment and health. Second, the ambition has been to develop a conceptual basis for an integrated framework potentially useful to all human sciences, for investigating human dimensions of environmental and health-oriented problems, and beyond. For reaching these two objectives, it has turned out to be crucial to add a third one: of shedding some light on the interests of human scientists themselves within their disciplines. The rest of this chapter briefly discusses these three objectives, followed by a couple of wider implications.

Three disciplines or two dimensions?

How the human sciences understand human interests is part of the axiology of the human sciences. It refers to the human values and interests that the disciplines identify, interpret, or ignore in their theoretical and empirical works. In previous research and courses where the axiology of the human sciences has been explored, this it has usually been done by studying one, or by comparing two, disciplines. Looking at only one discipline, however, is not likely to be very revealing, since insight, particularly into the values and partly hidden assumptions of one's own discipline, demands comparison. To compare the axiology of two disciplines is, of course, better. Still, this book has argued that it is time to bring in the three human sciences and their sub-disciplines into the process of comparative analysis and knowledge exchange. One among several reasons for this is that the human sciences (and all life sciences) have moved well into an era where any contemporary research still founded on the insistence on a binary understanding of nature and nurture can bluntly but safely be said to be merely a waste of time and money. Since the human sciences have several historical roots in such binary thinking, it becomes crucial that they engage in cross-disciplinary knowledge exchange and debate to overcome this binary.

The relation between the three disciplines

Was the claim made in this book's introduction exaggerated, as regards a minimal influence and knowledge exchange between the human sciences? By looking at the mainstreams of the disciplines, their dialogue, trialogue, and mutual influence have indeed been modest so far. There are several findings of human interests in the mainstreams of each of the human sciences that are well supported by ample data, explanation, and conceptualisation, yet subject to minimal knowledge exchange. Here are three examples:

The deeper problem of social and economic inequality for human wellbeing is striking. Social science, supported by evolutionary science, stresses its urgency for the human sciences. Traditional economics, however, usually perceives inequality as a 'political' and 'ideological' matter, irrelevant to scientific analysis and debate, once economic efficiency has been assessed.

The importance of examining human incentives and disincentives, and of fully understanding their implications, is emphasised by traditional economics, but is downplayed by vast areas of the social sciences. Yet, taking incentives and disincentives seriously, has been shown to be essential for reducing, for instance, the risk of environmental harm, caused by free riding of polluters. It should be noted that traditional economics certainly needs the findings in behavioural economics in order to correct several misunderstandings about incentives and disincentives. Moreover, the moral dimension surrounding new introductions of financial incentives and disincentives (through commodification) is also necessary from a perspective of human interests.

The genetic preparedness on the human slate is an indisputable lesson from the evolutionary sciences. Still, mainstream social science either ignores it or finds it irrelevant to its research domain. Mainstream economics accepts that there is genetic preparedness, but misunderstands the content of this readiness. Evolutionary science is continuously developing its insights about genetic preparedness. How this preparation works more precisely is subject to intensive and revising research. Learning how genetic preparedness is intertwined with cultural and social life is an enormous research area where all the human sciences should be involved, far beyond the advanced albeit limited methods and perspectives of evolutionary science. This will possibly help, for instance, to reduce the mismatches between our genetically evolved, universal interests, and social structures so that minimising harm to the environment and health may converge with our genetically evolved interests in social bonding and esteem.

The Apollonian and Dionysian dimensions of the human sciences

To be sure, one of the aspirations of this book has undoubtedly been to the many walls that exist between the human sciences. Several problems with environment and health are partly a result of a lack of absorption of fundamental insights in one discipline not being absorbed – or at least undogmatically scrutinised by the others. At the same time, I have found it vital to avoid making caricatures of the disciplines. Moreover, it has been important not to exaggerate their mutual exclusivity. The ancient dimensions of the Apollonian and Dionysian have turned out to be extremely useful for finding nuances and similarities across the three disciplines. These dimensions reflect two distinct but co-dependent types of cultural expression. Moreover, neuroscience has recently shown how something similar to this dual model can be found in the brain. Therefore, it is of little surprise that both Apollonian and Dionysian dimensions can be found in each of the human sciences. Searching for the Apollonian dimension, I have been able to elucidate several issues which parts of all the disciplines find crucial to investigate.

It is true that game-theoretical challenges of free riding and the tragedy of the commons are not mainstream endeavours of all the disciplines. Still, scholars and sub-disciplines with an Apollonian focus are active in all the human sciences in this area. This is a problem area that is critical to understanding and reducing environmental problems, and raises the issue of how the world may better govern the global commons. The focus on ways to improve health, comfort, and the general economic level of societies is an additional Apollonian area examined by all the sciences.

As to the Dionysian dimension, it is also represented by parts of all the human sciences. Human biases, conspicuous consumption, the latent and powerful interest in social bonding and esteem are recognised by parts of these sciences. Given that the evolutionary basis is particularly deep for Dionysian factors, the human sciences and policy makers should expect these factors to play an overriding role in motivating people and organisations at all levels of society to reduce their harm, for instance, to the environment and health.

Sharing a research area in the Apollonian or Dionysian dimensions does not necessarily mean that there are active dialogue and knowledge exchange between different disciplines within one dimension. In many cases, it seems to be a bigger step to incorporate insights from parts of the various disciplines that have their research focus within the same dimension, than to engage in discussions between Dionysian and Apollonian strands of thought within one and the same discipline. Behavioural economics appears to be an exception (so far) concerning where dialogue and knowledge exchange usually takes place. There are intensive dialogue and overlap between behavioural economics and evolutionary science. Meanwhile the relationship between behavioural and traditional economics, despite their contradictory views concerning human interests and motivations, is intriguingly one of complementarity and division of labour.

Social rationality

The second ambition of this book has been to provide a basis for an integrated framework about human interests. I have done this by offering a number of propositions throughout this book, propositions that can be used in such an integrated framework. The basis of such a framework and the common thread of its propositions is the overriding role of social rationality. That social rationality plays this important role for human interests is something that parts of all three human sciences indicate. For instance, the economic sociologist Granovetter echoes this fairly obvious recognition by incorporating social esteem (albeit in other words) into his idea of rationality: '[Actions are rational if they aim] not only at economic goals but also at sociability, approval, status, and power' (Granovetter 1985, 509–10).

However, Granovetter is overly cautious by merely adding esteem to an unhierarchical list of rationality factors. The human sciences, if they are to take social rationality seriously, ought to develop hypotheses and scrutinise explanations that social rationality often overrides, for instance, economic rationality, in cases where the two are in conflict. In light of the recent developments in Dionysian strands of thought in economics, this ought to be possible in this discipline as well. Behavioural and institutional economics, and neuroeconomics all recognise Dionysian traits, particularly the latent, often unconscious, level of humans and society. This is an essential element of social rationality.

An integrative framework of social rationality is not something that human scientists could, or should, try to use for explanation of everything. Instead, such a framework ought to be used for developing assumptions and hypotheses to be scientifically scrutinised, and that should be possible to falsify from time to time. To be useful, and to avoid tautology, expectations must be in principle falsifiable. I have criticised parts of rational choice scholarship in economics on this very point: This strand of thought runs the risk of circularity, by claiming that everything is an economically rational choice. Assumptions that socially rational activities are the roots to specific outcomes should be, in principle, falsifiable.

This means that it becomes critical to show examples of possible results in the human sciences that point towards social irrationality. Here are some overlapping examples. The most apparent example would be extensive efforts by individuals and organisations to operate as similarly as possibly to Homo economicus, with no active relationship to social norms, and conventions. Sen's notion of 'social moron' mentioned above expresses the social irrationality of such endeavours perfectly. Similar social irrationality is shown in empirical studies of how people and cultures where material accumulation alone is sought have a lower wellbeing than others. This may happen when consumerism is stripped of its social core, and disconnected from social bonding, culturally shared identity, and so forth. Second, even beyond the Homo economicus ideal, social irrationality may take place when actors and organisations are not helped or able to be responsive to social norms and conventions of the culture or sub-culture in which they find themselves. Third, social irrationality may stem from political, economic, or cultural preoccupation in society of favouring either only Apollonian or only Dionysian factors. A society with a preoccupation with Apollonian interests would refer to a fostering of a culture that always supports long-term planning, means to other means, individual decision making based on a systematic information processing of impartial facts, while ignoring latent, Dionysian processes or possible trade-offs between Apollonian problem solving and Dionysian outcomes. The concerns raised by the classical social thinkers can be traced here, a concern that continues in contemporary social science. On the other hand, a preoccupation with Dionysian interests would refer to a full focus on a human interest in impulse, immediate expression, on the relative levels of material and health standards, while downplaying the importance of absolute levels of health and material welfare. An over-emphasis of Dionysian interests would, furthermore, entail a downplaying of the importance of self-control and long-term planning, by extension downplaying long-term human interests. Economics points to the possibility of economic irrationality of this one-sidedness. The sociologist, Bell, indicates how particular groups of men have had a harder time making socially rational decisions in order to adapt to the societal transition to the service and knowledge society, much due to a lack of Apollonian planning and support.

In sum, there are many ways in which individuals, organisations at all level may act in a direction towards social irrationality. Importantly, however, identifications of socially rational or socially irrational activities and structure should not be interpreted as automatically normative statements. Even here, a four-field table would be possible. However, I will spare the reader another such table. A few examples will do. The book has shown several cases of activities and propensities that might be socially rational, yet seemingly undesirable, immoral, and so forth. Sadly, the striking inertia that prevailed before the child battering syndrome was recognised as a societal problem also by the community of paediatricians in general, is a case where paediatricians arguably acted out of social rationality, in (perhaps unconsciously) maintaining for a long time the status quo, which was beneficial to themselves. A wide range of other examples exists how people in the dominant segment of society have, consciously or unconsciously, preserved an oppressive order, a status quo that has benefitted their position and esteem. Another example is the social rationality of ecological inconsistency found in much of the well-educated middle class today. Many people in this segment perform certain conspicuously 'eco-friendly' acts, such as purchasing eco-labelled products, ecologically contradicted by exotic 'eco-tourism' to distant destinations by aeroplane. This might promote people's social esteem but is less beneficial from an ecological perspective. Reversely, certain activities seem socially irrational, but may nevertheless be highly valuable to society. Whistle-blowers, social movement actors, human rights or environmental activists, people and organisations who dare 'to speak truth' to power and challenge harmful cultural conventions, might act in socially irrational ways, unless they are part of a sub-group or sub-culture with strong social bonding. Still, such forces are necessary for a healthy, vibrant, and evolving society, and may turn out to have been socially rational at the end, elevating these activists to heroines and heroes. In sum, there is nothing intrinsically good with social rationality. Since social rationality is deeply rooted in human evolution, one would immediately fall into the trap of the naturalistic fallacy, if one claimed that social rationality is per definition good. Instead, I direct my normativity to human scientific treatment of social rationality. To ignore or downplay social rationality when doing human scientific analysis is certainly a bad thing. By extension, it is bad if policy makers or other 'practitioners' ignore or downplay social rationality. Or to reverse the matter: recognising social rationality as an overriding human – and organisational – force may provide society with an immense potential for developing schemes and policies designed in novel, powerful ways.

Interests within the human sciences

My ambitions mentioned above need to be supplemented by a third one: of bringing to the analysis some of the interests of the human scientists themselves. Admittedly, the eminent sociologist Bell, mentioned several times in this book, maintained himself to be 'a socialist in economics, a liberal in politics, and a conservative in culture' (Bell, 1976/1996, xi). As regards economics, he demanded that society provided financially for the whole population a material basis for human dignity. In politics, he stressed the importance of rewarding competence, hard work, and accomplishments. In culture, he thought that it was essential to take cultural heritage and identity seriously, for instance by preserving certain traditions. Although many, if not most, human scientists may be ideologically multifaceted in various ways, I argue that it is still meaningful to discuss, first, ideology of the human scientists themselves, and second, ideas that seem to be fairly fixed within the respective sciences.

Earlier in the book, I discussed seven 'moral foundations', that the moral psychologist, Haidt, has identified (Haidt, 2012). He describes, and provides support for, the universality of these moral foundations; they can be found in all cultures. Since human scientists are – after all – human, we should, informed by the Dionysian side of the human sciences, expect human scientists to have biases just like everyone else. One such bias is confirmation bias, making people motivated and highly capable of finding support for their already established beliefs and values. In this light, we can expect human scientists to stress the significance of those foundations that they hold dearest, and interpret these foundations in ways that do not contradict their ideology. In fact, Haidt implies a similar logic in his public engagement in what he perceives as a problem of ideological homogeneity in several of the human sciences. The reason that he finds such homogeneity problematic is that it may have, according to him, a direct impact on the research that is conducted, from research question to discussions about 'policy implications'. For instance, an economist may hold the view that capitalism falls within the moral foundation of oppression or its opposite, liberty. Whether the economist is to be open towards expanding or shrinking the regulatory state or welfare state is likely to depend on which moral foundations are strongest rooted in her or his values. In consequence, if most or all economists perceive capitalism as liberation, society is likely to see very little economic research that points towards nuances and unintended consequences related to the goal of shrinking the regulatory or welfare state. Through a survey of economists, combined with previous research, Randazzo and Haidt strongly confirm that the 'scientific' conclusions that economists draw about 'scientifically preferable' economic policies heavily correlated with the moral values that they hold, among both left- and right-oriented economists (Randazzo & Haidt, 2015). Together with several other psychologists, Haidt has done a similar survey with American social psychologists. They find, first, that an overwhelming majority of social psychologists are 'liberal' (in the American sense). This corresponded to the researchers' initial assumptions. More remarkable is that they found high correlations between the research that social psychologists do and their political conviction. Risks with this include that liberal values become embedded in method and theory, that scholars concentrate on issues that validate the progressive, liberal narrative, and so forth (Duarte *et al.*, 2014). To my knowledge, no similar studies have been done with the category of social scientists and evolutionary scientists. Moreover, these two categories are far less clear-cut than social psychology. Although my intuition is that 'social scientists', the way they have been categorised in this book, hold predominantly 'liberal', leftist, or green values, this is not my main point. Instead, like Haidt, I want to highlight the general phenomenon of homogeneity of underlying claims within each of the sciences. Although Haidt does not make full use of his conceptualisation of universal, moral foundations, I think that these could be utilised for searching for possible gaps in each of the human sciences, partly based on their homogeneity. One assumption, based on earlier discussions in this book, is that large parts of the economic sciences do not fully incorporate the moral foundation of sanctity and degradation when they are unreservedly positive to commodification of previously untradable things, activities, and ideas. Another assumption would be that the social sciences downplay the moral foundations of fairness and cheating as well as loyalty and betrayal when failing to fully understand and explain public scepticism to what parts of the public perceive as 'over-generous' immigration policies. Such failure to recognise the manifest and latent interests of groups in society leads to an unnecessarily low preparedness for how to reduce the risks of, for instance, violence between ethnic groups.

Haidt and his colleagues have done path-breaking work in highlighting the importance of political and ideological diversity in human scientific disciplines. At the same time, this book has tried to show how the problem of disciplinary homogeneity goes beyond ideology. A less profound basis can in some cases be the methodological and conceptual toolbox that differs between the human sciences. Take, for instance, how evolutionary science usually analyses and explains crime and violence. The typical focus is young men, low-status, unemployed, unmarried, whose Dionysian frustration with their low socio-economic status is manifested, often by influence of alcohol, drugs, and fatigue (more often at night), through crime and violence on the street. A social scientific gut reaction to such an analysis might be that it is ideologically conservative, by focusing on destructive and uncivilised behaviour of marginalised, disadvantaged groups. However, there does not have to be a conservative basis here.

First, focusing on this category of low-status young men could just as well trigger a broader debate about the responsibility of the welfare state to improve the conditions for more employment (Sapolsky, 2004). Second, the evolutionary focus on the ill deeds committed by low-status young men is partly methodological. Evolutionary scientists often measure hormones, scan brains, and analyse statistics of direct instances of crime and violence across space and time. They compare these data with data on other primates. Thus, unless they supplement their primary research with the ditto from the social and economic sciences, they are unlikely to reach explanatory factors of crime and violence at the structural level. Such factors might include latent interests of the leading segments of society in maintaining structures that entail continuous social and economic inequality, which, in turn, may give rise to resentment and violence.

Like all other scientists, human scientists usually search where their discipline's methodological light is. This alludes to the man who, in the darkness of night, searches for his lost keys. But he searches only under the streetlight, since this is where he can see. He does not search elsewhere, although the keys might just as well lie there. In addition to methodology, the intra-disciplinary concepts and theories restrict the analysis in each human science. It has become a cliché to state that scholars see things through the conceptual lens of their own science.

But there seems to be a more fundamental factor involved here, that can be reduced neither to personal ideology nor the 'innocent' limits of methods and concepts within each human science. This factor is the latent, Dionysian interests of human scientists and the scientific communities that their disciplines constitute. Part of our social rationality, for better or for worse, is a deeply rooted confirmation bias, the human inclination and high ability to confirm not just one's own view, but also the view of the community. If one's intellectual community is only one's specific discipline, it is usually socially rational to repeat its views (often unconsciously, by taking them for granted), searching for additional arguments that support these views, albeit with a small twist of critique and challenge.

Proposition 9: when isolated from the other human sciences, it can be expected to be socially rational most of the time for human scientists within each discipline to uncritically reconfirm (/to take as an unquestionable given) the most basic assumptions (disciplinary identity batch) of their discipline, albeit with a moderate twist of criticism at the detail level to mark distinction. By extension, lengthy disciplinary isolation is likely to lead to intellectual hair-splitting, as the intra-disciplinary issues of major and moderate significance will eventually be used up.

The proposal above alludes to Kuhn's notion of scientific paradigms. Under long periods of 'normal science', Kuhn argues, scientists within the dominant paradigm mainly confirm it (Kuhn, 1962/2012). In the human sciences, there have been misunderstandings about the notion of paradigms. For instance, in sociology, the concept of paradigms has been watered down and inflated, ever since Ritzer claimed that sociology is a multi-paradigm science. He distinguishes, for instance, between the social facts paradigm, social definitions paradigm, and the social behaviour paradigm. This is particularly odd given his own definition of paradigms, as 'the broadest unit of consensus within science' (Ritzer, 1975, 157). Even if the difference between these so-called paradigms may seem enormous to the sociologists involved there is still a high degree of consensus among them. There are several, more appropriate terms, such as traditions or perspectives. The reason is that the traditions of social facts, social definitions, and social behaviour all fit reasonably well within the 'Standard Social Science Model' (Tooby & Cosmides, 1992), or what this book simply labels 'social science'. I argue that the same applies to what this book calls traditional economics and evolutionary science. It is in this light that Proposition 9 should be understood.

Summing up the bases for intellectual homogeneity, taking ideological, methodological, conceptual, and esteem-oriented factors into account it stands clear that Haidt's call for political diversity within each of the sciences is certainly important, but not sufficient. With political diversity within each human science, the intellectual homogeneity will probably be reduced to some extent, opening for the recognition of more of Haidt's moral foundations in each of the sciences. At the same time, the tribal traits of isolation and even xenophobia between the human sciences would most likely not go away with this improvement. Additional, in part top-down measures would probably be needed, such as research policies and funding that stimulates not just interdisciplinary collaboration, but more specifically human scientific inter- and cross-disciplinary research collaboration. New ways of thinking about how to organise thematic research groups in the universities will also be instrumental here. I hope, moreover, that this book will contribute to facilitating such changes, both in new research constellations and in human scientific courses on axiology and theories of science where human interests are in focus. The ideal should never be full consensus between the human sciences. As I mentioned early in the book, a better ideal is a transition from sling shooting at a far distance to wrestling. This way, myths and misunderstandings about human interests and social problems would become far less resistant to scrutiny and dispelling. The continued societal relevance of the human sciences depends on how well its disciplines can find a constructive balance between competition and collaboration.

References

Ahlquist, John S., & Margaret Levi. 2013. *In the Interest of Others: Organizations and Social Activism*. Princeton, NJ: Princeton University Press.

Ansari, Daniel. 2012. 'Culture and Education: New Frontiers in Brain Plasticity.' *Trends in Cognitive Sciences* 16(2):93–5.

Antoci, Angelo, & Luca Zarri. 2015. 'Punish and Perish?' *Rationality and Society* 27(2):195–223.

Archer, Margaret, Roy Bhaskar, Andrew Collier, Tony Lawson, & Alan Norrie. 2013. *Critical Realism: Essential Readings*. London: Routledge.

Ariely, Dan. 2009. *Predictably Irrational: The Hidden Forces That Shape Our Decisions*. London: Harper.

Arnhart, Larry. 2005. 'Natural Law and the Darwinian Conservatism of Sex Differences.' *Perspectives on Political Science* 34(3):135–43.

Atkinson, Anthony B. 2009. 'Economics as a Moral Science.' *Economica* 76:791–804.

Axelrod, Robert M. 2006. *The Evolution of Cooperation*. New York, NY: Basic Books.

Baldursson, Fridrik M., & Jon Thor Sturluson. 2011. 'Fees and the Efficiency of Tradable Permit Systems: An Experimental Approach.' *Environmental & Resource Economics* 48(1):25–41.

Barash, David P. 2000. 'Evolutionary Existentialism, Sociobiology, and the Meaning of Life.' *BioScience* 50(11):1012–17.

Barkow, Jerome. 2003. 'Biology Is Destiny Only if We Ignore it.' *World Futures* 59(3):173–88.

Barkow, Jerome H., ed. 2005. *Missing the Revolution: Darwinism for Social Scientists*. 1st ed. Oxford, UK: Oxford University Press.

Barnett, Mark W., & Philip M. Larkman. 2007. 'The Action Potential.' *Practical Neurology* 7(3):192–7.

Baron-Cohen, Simon. 2001. 'Adult "Reading the Mind in the Eyes" Test – Revised.' *PsycTESTS*.

Bauman, Zygmunt. 1993. *Modernity and Ambivalence*. New ed. Cambridge, UK: Polity.

Baumeister, Roy F. 2005. *The Cultural Animal*. Oxford, UK: Oxford University Press.

Beck, Ulrich. 1999. *World Risk Society*. Cambridge, UK: Polity.

Becker, Gary S., & Kevin M. Murphy. 1988. 'A Theory of Rational Addiction.' *Journal of Political Economy* 96(4):675–700.

Bell, Daniel. 1976/2008. *The Coming of Post-Industrial Society*. New York, NY: Basic Books.

Benford, R. D., & D. A. Snow. 2000. 'Framing Processes and Social Movements: An Overview and Assessment.' *Annual Review of Sociology* 26:611–39.

Bennett, James T., & Bruce E. Kaufman, eds. 2007. *What Do Unions Do?: A Twenty-Year Perspective*. New Brunswick, NJ: Transaction Publishers.

Bentley, Alex, Mark Earls, & Michael J. O'Brien. 2011. *I'll Have What She's Having: Mapping Social Behavior*. Cambridge, MA: MIT Press.

Berger, Peter L. 2011. *Adventures of an Accidental Sociologist*. Amherst, NY: Prometheus Books.

Berlin, Isaiah. 1958. *Two Concepts of Liberty: An Inaugural Lecture, Delivered before the University of Oxford on 31 October 1958*. Oxford: Clarendon Press.

Berman, Marshall. 1983. *All That Is Solid Melts Into Air: The Experience of Modernity*. London: Verso.

Berridge, Kent C., & Terry E. Robinson. 1998. 'What Is the Role of Dopamine in Reward: Hedonic Impact, Reward Learning, or Incentive Salience?' *Brain Research Reviews* 28(3):309–69.

Bingham, Paul M., & Joanne Souza. 2012. 'Ultimate Causation in Evolved Human Political Psychology: Implications for Public Policy.' *Journal of Social, Evolutionary & Cultural Psychology* 6(3):360–83.

Binmore, Ken. 2005. 'Economic Man – or Straw Man?' *Behavioral and Brain Sciences* 28(6):817–18.

Blanchflower, David G., & Andrew J. Oswald. 2011. 'International Happiness: A New View on the Measure of Performance.' *Academy of Management Perspectives* 25(1):6–22.

Blasch, Julia, & Markus Ohndorf. 2015. 'Altruism, Moral Norms and Social Approval: Joint Determinants of Individual Offset Behavior.' *Ecological Economics* 116:251–60.

Blau, Peter M. 1997. 'On Limitations of Rational Choice Theory for Sociology.' *American Sociologist* 28(2):16–21.

Boardman, Helen E. 1962. 'A Project to Rescue Children from Inflicted Injuries.' *Social Work* 7(1):43–51.

Bok, Derek. 2010. *The Politics of Happiness: What Government Can Learn from the New Research on Well-Being*. 1st ed. Princeton, NJ: Princeton University Press.

Bolsen, Toby, Thomas. J. Leeper, & Matthiew. A. Shapiro. 2014. 'Doing What Others Do: Norms, Science, and Collective Action on Global Warming.' *American Politics Research* 42(1):65–89.

Bone, Jonathan E., & Nichola J. Raihani. 2015. 'Human Punishment Is Motivated by Both a Desire for Revenge and a Desire for Equality.' *Evolution & Human Behavior* 36(4):323.

Boström, Magnus, & Mikael Klintman. 2011. *Eco-Standards, Product Labelling and Green Consumerism*. Houndmills, Basingstoke, UK: Palgrave Macmillan.

Boström, Magnus, Åsa Casula Vifell, Mikael Klintman, Linda Soneryd, Kristina Tamm Hallström, & Renita Thedvall. 2015. 'Social Sustainability Requires Social Sustainability: Procedural Prerequisites for Reaching Substantive Goals.' *Nature & Culture* 10(2).

Bourdieu, Pierre. 1990. *The Logic of Practice*. Stanford, CA: Stanford University Press.

Bowles, Samuel, Eric Alden Smith, & Monique Borgerhoff Mulder. 2010. 'The Emergence and Persistence of Inequality in Premodern Societies.' *Current Anthropology* 51(1):7–17.

Boyd, Robert. 2006. 'Evolution: The Puzzle of Human Sociality.' *Science* 314:1555–6.

Boyd, Robert, & Joan Silk. 2006. *How Humans Evolved*. 4th ed. New York, NY: W. W. Norton & Company.

Brennan, Geoffrey, & Philip Pettit. 2004. *The Economy of Esteem: An Essay on Civil and Political Society*. Oxford, UK; New York, NY: Oxford University Press.

Briggs, Jean. 1971. *Never in Anger: Portrait of an Eskimo Family*. New ed. Cambridge, MA: Harvard University Press.

Brouwer, R., L. Brander, & P. Van Beukering. 2008. ' "A Convenient Truth": Air Travel Passengers' Willingness to Pay to Offset Their CO_2 Emissions.' *Climatic Change* 90(3):299–313.

Brown, Donald. 1991. *Human Universals*. 1st ed. New York, NY: McGraw-Hill Humanities/ Social Sciences/Languages.

Brown, Donald E. 2004. 'Human Universals, Human Nature & Human Culture.' *Daedalus* 133(4):47–54.

Buchanan, James M. 1977/2000. *Democracy in Deficit*. Indianapolis, IN: Liberty Fund.

Bunge, Mario. 1996. *Finding Philosophy in Social Science*. New Haven, CT: Yale University Press.

Burawoy, Michael. 2014. 'Sociology as a Vocation: Moral Commitment and Scientific Imagination.' *Current Sociology* 62(2):279–84.

Burt, S. Alexandra. 2009. ' "A Mechanistic Explanation of Popularity: Genes, Rule Breaking, and Evocative Gene-Environment Correlations": Correction to Burt (2009).' *Journal of Personality and Social Psychology* 97(1):57–57.

Buss, David M. 1989. 'Sex Differences in Human Mate Preferences: Evolutionary Hypotheses Tested in 37 Cultures.' *Behavioral and Brain Sciences* 12(1):1–14.

Buss, D. M. 2000. 'The Evolution of Happiness.' *The American Psychologist* 55(1):15–23.

Butler, Samuel. 1877. *Life and Habit*. London: A.C. Fifield.

Cacioppo, John T., Stephanie Cacioppo, & Dorret I. Boomsma. 2014. 'Evolutionary Mechanisms for Loneliness.' *Cognition & Emotion* 28(1):3–21.

Camerer, Colin F., George Loewenstein, & Matthew Rabin. 2011. *Advances in Behavioral Economics (The Roundtable Series in Behavioral Economics)*. New Haven, CT: Princeton University Press.

Campbell, Anne. 2012. 'The Study of Sex Differences: Feminism and Biology.' *Zeitschrift für Psychologie* 220(2):137–43.

Campbell, Colin. 1982. 'A Dubious Distinction? An Inquiry into the Value and Use of Merton's Concepts of Manifest and Latent Function.' *American Sociological Review* 47(1):29–44.

Camus, Albert. 1942/1955. *The Myth of Sisyphus and Other Essays*. New York, NY: Vintage Books.

Carothers, Bobbi J., & Harry T. Reis. 2013. 'Men and Women Are from Earth: Examining the Latent Structure of Gender.' *Journal of Personality and Social Psychology* 104(2):385–407.

Chaiken, Shelly, & Yaacov Trope. 1999. *Dual-Process Theories in Social Psychology*. New York, NY: Guilford Press.

Chomsky, Noam. 2007. *On Language*. New York, NY: New Press.

Chuah, Swee-Hoon, Robert Hoffmann, Martin Jones, and Geoffrey Williams. 2007. 'Do Cultures Clash? Evidence from Cross-National Ultimatum Game Experiments.' *Journal of Economic Behavior & Organization* 64(1):35–48.

Clements, Matthew T. 2013. 'Self-Interest vs. Greed and the Limitations of the Invisible Hand.' *American Journal of Economics and Sociology* 72(4):949–65.

Cobb-Clark, Deborah A., & Stefanie Schurer. 2012. 'The Stability of Big-Five Personality Traits.' *Economics Letters* 115(1):11–15.

Cohas, A., & D. Allaine. 2009. 'Social Structure Influences Extra-Pair Paternity in Socially Monogamous Mammals.' *Biology Letters* 5(3):313–16.

Cohen, Dov, Richard E. Nisbett, Brian F. Bowdle, & Norbert Schwarz. 1996. 'Insult, Aggression, and the Southern Culture of Honor: An "Experimental Ethnography".' *Journal of Personality and Social Psychology* 70(5):945–60.

Cole, G. D. H. 1952. 'Review of Imperialism and Social Classes.' *The Economic Journal* 62(245):177–80.

Coleman, James Samuel. 1990. *Foundations of Social Theory*. Cambridge, MA: Harvard University Press.

Collins, Randall. 2005. *Interaction Ritual Chains*. Princeton, NJ: Princeton University Press.

Compton, Janice, & Robert A. Pollak. 2009. *Proximity and Coresidence of Adult Children and Their Parents: Description and Correlates*. Ann Arbor: Michigan Retirement Research Center, University of Michigan.

Confer, Jaime C., Judith A. Easton, Diana S. Fleischman, Cari D. Goetz, David M. G. Lewis, Carin Perilloux, & David M. Buss. 2010. 'Evolutionary Psychology: Controversies, Questions, Prospects, and Limitations.' *American Psychologist* 65(2):110–26.

Constant, Benjamin. 1816/1988. *Constant: Political Writings*. Cambridge, UK: Cambridge University Press.

Cook, Scott. 1966. 'The Obsolete "Anti-Market" Mentality: A Critique of the Substantive Approach to Economic Anthropology.' *American Anthropologist* 68(2):323–45.

Crane, William. 2010. *Theories of Development: Concepts and Applications*. 6th ed. London: Routledge.

Cronk, Lee. 2005. 'Behavioral Ecology and the Social Sciences.' In J. H. Barkow (ed.), *Missing the Revolution: Darwinism for Social Scientists*. Oxford, UK: Oxford University Press.

Cummins, Denise, & Robert Cummins. 1999. 'Biological Preparedness and Evolutionary Explanation.' *COGNITION* 73(3):B37–53.

Czaran, Tamas L., & Rolf F. Hoekstra. 2004. 'Evolution of Sexual Asymmetry.' *BMC Evolutionary Biology* 4(1):34.

Dahl, Melissa. 2015. 'If Daniel Kahneman Had a Magic Wand He'd Rid the Human Race of Overconfidence.' *Science of Us*. Retrieved 17 August 2015 (http://nymag.com/scienceofus/2015/07/bias-one-scientist-wishes-he-could-eliminate.html).

Dahms, Harry F. 1995. 'From Creative Action to the Social Rationalization of the Economy: Joseph A. Schumpeter's Social Theory.' *Sociological Theory* 13(1):1–13.

Dallongeville, Jean, Luc Dauchet, Olivier de Mouzon, Vincent Requillart, and Louis Georges Soler. 2011. 'Increasing Fruit and Vegetable Consumption: A Cost-Effectiveness Analysis of Public Policies.' *European Journal of Public Health* 21(1):69–73.

Darby, Michael R., & Edi Karni. 1973. 'Free Competition and the Optimal Amount of Fraud.' *Journal of Law and Economics* (1):67.

Darwin, Charles. 1872. *The Expression of the Emotions in Man and Animals*. London: John Murray.

Dawkins, Richard. 2005. *The Ancestor's Tale: A Pilgrimage to the Dawn of Evolution*. Boston, MA: Mariner Books.

Dawkins, Richard. 2006. *The Selfish Gene*. 30th anniversary ed. Oxford, UK: Oxford University Press.

De Vries, P., H. Aarts, & C. J. H. Midden. 2011. 'Changing Simple Energy-Related Consumer Behaviors: How the Enactment of Intentions Is Thwarted by Acting and Non-Acting Habits.' *Environment and Behavior* 43(5):612–33.

De Waal, Frans. 2005. *Our Inner Ape: A Leading Primatologist Explains Why We Are Who We Are*. New York, NY: Riverhead Books.

De Waal, Frans. 2009. *Primates and Philosophers: How Morality Evolved*. 5th ed. (S. Macedo and J. Ober (eds.). Princeton, NJ: Princeton University Press.

Diamond, Marian Cleeves. 1988. *Enriching Heredity: The Impact of the Environment on the Anatomy of the Brain.* New York, NY: Free Press.

Dimijian, Gregory G. 2005. 'Evolution of Sexuality: Biology and Behavior.' *Proceedings (Baylor University Medical Center)* 18(3):244–58.

Duarte, Jose L., Jarret T. Crawford, Charlotte Stern, Jonathan Haidt, Lee Jussim, & Philip E. Tetlock. 2014. 'Political Diversity Will Improve Social Psychological Science.' *Behavioral and Brain Sciences* 1–54.

Duesenberry, James S. 1949. *Income, Saving, and the Theory of Consumer Behavior.* 1st ed. Cambridge, MA: Harvard University Press.

Duesenberry, James S. 1960. 'Comment.' In *Demographic and Economic Change in Developed Countries.* Princeton, NJ: Princeton University Press.

Dufour, D. L., & M. L. Sauther. 2002. 'Comparative and Evolutionary Dimensions of the Energetics of Human Pregnancy and Lactation.' *American Journal of Human Biology: The Official Journal of The Human Biology Council* 14(5):584–602.

Durkheim, Emile. 1895/1982. *The Elementary Forms of Religious Life.* New York, NY: Free Press.

Eagly, Alice H., & Shelly Chaiken. 1993. *The Psychology of Attitudes.* Belmont, CA: Wadsworth Publishing Co Inc.

Ehrlich, Paul R. 2002. *Human Natures: Genes, Cultures, and the Human Prospect.* 1st ed. New York, NY: Penguin Books.

Ehrlich, Paul R., & Anne H. Ehrlich. 2008. *The Dominant Animal: Human Evolution and the Environment.* Washington, DC: Island Press.

Ekman, Paul. 2007. *Emotions Revealed: Recognizing Faces and Feelings to Improve Communication and Emotional Life.* 2nd ed. New York, NY: Holt Paperbacks.

Eltis, David, Keith Bradley, & Paul Cartledge. 2011. *The Cambridge World History of Slavery: Volume 3, AD 1420–AD 1804.* Cambridge, UK: Cambridge University Press.

Eriksson, Lina. 2011. *Rational Choice Theory: Potential and Limits.* London: Palgrave Macmillan.

EUROSTAT. 2014. *Passenger Transport Statistics.* Retrieved 15 September 2014 (http://epp.eurostat.ec.europa.eu/statistics_explained/index.php/Passenger_transport_statistics).

Evans, Dylan, & Pierre Cruse. 2004. *Emotion, Evolution and Rationality.* 1st ed. Oxford, UK: Oxford University Press.

Evans, Jonathan St B. T., & Keith E. Stanovich. 2013. 'Theory and Metatheory in the Study of Dual Processing Reply to Comments.' *Perspectives on Psychological Science* 8(3):263–71.

Fang, Christina, Steven Orla Kimbrough, Stefano Pace, Annapurna Valluri, & Zhiqiang Zheng. 2002. 'On Adaptive Emergence of Trust Behavior in the Game of Stag Hunt.' *Group Decision and Negotiation* 11(6):449–67.

Fehr, Ernst, & Urs Fischbacher. 2005. 'Human Altruism – Proximate Patterns and Evolutionary Origins.' *Analyse & Kritik* 27:6–47.

Ferguson, Brian S. 2000. 'Interpreting the Rational Addiction Model.' *Health Economics* 9(7):587–98.

Fischer, Agneta H., Antony S. R. Manstead, & Patricia M. Rodriguez Mosquera. 1999. 'The Role of Honour-Related vs. Individualistic Values in Conceptualising Pride, Shame, and Anger: Spanish and Dutch Cultural Prototypes.' *Cognition & Emotion* 13(2):149–79.

Fiske, Alan. 1992. 'The Four Elementary Forms of Sociality: Framework for a Unified Theory of Social Relations.' *Psychological Review* 99(4):689–723.

Fligstein, Neil, & Doug McAdam. 2011. 'Toward a General Theory of Strategic Action Fields.' *Sociological Theory* 29(1):1–26.

Folmer, H. 2009. 'Why Sociology Is Better Conditioned to Explain Economic Behaviour than Economics.' *Kyklos* 62(2):258–74.

Fonseca-Azevedo, Karina, & Suzana Herculano-Houzel. 2012. 'Metabolic Constraint Imposes Tradeoff between Body Size and Number of Brain Neurons in Human Evolution.' *Proceedings of the National Academy of Sciences of the United States of America* 109(45):18571–6.

Fourcade, Marion, & Kieran Healy. 2007. 'Moral Views of Market Society.' *Annual Review of Sociology* 33:285–311.

Fournier, Marc A. 2009. 'Adolescent Hierarchy Formation and the Social Competition Theory of Depression.' *Journal of Social & Clinical Psychology* 28(9):1144–72.

Frank, Robert H. 2012. 'The Easterlin Paradox Revisited.' *Emotion* 12(6):1188–91.

Frankish, Keith. 2010. 'Dual-Process and Dual-System Theories of Reasoning.' *Philosophy Compass* 5(10):914–26.

Frederick, David A., Tania A. Reynolds, & Maryanne L. Fisher. 2013. 'The Importance of Female Choice.' In Maryanne L. Fisher, Justin R. Garcia, and Rosemarie S. Chang (eds.), *Evolution's Empress* (pp. 304–29). Oxford, UK: Oxford University Press.

Freese, Jeremy, Jui-Chung Allen Li, & Lisa D. Wade. 2003. 'The Potential Relevances of Biology to Social Inquiry.' *Annual Review of Sociology* 29(1):233–56.

Freud, Anna. 1936. *The Ego and the Mechanisms of Defense: The Writings of Anna Freud.* Revised ed. Madison, CT: International Universities Press.

Freud, Sigmund. 1930. *Civilization and Its Discontents.* New York, NY: W. W. Norton & Co.

Frewer, L. J., A. Kole, S. M. A. Van de Kroon, & C. de Lauwere. 2005. 'Consumer Attitudes Towards the Development of Animal-Friendly Husbandry Systems.' *Journal of Agricultural and Environmental Ethics* 18(4):345–67.

Friedman, Milton. 1953. *Essays in Positive Economics.* 1st ed. Chicago: University of Chicago Press.

Friedman, Milton. 2002. *Capitalism and Freedom.* 40th anniversary ed. Chicago: University of Chicago Press.

Frödin, Olle. 2015. 'Researching Governance for Sustainable Development: Some Conceptual Clarifications.' *Journal of Developing Societies* 31(4):447–66.

Gallup. 2015. 'Union Members Less Content With Safety, Recognition at Work.' *Gallup.com.* Retrieved 15 January 2016 (www.gallup.com/poll/185417/union-members-less-content-safety-recognition-work.aspx).

Gamson, William A. 1992. *Talking Politics.* Cambridge, UK: Cambridge University Press.

Gans, Joshua S., & Vivienne Groves. 2012. 'Carbon Offset Provision with Guilt-Ridden Consumers.' *Journal of Economics & Management Strategy* 21(1):243–69.

Gat, A. 2000. 'The Human Motivational Complex: Evolutionary Theory and the Causes of Hunter-Gatherer Fighting, Part II. Proximate, Subordinate, and Derivative Causes.' *Anthropological Quarterly* 74–88.

Geary, David C. 2010. 'Competing for Mates.' In David C. Geary (ed.), *Male, Female: The Evolution of Human Sex Differences.* 2nd ed. (pp. 213–45). Washington, DC: American Psychological Association.

Gellner, Ernest. 1983. *Nations and Nationalism.* 2nd ed. Ithaca, NY: Cornell University Press.

Giddens, Anthony. 1991. *Modernity and Self-Identity: Self and Society in the Late Modern Age.* Palo Alto, CA: Stanford University Press.

Gigerenzer, Gerd. 2015. *Simply Rational: Decision Making in the Real World.* 1st ed. Oxford, UK; New York, NY: Oxford University Press.

Gilbert, Paul, & Bernice Andrews. 1998. *Shame: Interpersonal Behavior, Psychopathology, and Culture*. Oxford, UK: Oxford University Press.

Gilovich, Thomas, Dale Griffin, & Daniel Kahneman. 2002. *Heuristics and Biases: The Psychology of Intuitive Judgment*. 1st ed. Cambridge, UK; New York, NY: Cambridge University Press.

Gneezy, Uri, & Aldo Rustichini. 2000. 'A Fine Is a Price.' *Journal of Legal Studies* 29:1.

Goffman, Erving. 1974/1986. *Frame Analysis: An Essay on the Organization of Experience*. Boston: Northeastern University Press.

Gowaty, Patricia Adair. 2013. 'A Sex-Neutral Theoretical Framework for Making Strong Inferences about the Origins of Sex Roles.' In M. L. Fisher, J. R. Garcia, and R. Sokol Chang (eds.), *Evolution's Empress: Darwinian Perspectives on the Nature of Women* (pp. 85–111). New York, NY: Oxford University Press.

Granovetter, Mark. 1985. 'Economic Action and Social Structure: The Problem of Embeddedness.' *American Journal of Sociology* 91(3):481–510.

Gruen, Lori, Dale Jamieson, & Christopher Schlottmann. 2013. *Reflecting on Nature: Readings in Environmental Ethics and Philosophy*. New York, NY: Oxford University Press.

Haidt, Jonathan. 2008. 'Morality.' *Perspectives on Psychological Science* 3(1):65–72.

Haidt, Jonathan. 2012. *The Righteous Mind: Why Good People Are Divided by Politics and Religion*. New York, NY: Knopf Doubleday Publishing Group.

Haisley, Emily, Romel Mostafa, & George Loewenstein. 2008. 'Myopic Risk-Seeking: The Impact of Narrow Decision Bracketing on Lottery Play.' *Journal of Risk and Uncertainty* 37(1):57–75.

Hardin, Garrett. 1968. 'The Tragedy of the Commons.' *Science* 162(3859):1243–8.

Harvey, David. 2011. *A Brief History of Neoliberalism*. Oxford, UK; New York, NY: Oxford University Press.

Hayek, F. A. 1944/1994. *The Road to Serfdom*. Fiftieth anniversary ed. Chicago: University of Chicago Press.

Hechter, Michael, & Satoshi Kanazawa. 1997. 'Sociological Rational Choice Theory.' *Annual Review of Sociology* 23(1):191–214.

Heise, Lori L., & Andreas Kotsadam. 2015. 'Cross-National and Multilevel Correlates of Partner Violence: An Analysis of Data from Population-Based Surveys.' *The Lancet Global Health* 3(6):e332–40.

Helms, Janet E., Maryam Jernigan, & Jackquelyn Mascher. 2005. 'The Meaning of Race in Psychology and How to Change It: A Methodological Perspective.' *American Psychologist* 60(1):27–36.

Henrich, Joseph, Jean Ensminger, Richard McElreath, Abigail Barr, Clark Barrett, Alexander Bolyanatz, Juan Camilo Cardenas, Michael Gurven, Edwins Gwako, Natalie Henrich, Carolyn Lesorogol, Frank Marlowe, David Tracer, & John Ziker. 2010. 'Markets, Religion, Community Size, and the Evolution of Fairness and Punishment.' *Science* 327(5972):1480–4.

Heyman, Gene M. 2010. *Addiction: A Disorder of Choice*. Reprint ed. Cambridge, MA; London: Harvard University Press.

Hirschman, Albert O. 1997/2013. *The Passions and the Interests: Political Arguments for Capitalism before Its Triumph*. With a new afterword by Jeremy Adelman. Princeton, NJ: Princeton University Press.

Hobbes, Thomas. 1651/1982. *Leviathan*. Harmondsworth, UK: Penguin Classics.

Holzer, Boris. 2007. 'Framing the Corporation: Royal Dutch/Shell and Human Rights Woes in Nigeria.' *Journal of Consumer Policy* 30(3):281–301.

Holzer, Boris. 2010. *Moralizing the Corporation: Transnational Activism and Corporate Accountability*. Cheltenham, UK: Edward Elgar.

Hopf, Ted. 2010. 'The Logic of Habit in International Relations.' *European Journal of International Relations* 16(4):539–61.

Horowitz, Mark, William Yaworsky, & Kenneth Kickham. 2014. 'Whither the Blank Slate? A Report on the Reception of Evolutionary Biological Ideas among Sociological Theorists.' *Sociological Spectrum* 34(6):489–509.

Huber, John D., & Michael M. Ting. 2013. 'Redistribution, Pork, and Elections.' *Journal of the European Economic Association* 11(6):1382–1403.

Hyland, Andrew, Joaquin Barnoya, & Juan E. Corral. 2012. 'Smoke-Free Air Policies: Past, Present and Future.' *Tobacco Control* 21(2):154–61.

Jagger, Mackenzie. 2013. *The Paleolithic Diet: What It Is and Why It Works*. 1st ed. Victoria, BC: First Choice Publishing.

Johnson, Allen W., & Timothy K. Earle. 1987. *The Evolution of Human Societies: From Foraging Group to Agrarian State*. Stanford, CA: Stanford University Press.

Johnson, Dirk R. 2010. *Nietzsche's Anti-Darwinism*. Cambridge, UK: Cambridge University Press.

Johnson, Dominic D. P. 2015. 'Survival of the Disciplines: Is International Relations Fit for the New Millennium?' *Millennium – Journal of International Studies* 43(2):749–63.

Johnson, Dominic. 2016. *God Is Watching You: How the Fear of God Makes Us Human*. Oxford, UK: Oxford University Press.

Johnson, Dominic D. P., & James H. Fowler. 2011. 'The Evolution of Overconfidence.' *Nature* 477(7364):317–20.

Johnson, Dominic D. P., Michael E. Price, & Mark Van Vugt. 2013. 'Darwin's Invisible Hand: Market Competition, Evolution and the Firm.' *Journal of Economic Behavior & Organization* 90:S128–40.

Judson, Olivia. 2002. *Dr. Tatiana's Sex Advice to All Creation: The Definitive Guide to the Evolutionary Biology of Sex*. New York, NY: Metropolitan Books.

Kahneman, Daniel. 2011. *Thinking, Fast and Slow*. Reprint edition. New York, NY: Farrar, Straus and Giroux.

Kahneman, Daniel, Dan Lovallo, & Olivier Sibony. 2011. 'The Big Idea: Before You Make That Big Decision…' *Harvard Business Review* 89(6).

Kahneman, Daniel, Peter P. Wakker, & Rakesh Sarin. 1997. 'Back to Bentham? Explorations of Experienced Utility.' *The Quarterly Journal of Economics*, 375.

Kalberg, Stephen. 1980. 'Max Weber's Types of Rationality: Cornerstones for the Analysis of Rationalization Processes in History.' *The American Journal of Sociology* 85(5):1145–79.

Kaplan, Hillard S., Paul L. Hooper, & Michael Gurven. 2009. 'The Evolutionary and Ecological Roots of Human Social Organization.' *Philosophical Transactions of the Royal Society of London B: Biological Sciences* 364(1533):3289–99.

Kaplan, Stephen. 2000. 'New Ways to Promote Proenvironmental Behavior: Human Nature and Environmentally Responsible Behavior.' *Journal of Social Issues* 56(3):491–508.

Kasser, Tim. 2001. *The High Price of Materialism*. 1st ed. Cambridge, MA: A Bradford Book.

Kehlbacher, A., R. Bennett, & K. Balcombe. 2012. 'Measuring the Consumer Benefits of Improving Farm Animal Welfare to Inform Welfare Labelling.' *Food Policy* 37(6):627–33.

Keyes, Corey L. M., Kenneth S. Kendler, John M. Myers, & Chris C. Martin. 2014. 'The Genetic Overlap and Distinctiveness of Flourishing and the Big Five Personality Traits.' *Journal of Happiness Studies* 16(3):655–68.

Kingsbury, Paul, & John Paul Jones. 2009. 'Walter Benjamin's Dionysian Adventures on Google Earth.' *Geoforum* 40(4):502–13.

Klintman, Mikael. 2002. 'Arguments Surrounding Organic and Genetically Modified Food Labelling: A Few Comparisons.' *Journal of Environmental Policy and Planning* 4(3):247–59.

Klintman, Mikael. 2006. 'Ambiguous Framings of Political Consumerism: Means or End, Product or Process Orientation?' *International Journal of Consumer Studies* 30(5):427–38.

Klintman, Mikael. 2012a. 'Issues of Scale in the Global Accreditation of Sustainable Tourism Schemes: Toward Harmonized Re-Embeddedness?' *Sustainability: Science, Practice, & Policy* 8(1):1008–40.

Klintman, Mikael. 2012b. *Citizen-Consumers and Evolution: Reducing Environmental Harm through our Social Motivation.* Houndmills, Basingstoke, UK: Palgrave.

Klintman, Mikael, & Magnus Boström. 2015. 'Citizen-Consumers.' In K. Backstrand and E. Lovbrand (eds.), *Research Handbook on Climate Governance* (pp. 309–19). London: Edward Elgar.

Knafo, Ariel, Sara Jaffee, Frances Rice, Gemma Lewis, Gordon Harold, & Anita Thapar. 2013. 'Examining the Role of Passive Gene–Environment Correlation in Childhood Depression Using a Novel Genetically Sensitive Design.' *Development & Psychopathology* 25(1):37–50.

Kock, Carl J., Juan Santalo, & Luis Diestre. 2012. 'Corporate Governance and the Environment: What Type of Governance Creates Greener Companies?' *Journal of Management Studies* 49(3):492–514.

Kohlberg, Lawrence. 1981. *The Meaning and Measurement of Moral Development.* Worcester, MA: Clark University Heinz Werner Institute.

Komter, Aafke. 2010. 'The Evolutionary Origins of Human Generosity.' *International Sociology* 25(3):443–64.

Konisky, David. M., Jeffrey Milyo, & Lilliard E. Richardson. 2008. 'Environmental Policy Attitudes: Issues, Geographical Scale, and Political Trust.' *Social Science Quarterly* 89(5):1066–85.

Kourvetaris, George A. 1997. 'The Dionysian and Apollonian Dimensions of Ethnicity: A Convergence Model.' *International Review of Sociology* 7(2):229–37.

Krugman, Paul, 2007. *The Conscience of a Liberal.* New York, NY: W. W. Norton.

Kuhn, T. S. 1962/2012. *The Structure of Scientific Revolutions.* Fiftieth anniversary ed. Chicago: University of Chicago Press.

Layard, Richard. 2007. 'Rethinking Public Economics: The Implications of Rivalry and Habit.' In L. Bruni and P. L. Porta (eds.), *Economics and Happiness: Framing the Analysis.* Oxford, UK: Oxford University Press.

Leary, Mark R., & Ashley Batts Allen. 2011. 'Self-Presentational Persona: Simultaneous Management of Multiple Impressions.' *Journal of Personality and Social Psychology* 101(5):1033–49.

Leary, Mark R., Alison L. Haupt, Kristine S. Strausser, & Jason T. Chokel. 1998. 'Calibrating the Sociometer: The Relationship between Interpersonal Appraisals and the State Self-Esteem.' *Journal of Personality and Social Psychology* 74(5):1290–9.

Lewens, Tim. 2006. *Darwin.* London: Routledge.

Lidskog, Rolf, Arthur P. J. Mol, & Peter Oosterveer. 2015. 'Towards a Global Environmental Sociology? Legacies, Trends and Future Directions.' *Current Sociology* 63(3):339–68.

Liebe, Ulf, P. Preisendorfer, & Jürgen Meyerhoff. 2010. 'To Pay or Not to Pay: Competing Theories to Explain Individuals' Willingness to Pay for Public Environmental Goods.' *Environment and Behavior* 43(1):106–30.

Linquist, Stefan. 2015. 'Which Evolutionary Model Best Explains the Culture of Honour?' *Biology & Philosophy* 1–23.

Lippold, Sebastian, Hongyang Xu, Albert Ko, Mingkun Li, Gabriel Renaud, Anne Butthof, Roland Schroeder, & Mark Stoneking. 2014. 'Human Paternal and Maternal Demographic Histories: Insights from High-Resolution Y Chromosome and mtDNA Sequences.' *Investigative Genetics* 5(1):13.

Long, Lynellyn D., & Ellen Oxfeld, eds. 2004. *Coming Home?: Refugees, Migrants, and Those Who Stayed Behind*. Philadelphia: University of Pennsylvania Press.

Lopreato, Joseph, & Timothy Alan Crippen. 2002. *Crisis in Sociology: The Need for Darwin*. New Brunswick, NJ: Transaction Publishers.

Lorenz, Edward C. 2012. *Civic Empowerment in an Age of Corporate Greed*. East Lansing: Michigan State University Press.

Luthar, Suniya S., & Bronwyn E. Becker. 2002. 'Privileged but Pressured? A Study of Affluent Youth.' *Child Development* 73(5):1593–1610.

Machalek, Richard, & Michael W. Martin. 2004. 'Sociology and the Second Darwinian Revolution: A Metatheoretical Analysis.' *Sociological Theory* 22(3):455–76.

Machiavelli, Niccolo. 1532/2003. *The Prince*. Penguin Classics ed. New York, NY: Penguin Classics.

Mandeville, Bernard. 1714/1989. *The Fable of the Bees: Or Private Vices, Publick Benefits*. Penguin Classics ed. New York, NY: Penguin Classics.

Manuck, Stephen B., & Jeanne M. McCaffery. 2014. 'Gene-Environment Interaction.' *Annual Review of Psychology* 65(1):41–70.

Marcuse, Herbert. 1964/2002. *One-Dimensional Man: Studies in the Ideology of Advanced Industrial Society*. New ed. London: Routledge.

Marcuse, Herbert. 1968. 'Liberation from the Affluent Society.' In D. Cooper (ed.), *The Dialectics of Liberation*. London: Verso Books.

Marechal, Kevin. 2009. 'An Evolutionary Perspective on the Economics of Energy Consumption: The Crucial Role of Habits.' *Journal of Economic Issues* 43(1):69–88.

Marmot, Michael. 2005. *The Status Syndrome: How Social Standing Affects Our Health and Longevity*. New York, NY: Owl Books.

Marmot, Michael, & Eric Brunner. 2005. 'Cohort Profile: The Whitehall II Study.' *International Journal of Epidemiology* 34(2):251–6.

Marx, Karl. 1844/2007. *Economic and Philosophic Manuscripts of 1844*. North Chelmsford, MA: Courier Corporation.

Marx, Karl. 1867/1992. *Capital: Volume 1: A Critique of Political Economy*. Reprint ed. London: Penguin Classics.

MasColell, Andreu, Michael Dennis Whinston, & Jerry R. Green. 2006. *Microeconomic Theory*. New York, NY: Oxford University Press.

Mateo, Jill M. 2015. 'Perspectives: Hamilton's Legacy: Mechanisms of Kin Recognition in Humans.' *Ethology* 121(5):419–27.

Mazur, Allan. 2005. *Biosociology of Dominance and Deference*. New York, NY: Rowman & Littlefield.

McCall, Cade, Christine M. Tipper, Jim Blascovich, & Scott T. Grafton. 2012. 'Attitudes Trigger Motor Behavior through Conditioned Associations: Neural and Behavioral Evidence.' *Social Cognitive & Affective Neuroscience* 7(7):841–9.

McCright, Aaron M., Chenyang Xiao, & Riley E. Dunlap. 2014. 'Political Polarization on Support for Government Spending on Environmental Protection in the USA, 1974–2012.' *Social Science Research* 48:251–60.

McKie, Linda. 2006. 'Sociological Work on Violence: Gender, Theory and Research.' *Sociological Research Online* 11(2).

McKinnon, Susan, & Sydel Silverman. 2005. *Complexities: Beyond Nature and Nurture.* Chicago: University of Chicago Press.

McMahon, John. 2015. 'Training for Neoliberalism.' *Boston Review*, 15 July. Retrieved 17 August 2015 (http://bostonreview.net/books-ideas/john-mcmahon-richard-thaler-misbehaving-behavioral-economics).

McManus, Phil, & Graham Haughton. 2006. 'Planning with Ecological Footprints: A Sympathetic Critique of Theory and Practice.' *Environment and Urbanization* 18(1):113–27.

Mecca, Andrew, Neil J. Smelser, & John Vasconcellos, eds. 1989. *The Social Importance of Self-Esteem.* Berkeley: University of California Press.

Mercier, Hugo. 2011. 'On the Universality of Argumentative Reasoning.' *Journal of Cognition and Culture* 11(1):85–113.

Mercier, Hugo. 2013. 'Using Evolutionary Thinking to Cut Across Disciplines.' In T. R. Zentall and P. H. Crowley (eds.), *Comparative Decision Making* (pp. 279–304). Oxford, UK: Oxford University Press.

Mercier, Hugo, & Helene E. Landemore. 2012. 'Reasoning Is for Arguing: Understanding the Successes and Failures of Deliberation.' *Political Psychology*: 243–58.

Merton, Robert. 1959. *Social Theory and Social Structure.* New York, NY: Free Press.

Merton, Robert K. 1942/1973. 'The Normative Structure of Science.' In Robert K. Merton, *The Sociology of Science: Theoretical and Empirical Investigations* (pp. 267–78). Chicago: University of Chicago Press.

Mesoudi, Alex. 2011. *Cultural Evolution: How Darwinian Theory Can Explain Human Culture and Synthesize the Social Sciences.* Chicago: University of Chicago Press.

Mill, John Stuart. 1844. *Essays on Some Unsettled Questions of Political Economy.* London: John W. Parker.

Mill, John Stuart. 1869. *On Liberty.* 4th ed. London: Longmans, Green, Reader, and Dyer.

Miller, Henry I., & Susanne L. Huttner. 1995. 'Food Produced with New Biotechnology: Can Labeling Be Anti-Consumer?' *Journal of Public Policy & Marketing*, 330–3.

Mischel, Walter, Ebbe B. Ebbesen, & Antonette Raskoff Zeiss. 1972. 'Cognitive and Attentional Mechanisms in Delay of Gratification.' *Journal of Personality & Social Psychology* 21(2):204–18.

Molenberghs, Pascal. 2013. 'The Neuroscience of in-Group Bias.' *Neuroscience & Biobehavioral Reviews* 37(8):1530–6.

Moll, Ian. 2004. 'Psychology, Biology and Social Relations.' *Journal of Critical Realism* 3(1):49–76.

Moore, George. E. 1903. *Principia Ethica.* Buffalo, NY: Prometheus Books.

Moseley, William G. 2004. *Taking Sides: Clashing Views on Controversial African Issues.* New York, NY: McGraw-Hill/Dushkin.

Moskowitz, Gordon A., Ian Skurnik, & Adam Galinsky. 1999. 'The History of Dual-Process Notions and the Future of Preconscious Control.' In S. Chaiken and Y. Trope (eds.), *Dual-process Theories in Social Psychology* (pp. 12–36). New York, NY: Guilford Press.

Muller, Jerry Z. 2007. *The Mind and the Market: Capitalism in Western Thought*. New York, NY: Knopf Doubleday Publishing Group.

Nagel, Thomas. 2012. *Mind and Cosmos: Why the Materialist Neo-Darwinian Conception of Nature Is Almost Certainly False*. 1st ed. New York, NY: Oxford University Press.

Narvaez, Darcia, Kristin Valentino, Agustin Fuentes, James J. McKenna, & Peter Gray, eds. 2014. *Ancestral Landscapes in Human Evolution: Culture, Childrearing and Social Wellbeing*. Oxford, UK: Oxford University Press.

Nesse, Randolph M. 2005. 'Natural Selection and the Elusiveness of Happiness.' In F. A. Huppert, N. Baylis, and B. Keverne (eds.), *The Science of Well-Being* (pp. 2–33). Oxford, UK: Oxford University Press.

Nietzsche, Friedrich. 1872/2010. *The Birth of Tragedy*. Whitefish, MT: Kessinger Publishing, LLC.

Nietzsche, Friedrich. 1908/2009. *Ecce Homo: How One Becomes What One Is*. Reissue ed. Oxford: Oxford University Press.

Niiya, Yu, Phoebe C. Ellsworth, & Susumu Yamaguchi. 2006. 'Amae in Japan and the United States: An Exploration of a "Culturally Unique" Emotion.' *Emotion* 6(2):279–95.

Nussbaum, Martha C. 2012. *The New Religious Intolerance: Overcoming the Politics of Fear in an Anxious Age*. Cambridge, MA: Harvard University Press.

Ott, Jan. 2010. 'Happiness, Economics and Public Policy: A Critique.' *Journal of Happiness Studies* 11(1):125–30.

Parsons, Talcott. 1966. *Societies: Evolutionary and Comparative Perspectives*. New York, NY: Prentice-Hall, Inc.

Paul, Joanne. 2012. *Governing Diversities: Democracy, Diversity and Human Nature*. Newcastle upon Tyne, UK: Cambridge Scholars Publishing.

Peltzman, Sam. 1993. 'George Stigler's Contribution to the Economic Analysis of Regulation.' *Journal of Political Economy* 101(5):818–32.

Pervin, Lawrence A. 1989. *Goal Concepts in Personality and Social Psychology*. Hillsdale, NJ: L. Erlbaum Associates.

Piaget, Jaques. 1932/1997. *The Moral Judgment of the Child*. New York, NY: Free Press.

Pickett, Kate, & Richard G. Wilkinson. 2008. *Health and Inequality: Health Inequalities – Interventions and Evaluations*. London: Routledge.

Pillas, Demetris, M. Marmot, Kiyuri Naicker, Peter Goldblatt, Joana Morrison, & Hynek Pikhart. 2014. 'Social Inequalities in Early Childhood Health and Development: A European-Wide Systematic Review.' *Pediatric Research* 76(5):418–24.

Pinker, Steven. 2002. *The Blank Slate: The Modern Denial of Human Nature*. 1st ed. New York, NY: Viking Press.

Pinker, Steven. 2009. *How the Mind Works*. Reissue. New York, NY: W. W. Norton & Co.

Pinker, Steven. 2011. *The Better Angels of Our Nature: Why Violence Has Declined*. 1st ed. New York, NY: Viking Adult.

Polanyi, Karl. 1944. *The Great Transformation: The Political and Economic Origins of Our Time*. 2nd ed. Boston, MA: Beacon Press.

Polanyi, Michael. 1968. 'Life's Irreducible Structure.' *Science* 160(3834):1308–12.

Polites, Greta L., & Elena Karahanna. 2012. 'Shackled to the Status Quo: The Inhibiting Effects of Incumbent System Habit, Switching Costs, and Inertia on New System Acceptance.' *MIS Quarterly* 36(1):21–A13.

Polley, William J. 2015. 'The Rhetoric of Opportunity Cost.' *American Economist* 60(1):9–19.

Popper, Karl. 1959. *The Logic of Scientific Discovery*. 2nd ed. London: Routledge.

Pratten, Stephen. 2013. 'Critical Realism and the Process Account of Emergence.' *Journal for the Theory of Social Behaviour* 43(3):251–79.

Quintelier, Katinka, & Daniel Fessler. 2012. 'Varying Versions of Moral Relativism: The Philosophy and Psychology of Normative Relativism.' *Biology & Philosophy* 27(1):95.

Radcliff, Benjamin. 2013. *The Political Economy of Human Happiness: How Voters' Choices Determine the Quality of Life*. Cambridge, UK: Cambridge University Press.

Randazzo, Anthony, & Jonathan Haidt. 2015. 'The Moral Narratives of Economists.' *Econ Journal Watch* 12(1):49.

Reyna, Valerie F., & Vivian Zayas. 2014. 'Introduction to the Neuroscience of Risky Decision Making'. In V. F. Reyna and V. Zayas (eds.), *The Neuroscience of Risky Decision Making, Bronfenbrenner Series on the Ecology of Human Development* (pp. 3–8). Washington, DC: American Psychological Association.

Richards, Timothy J., Paul M. Patterson, & Abebayehu Tegene. 2007. 'Obesity and Nutrient Consumption: A Rational Addiction?' *Contemporary Economic Policy* 25(3):309–24.

Rigby, Nichole, & Rob J. Kulathinal. 2015. 'Genetic Architecture of Sexual Dimorphism in Humans.' *Journal of Cellular Physiology* 230(10):2304–10.

Rilling, James. K., Gutman, David. A., Zeh, Thorsten. R., Pagnoni, Giuseppe, Berns, Gregory S., & Kilts, Clinton D. 2002. 'A Neural Basis for Social Cooperation.' *Neuron*, 35:395–405.

Ritzer, George. 1975. 'Sociology: A Multiple Paradigm Science.' *American Sociologist* 10(3):156–67.

Robbins, Lionel. 1932. *An Essay on the Nature and Significance of Economic Science*. 1st ed. London: Macmillan.

Rol, Menno. 2008. 'Idealization, Abstraction, and the Policy Relevance of Economic Theories.' *Journal of Economic Methodology* 15(1):69–97.

Rosen, Michael. 2013. *On Voluntary Servitude: False Consciousness and the Theory of Ideology*. Hoboken, NJ: John Wiley & Sons.

Rothgerber, Hank. 2013. 'Real Men Don't Eat (Vegetable) Quiche: Masculinity and the Justification of Meat Consumption.' *Psychology of Men & Masculinity* 14(4):363–75.

Rousseau, Jean-Jacques. 1755/2004. *Discourse on the Origin of Inequality*. Mineola, NY: Dover Publications.

Ruff, Christian C., & Ernst Fehr. 2014. 'The Neurobiology of Rewards and Values in Social Decision Making.' *Nature Reviews Neuroscience* 15(8):549–62.

Runciman, Walter. G. 2005. 'Stone Age Sociology.' *Journal of the Royal Anthropological Institute* 11(1):129–42.

Runciman, Walter. G. 2009. *The Theory of Cultural and Social Selection*. Cambridge, UK; New York, NY: Cambridge University Press.

Sabbagh, Clara. 2010. 'Review Essays: Human Motives and Social Cooperation Towards Integrating Sociological, Economic and (Social) Psychological Perspectives.' *International Sociology* 25(5):639–53.

Salthe, Stanley. 1989. *Evolving Hierarchical Systems*. New York, NY: Columbia University Press.

Samuelson, William, & Richard Zeckhauser. 1988. 'Status Quo Bias in Decision Making.' *Journal of Risk and Uncertainty* 1(1):7–59.

Sandel, Michael J. 2013. *What Money Can't Buy: The Moral Limits of Markets*. Reprint ed. New York, NY: Farrar, Straus and Giroux.

Sanderson, Stephen. 2014. *Human Nature and the Evolution of Society*. Boulder, CO: Westview Press.

Sapolsky, Robert. 2004. *Why Zebras Don't Get Ulcers*. 3rd ed. New York, NY: Holt Paperbacks.

Sapolsky, Robert. 2005. 'Sick of Poverty.' *Scientific American* 293(6):92–9.

Sapolsky, Robert. 2012. *Being Human: Life Lessons from the Frontiers of Science*. Chantilly, VA: The Great Courses.

Sapolsky, Robert. 2013. 'Rousseau with a Tail: Maintaining a Tradition of Peace among Baboons.' In D. P. Fry (ed.), *War, Peace, and Human Nature: The Convergence of Evolutionary and Cultural Views* (pp. 421–38). New York, NY: Oxford University Press.

Sarkar, Runa. 2008. 'Public Policy and Corporate Environmental Behaviour: A Broader View.' *Corporate Social Responsibility and Environmental Management* 15(5):281–97.

Sartre, Jean-Paul, 1945/2007. *Existentialism Is a Humanism*. Trade Paperback ed. New Haven, CT: Yale University Press.

Sauer, Uta, & Anke Fischer. 2010. 'Willingness to Pay, Attitudes and Fundamental Values – On the Cognitive Context of Public Preferences for Diversity in Agricultural Landscapes.' *Ecological Economics* 70(1):1–9.

Scheiner, Joachim, & Christian Holz Rau. 2012. 'Gendered Travel Mode Choice: A Focus on Car Deficient Households.' *Journal of Transport Geography* 24:250–61.

Schelling, Thomas C. 1977/2006. *Micromotives and Macrobehavior*. Revised ed. New York, NY: W. W. Norton & Company.

Schmitt, Carl. 1932/2007. *The Concept of the Political*. Expanded ed. Chicago: University of Chicago Press.

Schmitz, Sigrid, & Grit Hoppner. 2014. 'Neurofeminism and Feminist Neurosciences: A Critical Review of Contemporary Brain Research.' *Frontiers in Human Neuroscience* 8:546.

Schön, Donald A., & Martin Rein. 1994. *Frame Reflection: Toward the Resolution of Intractable Policy Controversies*. New York, NY: Basic Books.

Schumpeter, Joseph A. 1942/2010. *Capitalism, Socialism and Democracy*. London: Routledge.

Schumpeter, Joseph A. 1949/2012. *The Theory of Economic Development*. New Brunswick, NJ: Transaction Publishers.

Schumpeter, Joseph A., & John E. Elliott. 1911. *The Theory of Economic Development: An Inquiry into Profits, Capital, Credit, Interest, and the Business Cycle*. 1st ed. New Brunswick, NJ: Transaction Publishers.

Scully, Diana. 1990. *Understanding Sexual Violence: A Study of Convicted Rapists*. New York, NY: Routledge.

Segal, Nancy L., & Franchesca A. Cortez. 2014. 'Born in Korea-Adopted Apart: Behavioral Development of Monozygotic Twins Raised in the United States and France.' *Personality and Individual Differences* 70:97–104.

Sen, Amartya K. 1977. 'Rational Fools: A Critique of the Behavioral Foundations of Economic Theory.' *Philosophy & Public Affairs* 6(4):317–44.

Sen, Amartya. 1999. *Development as Freedom*. Oxford, UK: Oxford University Press.

Shadish, William R., & Steve Fuller. 1994. *The Social Psychology of Science*. New York, NY: Guilford Press.

Shaw, Rachel L., & David C. Giles. 2009. 'Motherhood on Ice? A Media Framing Analysis of Older Mothers in the UK News.' *Psychology & Health* 24(2):221–36.

Shepherd, Lee, Ronan E. O'Carroll, & Eamonn Ferguson. 2014. 'An International Comparison of Deceased and Living Organ Donation/Transplant Rates in Opt-in and Opt-out Systems: A Panel Study.' *BMC Medicine* 12(1):131.

Sherman, Jeffrey W., Bertram Gawronski, & Yaacov Trope. 2014. *Dual-Process Theories of the Social Mind*. 1st ed. New York, NY: The Guilford Press.

Shermer, Michael. 1996. 'History at the Crossroads: Can History Be a Science? Can It Afford Not to Be?' *Sceptic*, 56–67.

Shove, Elizabeth. 2010. 'Social Theory and Climate Change: Questions Often, Sometimes and Not Yet Asked.' *Theory Culture Society* 27(2–3):277–88.

Siegel, Ronald D. 2010. *The Mindfulness Solution: Everyday Practices for Everyday Problems*. 1st ed. New York, NY: The Guilford Press.

Silhon, Jean de. 1661. *De la certitude des connaissances humaines, 1661*. Paris: Fayard.

Silverman, Frederic. N. 1953. 'The Roentgen Manifestations of Unrecognized Skeletal Trauma in Infants.' *The American Journal of Roentgenology, Radium Therapy, and Nuclear Medicine* 69(3):413–27.

Simmel, Georg. 1898. *Essays on Religion*. New Haven, CT: Yale University Press.

Simmel, Georg. 1900/2004. *Philosophy of Money*. London: Taylor & Francis.

Simmel, Georg. 1903. 'The Metropolis and Mental Life.' In G. Bridge and S. Watson (eds.), *The Blackwell City Reader* (pp. 103–10). New York, NY: Wiley.

Simonton, Dean Keith. 1999. *Origins of Genius: Darwinian Perspectives on Creativity*. 1st ed. Oxford, UK: Oxford University Press.

Smiles, Samuels. 1859. *Self Help; with Illustrations of Conduct and Perseverance*. San Rafael, CA: CreateSpace Independent Publishing Platform.

Smith, Adam. 1776/1843. *An Inquiry into the Nature and Causes of the Wealth of Nations*. Edinburgh: Thomas Nelson.

Smith, Adam. 1790/2013. *The Theory of Moral Sentiments*. New York, NY: Augustus M. Kelley: Reprints of Economic Classics.

Snowdon, David. 2008. *Aging with Grace: What the Nun Study Teaches Us About Leading Longer, Healthier, and More Meaningful Lives*. New York, NY: Random House Publishing Group.

Solomon, Robert. 2008. *True to Our Feelings: What Our Emotions Are Really Telling Us*. Oxford, UK: Oxford University Press.

Sombart, Werner. 1913/2015. *The Jews and Modern Capitalism*. Eastford, CT: Martino Fine Books.

Soper, Kate. 2008. 'Alternative Hedonism, Cultural Theory and the Role of Aesthetic Revisioning.' *Cultural Studies* 22(5):567–87.

Spaargaren, Gert. 2011. 'Theories of Practices: Agency, Technology, and Culture: Exploring the Relevance of Practice Theories for the Governance of Sustainable Consumption Practices in the New World-Order.' *Global Environmental Change* 21(3):813–22.

Spencer, Herbert, & J. D. Y. Peel. 1983. *On Social Evolution: Selected Writings*. Chicago: University of Chicago Press.

Spiro, Melford E. 1986. 'Cultural Relativism and the Future of Anthropology.' *Cultural Anthropology* 1(3):259–86.

Squire, Larry R., & Stephen Michael Kosslyn. 1998. *Findings and Current Opinion in Cognitive Neuroscience*. Cambridge, MA: MIT Press.

Stanley, Damian, Elizabeth Phelps, & Mahzarin Banaji. 2008. 'The Neural Basis of Implicit Attitudes.' *Current Directions in Psychological Science* 17(2):164–70.

Stern, Charlotta, & Peter Hedström. 2008. 'Rational Choice and Sociology'. In S. N. Durlauf and L. E. Blume (eds.), *The New Palgrave Dictionary of Economics* (pp. 872–7). Basingstoke: Palgrave.

Stevenson, Betsey, & Justin Wolfers. 2008. 'Economic Growth and Subjective Well-Being: Reassessing the Easterlin Paradox.' *Brookings Papers on Economic Activity* 2008:1–87.

Stoker, Gerry. 2014. *The Politics of Nudge: Dilemmas in Implementing Policies for Sustainable Consumption*. Oxford, UK: Oxford University Press.

Stone, Emily A., Todd K. Shackelford, & David M. Buss. 2007. 'Sex Ratio and Mate Preferences: A Cross-Cultural Investigation.' *European Journal of Social Psychology* 37(2):288–96.

Suddendorf, Thomas. 2011. 'Evolution, Lies, and Foresight Biases.' *Behavioral and Brain Sciences* 34(1).

Sweetman, Caroline. 1998. *Violence Against Women*. Oxford, UK: Oxfam.

Tamm Hallström, Kristina, & Magnus Boström. 2010. *Transnational Multi-Stakeholder Standardization: Organizing Fragile Non-State Authority*. Cheltenham, UK: Edward Elgar.

TenEyck, M., & J. C. Barnes. 2015. 'Examining the Impact of Peer Group Selection on Self-Reported Delinquency: A Consideration of Active Gene–Environment Correlation.' *Criminal Justice and Behavior* 42(7):741–62.

Thaler, Richard H. 2015. *Misbehaving: The Making of Behavioral Economics*. 1st ed. New York: W. W. Norton & Company.

Thaler, Richard H., & Prof. Cass R. Sunstein. 2008. *Nudge: Improving Decisions About Health, Wealth, and Happiness*. 1st ed. New Haven, CT: Yale University Press.

The Economist. 2014. 'A Personal Choice.' *The Economist*, August. Retrieved 14 August 2015 (www.economist.com/news/leaders/21611063-internet-making-buying-and-selling-sex-easier-and-safer-governments-should-stop?zid=319&ah=17af09b0281b01505c226b1e574f5cc1).

The Universal Declaration of Human Rights. 2013. *The Universal Declaration of Human Rights*. Cambridge, UK: Cambridge University Press.

Tönnies, Ferdinand. 1887/1988. *Community & Society (Gemeinschaft Und Gesellschaft)*. New Brunswick, NJ: Transaction Publishers.

Tooby, John, & Leda Cosmides. 1992. 'The Psychological Foundations of Culture.' In *The Adapted Mind: Evolutionary Psychology and the Generation of Culture* (pp. 19–136). Oxford, UK: Oxford University Press.

Tool, Marc R. 1988. *Evolutionary Economics: Institutional Theory and Policy*. London: M.E. Sharpe.

Trivers, Robert. 1971. 'The Evolution of Reciprocal Altruism.' *The Quarterly Review of Biology* 46(1):35–57.

Trivers, Robert. 1972. 'Parental Investment and Sexual Selection.' In B. Campbell (ed.), *Sexual Selection and the Descent of Man* (pp. 136–79). London: Heinemann.

Trivers, Robert. 2011. *Deceit and Self-Deception: Fooling Yourself the Better to Fool Others*. New York, NY: Penguin.

Tullberg, Jan. 2006. 'Group Egoism; Investigating Collective Action and Individual Rationality.' *Journal of Socio-Economics* 35:1014–31.

Turnbull, Colin M. 1987. *The Mountain People*. New York, NY: Simon & Schuster.

Turner, Jonathan H., & David E. Boyns. 2001. 'The Return of Grand Theory.' In Jonathan H. Turner (ed.), *Handbook of Sociological Theory* (pp. 353–78). New York, NY: Springer Science & Business Media B.V./Books.

Turner, Jonathan H., & Alexandra Maryanski. 2016. *On the Origin of Societies by Natural Selection*. London: Routledge.

Tuschman, Avi. 2013. *Our Political Nature: The Evolutionary Origins of What Divides Us*. Amherst, NY: Prometheus Books.

Tversky, Amos, & Daniel Kahneman. 1974. 'Judgment under Uncertainty: Heuristics and Biases.' *Science* 185(4157):1124–31.

Tylor, Edward Burnett. 1873/2010. *Primitive Culture: Researches into the Development of Mythology, Philosophy, Religion, Art, and Custom*. Cambridge, UK: Cambridge University Press.

Uher, Rudolf, Silvia Alemany, & Ruud VanWinkel. 2014. 'Gene–Environment Interactions in Severe Mental Illness.' *Frontiers in Psychiatry* 5:1–9.

van Hooff, Jan A. R. A. M. 2011. 'Males and Females: The Big Little Difference.' *Future of Motherhood in Western Societies* 17.

Van Kempen, Luuk, Roldan Muradian, Cesar Sandoval, & Juan Pablo Castaneda. 2009. 'Too Poor to Be Green Consumers? A Field Experiment on Revealed Preferences for Firewood in Rural Guatemala.' *Ecological Economics* 68(7):2160–7.

Veblen, Thorstein. 1899/1967. *The Theory of the Leisure Class: An Economic Study of Institutions.* New York, NY: Funk & Wagnalls.

Verma, Meghna. 2014. 'Growing Car Ownership and Dependence in India and Its Policy Implications.' *Case Studies on Transport Policy.*

Voltaire, Francois M. A. 1733/2003. *Philosophical Letters: Letters Concerning the English Nation.* Mineola, NY: Dover Publications.

Voltaire, Francois M. A. 1764/2012. *Philosophical Dictionary.* New York, NY: Carlton House.

von Hippel, William, & Robert Trivers. 2011. 'The Evolution and Psychology of Self-Deception.' *Behavioral and Brain Sciences* 34(1):1–16.

Walla, Peter, Monika Koller, & Julia L. Meier. 2014. 'Consumer Neuroscience to Inform Consumers – Physiological Methods to Identify Attitude Formation Related to Over-Consumption and Environmental Damage.' *Frontiers in Human Neuroscience* 8:304.

Wallace, Gregory L., Nancy Raitano Lee, Elizabeth C. Prom-Wormley, Sarah E. Medland, Rhoshel K. Lenroot, Liv S. Clasen, James E. Schmitt, Michael C. Neale, & Jay N. Giedd. 2010. 'A Bivariate Twin Study of Regional Brain Volumes and Verbal and Nonverbal Intellectual Skills during Childhood and Adolescence.' *Behavior Genetics* 40(2):125–34.

Ward, Tony, & Russil Durrant. 2011. 'Evolutionary Behavioural Science and Crime: Aetiological and Intervention Implications.' *Legal and Criminological Psychology* 16(2):193–210.

Watson, John Broadus. 1930. *Behaviorism.* New Brunswick, NJ: Transaction Publishers.

Weber, Max. 1922/1978. *Economy and Society: An Outline of Interpretive Sociology* (G. Roth and C. Wittich, eds.). Berkeley: University of California Press.

Whitford, Josh. 2002. 'Pragmatism and the Untenable Dualism of Means and Ends: Why Rational Choice Theory Does Not Deserve Paradigmatic Privilege.' *Theory & Society* 31(3):325.

Whitmarsh, Lorraine, Gill Seyfang, & Saffron O'Neill. 2011. 'Public Engagement with Carbon and Climate Change: To What Extent Is the Public "Carbon Capable"?' *Global Environmental Change-Human and Policy Dimensions* 21(1):56–65.

Wilk, Richard R., & Lisa Cliggett. 2007. *Economies and Cultures: Foundations of Economic Anthropology.* Boulder, CO: Westview Press.

Wilkinson, Richard. 2001. *Mind the Gap: Hierarchies, Health, and Human Evolution.* New Haven, CT: Yale University Press.

Wilkinson, Richard, & Kate Pickett. 2006. 'Health Inequalities and the UK Presidency of the EU.' *LANCET* 367(9517):1126–8.

Wilson, David Sloan, Eric Dietrich, & Anne B. Clark. 2003. 'On the Inappropriate Use of the Naturalistic Fallacy in Evolutionary Psychology.' *Biology and Philosophy* 18(5):669–81.

Wilson, Edward O. 2012. *The Social Conquest of Earth.* 1st ed. New York, NY: W. W. Norton & Co.

Witt, Ulrich. 2006. 'Evolutionary Concepts in Economics and Biology.' *Journal of Evolutionary Economics* 16(5):473–76.

Wood, John Cunningham. 1993. *Thorstein Veblen: Critical Assessments*. London: Routledge.

Woods, Matthew. 2002. 'Reflections on Nuclear Optimism: Waltz, Burke and Proliferation.' *Review of International Studies* 28(1):163–89.

Woolley, Paul. V., & William. A. Evans. 1955. 'Significance of Skeletal Lesions in Infants Resembling Those of Traumatic Origin.' *Journal of the American Medical Association* 158(7):539–43.

Wright, Robert. 2001. *Nonzero: The Logic of Human Destiny*. New York, NY: Vintage.

Yurgelun-Todd, D. A., & W. D. S. Killgore. 2006. 'Fear-Related Activity in the Prefrontal Cortex Increases with Age during Adolescence: A Preliminary fMRI Study.' *Neuroscience Letters* 406(3):194–99.

Zafirovski, Milan. 2003. 'Human Rational Behavior and Economic Rationality.' *Electronic Journal of Sociology* 7(2):1–34.

Zechenter, Elizabeth M. 1997. 'In the Name of Culture: Cultural Relativism and the Abuse of the Individual.' *Journal of Anthropological Research* 53(3):319–47.

Zmora, Hillay. 2007. 'A World without a Saving Grace: Glory and Immortality in Machiavelli.' *History of Political Thought* 28(3):449–68.

Index

Page numbers in *italics* denote tables.

Taylor & Francis eBooks

Helping you to choose the right eBooks for your Library

Add Routledge titles to your library's digital collection today. Taylor and Francis ebooks contains over 50,000 titles in the Humanities, Social Sciences, Behavioural Sciences, Built Environment and Law.

Choose from a range of subject packages or create your own!

Benefits for you

» Free MARC records
» COUNTER-compliant usage statistics
» Flexible purchase and pricing options
» All titles DRM-free.

REQUEST YOUR FREE INSTITUTIONAL TRIAL TODAY

Free Trials Available
We offer free trials to qualifying academic, corporate and government customers.

Benefits for your user

» Off-site, anytime access via Athens or referring URL
» Print or copy pages or chapters
» Full content search
» Bookmark, highlight and annotate text
» Access to thousands of pages of quality research at the click of a button.

eCollections – Choose from over 30 subject eCollections, including:

Archaeology	Language Learning
Architecture	Law
Asian Studies	Literature
Business & Management	Media & Communication
Classical Studies	Middle East Studies
Construction	Music
Creative & Media Arts	Philosophy
Criminology & Criminal Justice	Planning
Economics	Politics
Education	Psychology & Mental Health
Energy	Religion
Engineering	Security
English Language & Linguistics	Social Work
Environment & Sustainability	Sociology
Geography	Sport
Health Studies	Theatre & Performance
History	Tourism, Hospitality & Events

For more information, pricing enquiries or to order a free trial, please contact your local sales team:
www.tandfebooks.com/page/sales

 Routledge
Taylor & Francis Group

The home of
Routledge books

www.tandfebooks.com